DIVISION AND REUNION: AMERICA 1848-1877

AMERICAN REPUBLIC SERIES

EDITED BY DON E. FEHRENBACHER

DIVISION AND REUNION: AMERICA 1848-1877

LUDWELL H. JOHNSON
College of William and Mary

John Wiley & Sons

NEW YORK ● SANTA BARBARA ● CHICHESTER ●
BRISBANE ● TORONTO

Library of Congress Cataloging in Publication Data:

Johnson, Ludwell H
   Division and reunion.

   (American Republic series)
   Includes index.
   1. United States—History—1849-1877. 2.   Slavery in the United States—History.
3. Reconstruction. I. Title.
E415.7.J69   973   77-16330
ISBN 0-471-44349-2
ISBN 0-471-44350-6 pbk.

Printed in the United States of America

10 9 8 7 6 5 4 3 2 1

To PCJ and ACJ

Editor's Preface

Division and Reunion is a volume in the "Wiley American Republic Series," a joint effort at exploring the meaning of the past to the present, written in separate volumes by specialists in the fields. With admirable clarity this volume surveys the three decades of sectional conflict that began when the Mexican War reopened the issue of slavery in the territories, and ended with the collapse of Radical Reconstruction. But this is no routine retelling of a familiar story; each chapter is enlivened by the vigor and distinctiveness of the author's interpretation. It has more than once been pointed out that historians in their explanations of the Civil War have tended to fall into groups that more or less recapitulate the views of the major factions actually engaged in the sectional conflict. The orthodox interpretation over the years has been that of the so-called "nationalists," who generally approve of the course taken by Lincoln and his party throughout the sectional crisis and the Civil War, but look with less favor on the program of Radical Reconstruction. In the 1930s and 1940s, this orthodoxy was challenged by a group of revisionists who viewed the war as tragically unnecessary and who found their heroes in antebellum compromisers like Stephen A. Douglas and in the opponents of Radical Reconstruction like Andrew Johnson. More recently, orthodoxy has been challenged from the other side by a school of neoabolitionists, white and black, who identify with the militancy of a Wendell Phillips and a Frederick Douglass, and who say the main trouble with Radical Reconstruction was that it never became radical enough. Still another dissenting school, one that dates back to the Civil War itself, can be called "neo-Confederate" because of its disposition to vindicate the South. *Division and Reunion* is a modern, sophisticated version of this line of interpretation. Ludwell H. Johnson takes a dim view of the Republican party and its motives, for example; he prefers Lee to Grant as a military commander and Jefferson Davis to Lincoln as a war president; and he sees the South as defending itself against an aggressive North. Here, in short, is a controversial history of the Civil War era. But if learning begins with provocation, and I believe that it often does, readers of this book will be doubly educated —first, in the remarkable amount of information it contains; and second, in its challenge to orthodoxy and consequent stimulus to thought.

Don E. Fehrenbacher

Preface

Historians who study the Civil War era are like people who embark, perhaps imprudently, on the Niagara River. They see downstream a great plume of spray and hear the thunder of the falls; they cannot fully appreciate where they are without reference to what lies before them. Similarly, as historians survey the antebellum years, they cannot interpret the period without reference to the tragedy of the 1860s. As best they can, they must confront the problem of why there was a civil war. American history does not pose a more significant question. It is bound up with many issues that are still of fundamental importance, such as the malfunctioning of democratic institutions, the conflict between majority rule and minority rights, the Negro's place in American society, and the reconciliation of moral principles with political realities.

The search for an answer must be pursued into the war itself, which often reveals as nothing else can what the antagonists hoped to accomplish by taking up arms. This is a complicated task, because war aims change according to the demands and opportunities of the conflict. In 1861 President Lincoln disclaimed any intention of interfering with Southern slavery, yet some 18 months later he issued the preliminary proclamation of emancipation. Some war aims are avowed, others are not, and still others seem to appear spontaneously.

The consequences of the war are even more important than its causes, to which they are, of course, closely related. Because war takes on a logic and momentum of its own, the outcome is frequently surprising even to the victor. As Lincoln said in 1865, each side "looked for . . . a result less fundamental and astounding." In the case of the Civil War, the nature and significance of the result are especially difficult to grasp. For one thing, the war did not end by treaty, so the peace settlement did not take final shape until a dozen years after Lee's surrender. For another, that "fundamental and astounding" result is inseparable from what the nation has since become. Americans have long sensed that the Civil War era is the "Great Divide" in their history, with an older way of life on one side and modern America on the other. Perhaps that is why they return to it so often in search of their national identity.

Ludwell H. Johnson

Acknowledgments

This little book has profited from the pointed criticisms of Don E. Fehrenbacher, editor of the Wiley American Republic Series, the comments of Robert F. Durden, who read the entire manuscript, and the suggestions of Willie Lee Rose and C. Vann Woodward, who read sample chapters. Naturally none of these distinguished scholars is in any way responsible for the deficiencies of the final product. Thanks are due to the William and Mary faculty research committee and the history department for supplying valuable logistical support. Most of all I am endebted to Pamela C. Johnson for her expert editorial help and substantive criticisms, as well as for her loyalty and sympathy, sentiments vehemently seconded by Abigail.

Ludwell H. Johnson

Contents

List of Maps

Chapter I

The Fundamental Issues

SLAVERY

Slavery is an essential part of any examination of antebellum America or any attempt to analyze the causes of the Civil War. But the problems inherent in studying an institution so vast and complex are formidable. By 1860 there were 3,950,000 slaves in the country, spread through 15 states from Delaware to Texas, from Florida to Missouri. There were 384,000 slaveowners in a Southern white population of 7 million, holding from 1 to (in a single instance) 1000 bondsmen. The majority owned from 1 to 6; about 3 percent owned more than 100.

Slaves might work under close supervision in broad cotton fields as part of a highly disciplined gang, or in factories alongside whites. They might live in towns, hire themselves out for set fees, part of which they could keep, and enjoy a considerable degree of personal freedom. Slaves might be house servants, daily in close contact with whites, or "drivers" occupying positions of responsibility and exercising authority over other slaves. Slaves might be almost exclusively field laborers, as great numbers were, but they could also be wheelwrights, blacksmiths, painters, carpenters, coopers, cooks, seamstresses, or nurses (to either blacks or whites). Slaves might be kindly treated, have garden plots of their own, or even their own businesses; in rare cases they might be able to buy their freedom. Slaves were sometimes loved and cherished by their masters as if they were members of the family.

Hannah [a slave] continued sensible to the very last, and could speak until within five minutes. The last thing she said: "All the time you are all doing something for me and giving me something good." In a few minutes after, she died, surrounded by a weeping group, white and black, as we all knelt in prayer at her bedside. . . . . When we lose our servants, the loss of their services is the last thing we think of; it is the shadow on our household when an attached faithful one is removed. (From Robert M. Myers, *Children of Pride.*)

On the other hand, slaves might be miserably fed, housed, and clothed, brutally mistreated and worked to the limit of endurance, as the following newspaper advertisements show:

STOP THE RUNAWAY. FIFTY DOLLARS REWARD. Eloped from the subscriber, living near Nashville on the 25th of June last, [1804] a Mulatto Man Slave. . . . The above reward will be given any person that will take him and deliver him to me, or secure him in jail so I can get him. If taken out of the state, the above reward, and all reasonable expenses paid — and ten dollars extra for every hundred lashes any person will give him to the amount of three hundred.
  (signed) ANDREW JACKSON, near
Nashville, State of Tennessee

RUNAWAY SLAVE. Is detained in the public prison . . . a negro about twenty years of age, calls himself William, he is Black and has a down look, . . . when committed, had around his neck an Iron collar with three prongs extending upwards, has many scars on his back and shoulders from the whip. . . . Owners are requested to prove property and take him away. (From U. B. Phillips, *Plantation and Frontier.*)

How well can one generalize about an institution that involved millions of people and existed under such a variety of conditions? The perplexities of that question, when added to the ideological and political conflict over slavery, have produced a debate that is still going on, and that has made the history of slavery preeminently a problem in historiography.

Southern planters defended the institution as a humane and necessary means of controlling, civilizing, and Christianizing a semibarbarous people. Abolitionists charged that slavery itself was a "relic of barbarism," sinful, cruel, and degrading. About the only thing concerning blacks that the vast majority of antebellum Americans agreed on was that they were innately inferior to whites. After the war, most Southerners were willing to concede that slavery had been wrong, or at least that it had been a burden to the whites, although they continued to deny that it had been cruel. And the North, by its actions, eventually agreed that congressional Reconstruction had been a mistake, and that the South was right in segregating and disfranchising the Negro. Thus prevailing racial attitudes paved the way for a more favorable historical view of slavery in the early twentieth century, when it came to be seen as a mild, paternalistic social system generally acquiesced in by the slaves.

In the 1920s, however, there occurred a reexamination and subsequent repudiation of the concept of innate racial differences. The new attitude toward race, strengthened by reaction to the horrors of Nazi racism and the growing political influence of black voters, cleared the way for the civil rights movement of the 1950s. The sympathetic view of slavery that had been accepted by scholars for a generation was supplanted by what has been called the "Northern liberal" or sometimes "neoabolitionist" interpretation. It emphasized the profit motive, the harshness of slavery, the rebelliousness of the slaves, and denied the existence of inherent racial differences. This approach to slavery soon came under attack from several directions. Some historians complained that the Northern liberal school was merely prolonging the North-South debate of the 1850s, and urged that a comparative study of various slave societies be substituted for this parochial viewpoint. More striking was the rehabilitation, minus assumptions of racial inferiority, of an amplified and refined concept of slavery as a paternalistic system that was defended by Southerners for reasons other than monetary profit. Complementing this interpretation to some degree was the work of certain econometricians, that is, practitioners of a new economic history who reached their conclusions by using computer technology to gather and process their data, which they then elucidated by using sophisticated mathematical techniques. These econometricians concluded, among other things, that plantation slavery was efficient and profitable; that the material circumstances of the slaves compared favorably with those of free white workers in the North; that slaves were well-fed, well-housed, "well-paid," and rarely whipped; that slave families were seldom disrupted; and so forth. The validity of these conclusions was immediately and vehemently challenged by other econometricians as well as by more traditional historians. This confusion of the scholarly community as to the nature of slavery, especially as to its cruelty or benevolence, coincided with increasing racial turmoil and resistance to integration in various Northern cities during the 1960s and 1970s.

Fortunately, as the history of slavery swings back and forth between extremes of ideology and bias, it brings to light much additional information that will help to narrow the area of disagreement. In time perhaps the pendulum will come to rest, and a picture of slavery will emerge that can be generally accepted as accurate and comprehensive.

ABOLITION

Antebellum Americans, unlike modern historians, had few doubts as to what slavery was like or what it meant. This was especially true of its most militant opponents, the abolitionists, and its most determined defenders, Southern slaveowners. How could Americans who shared a common cultural, religious, and political tradition have come to differ so radically on such a fundamental question as the ownership of one person by another? The answer may lie in the fact that both slavery and abolition were rooted in the same great developments that gave rise to the modern world. Slavery was a child of the Commercial Revolution, which began in the fourteenth century and extended into the eighteenth century. That revolution consisted of the emergence of a capitalist economy and long-range trade, and resulted in a demand for colonies to produce the commodities that fed this extensive commerce. Because the native population was sparse in most parts of the New World, large numbers of African slaves were imported to cultivate sugar, rice, tobacco, and other valuable crops.

The Commercial Revolution was also the basis for intellectual and cultural changes that led ultimately to the eighteenth-century Enlightenment. The political philosophy of that period revolved around the idea of natural law and the natural rights of man, defined by John Locke as life, liberty, and property. Inevitably many came to believe that there was an inherent conflict between slavery and natural rights, that the right to own property did not extend to property in human beings.

Religion also became a major source of antislavery sentiment, largely because it had to adjust to the new order of things. This was especially true of Calvinism, which, in reacting against the corruption and lack of spirituality in the Catholic church, had adopted an other-worldly theology that emphasized predestination (the inability of the sinner to win salvation by good works) and dourly expected the great majority of mankind to suffer everlasting torment in the hereafter. This depressing outlook could not indefinitely withstand the growing optimism that swept the Western world in the seventeenth and eighteenth centuries. When the wealth of America and the Orient began to invigorate Europe, the idea of progress was born. Heaven no longer held the only hope for a better life. Now the world seemed filled with promise, and not only for the privileged few as had been the case in the static and stratified society of the Middle Ages. Western man began to concentrate on the now instead of the hereafter.

It was therefore particularly necessary for Calvinism, which was strong in England and in the Northern colonies, to change if it was to compete with the new-found charms of this life. It had to become more worldly, to devote itself to benevolent undertakings here below. It came under growing pressure to open heaven's door to all men and women. Salvation would no longer be confined to a predestined minority, but would depend more and more on the individual's volition and deeds.

This can be seen as a democratization of religion. Just as America promised the average man access to economic and political opportunities, so it would offer an equal chance for salvation. The promise of life in America, this other Eden, seemed so bright that many believed the second coming of Christ must be near, and they decided to improve society in order to prepare for the Kingdom of God on earth. For such people reform became a wide road to salvation. It was the responsibility of the whole community, the whole country, for God held society accountable for the sins of every member. It was especially the responsibility of religious leaders, who were the moral stewards of society. So, by the nineteenth century, as religion was secularized, many reform movements were filled with religious zeal. They became battles between good and evil, sin and salvation. They became crusades, such as the crusade against slavery.

Beginning in the eighteenth century, conversion — an overwhelming conviction of salvation — was more and more a phenomenon of religious revivals. Revivals were in turn the main feature of a religious "awakening." There were two "Great Awakenings" before the Civil War, the first, lasting approximately from 1725 to 1750, centered in New England; the second (1795 to 1835) centered in the part of New York that was heavily colonized from New England. Both spread far beyond their original boundaries. The most striking figure of the second awakening was Charles Grandison Finney, perhaps the greatest evangelist in American history. During the 1820s, anxious sinners flocked to Finney's revivals by the tens of thousands. His doctrine was a far cry from the pure Calvinism of earlier days; all people, he said, have heaven within their reach. Sin was merely selfishness; holiness consisted of "disinterested benevolence." Conversion, salvation, meant repenting of the sin of selfishness and then setting out "with a determination to aim at being useful in the highest degree possible." The tidal wave of religious fervor whipped up by the Great Revival was channeled into reform, most especially into the abolition movement.

The supremely eloquent Theodore Dwight Weld and other young ministerial students who, like Weld, had assisted Finney and had mastered his techniques, led an abolition revival that swept through many Northern states. Just as Finney had called on the people to repent of the sin of selfishness, so his disciples called on them to renounce the sin of slavery. By the late 1830s the American Antislavery Society claimed over 1300 local chapters and 250,000 members. William Lloyd Garrison, a pioneer abolitionist and founder of the famous *Liberator,* was for a time part of this movement. However, he drifted away from the mainstream of the antislavery impulse, and although recently some scholars have reaffirmed his importance, his notoriety was greater than his influence.

The dramatic increase in popular support for abolition guaranteed that slavery would quickly become a political issue, which it did just as the revivals reached their peak. The elimination of slavery in the District of Columbia had for years been a primary target of abolitionists, and petitions on that and other aspects of slavery were regularly presented to Congress. As the number increased, the House of Representatives adopted a rule in 1836 to prevent consideration of the petitions. This so-called "Gag Rule" was resented by some Northern members, led by ex-president John Quincy Adams, as an attack by a cabal of slaveowners on the constitutional liberties of all Americans. Recognizing the value of the controversy as a propaganda vehicle, abolitionists organized a gigantic campaign and sent antislavery petitions to Washington by the ton. The Gag Rule fight continued through one Congress after another: not until 1844 did the House repeal the rule.

Meanwhile, slavery had become a political issue in other ways. The same year that the Gag Rule was passed, Texas won its independence from Mexico. Many antislavery people concluded that this was part of a dark plot by "the slaveocracy" to acquire more land for the sinful institution. Belief in sinister conspiracies has always been a feature of American political psychology, and before many years had passed increasing numbers of Northerners were convinced that the "slaveocrats" designed to extend slavery not only into the Southwest, but into the free states as well. Having in this way become politically invincible, they would proceed to subvert the Constitution and set themselves up as a ruling oligarchy. The events of the 1840s and 1850s would render this idea plausible to still more Northerners, swelling the ranks of the antislavery forces.

ECONOMICS

The conflict over slavery was compounded by deep-seated differences on economic and constitutional theory going back to the eighteenth century. Under the Articles of Confederation the central government could not levy taxes or regulate commerce. When the framers of the Constitution granted those powers to Congress, they made a fundamental change in the nature of the government, for men of that day understood clearly that political power followed the taxing power. Thus the Constitution allowed a transfer of power from the states to the Federal government proportional to the latter's exercise of its new authority. This disturbed the many Southerners who had an abiding distrust of any government outside of or superior to the states. In particular they were reluctant to surrender control over their commerce to a potentially hostile majority, since the South lived by exporting its agricultural commodities. Finally, they knew that slavery was rapidly dying out in the North, where its unpopularity increased as the number of slaves dwindled. Therefore Southern delegates at the Philadelphia Convention accepted the Constitution only after insisting on several concessions, such as outlawing an export tariff and bolstering the South's political strength by counting three of every five slaves when apportioning seats in the House of Representatives.

Hamilton's economic program and the Federalists' political behavior in the 1790s confirmed Southern misgivings about the new system. Even James Madison, sometimes called the Father of the Constitution, must have felt rather like Baron Frankenstein the morning after. In reaction to the Federalists' centralizing policies, he and Jefferson founded the states' rights school of politics, whose main object was to restore the influence of the states by keeping the Federal government weak. This was to be done by allowing the latter to use only those powers expressly delegated to it by the Constitution, and by preventing it from levying more taxes than were absolutely necessary. Thus the flow of political power toward the center would be reversed. The common theme running through all the varieties of the states' rights philosophy was that of a small, frugal, passive central government whose main function was to represent the states in their dealings with foreign nations.

This philosophy reflected the South's economic needs as well as its political beliefs. By the 1830s several issues had come to dominate American economic thought: tariff policy; Federal funding of roads, canals, and river and harbor projects (all known as "internal improvements"); Federal subsidies to private business; public land policy; and financial policy, that is, whether or not the Federal government should charter a central bank. For present purposes the bank may be ignored because it was more a party than a sectional question.

During most of the antebellum period, the main bone of contention was the tariff, the chief source of Federal revenue. The growth of Northern manufacturing during and after the War of 1812 created a demand for protection against competition from cheap foreign goods. The South, on the other hand, opposed a high tariff because it increased the planter's cost of living and cost of production, restricted foreign markets for Southern commodities, and, through high profits and inequitable Federal expenditures, transferred wealth from South to North. The South also opposed Federal subsidies for internal improvements and private business. Most of these funds would be spent in the North, and the additional demands on the treasury would necessitate raising the tariff. That was also a reason for resisting legislation that would give away the vast public lands: a reduction in land revenues would tend to drive up the tariff. Moreover, given the facts of geography and the North's large and relatively mobile population, free land would mean new states settled by Northerners and would create more political problems for the South. There were, of course, Southerners who dissented from prevailing attitudes, but they were always a decided minority.

Northern support for these policies was not as solid as Southern opposition; otherwise the South could not have fought even a delaying action. But Northerners agreed more than they differed, and as the effects of the revolution in transportation and industry were felt, disagreement diminished while impatience with the South intensified. That section came to be seen as the chief obstacle in the way of Northern progress and prosperity. Eventually this resentment could combine with the antislavery impulse to produce a new political movement aimed at expelling Southern influence from the government.

TERRITORIAL SLAVERY: SYMBOL AND SUBSTANCE

The existence of intersectional political parties greatly enhanced the likelihood of compromising sectional differences. In ordinary times party unity was essential to winning elections. Therefore during the 1830s and early 1840s the Whigs and Democrats, who counted on support in both North and South, strove to keep intraparty hostilities to a minimum. But as abolition attracted new recruits it became more difficult to keep the most explosive issue of all out of the political arena. Abolitionists came to hold the balance of power in certain key states such as New York and Ohio, and to exert influence all out of proportion to their numbers by forcing both parties to bid for their support. Northern politicians encountered growing difficulty in justifying their alliance with Southerners when the latter clamored for the Gag Rule or Texas annexation.

The depression that followed the Panic of 1837 undermined support for President Martin Van Buren, leader of the Northeastern Democrats, and helped to prevent his reelection in 1840. His defeat caused the party's center of balance to move in a southerly direction. The party rejected Van Buren in 1844 and nominated a Southerner, James K. Polk of Tennessee. The Van Buren faction, angered and humiliated by their leader's repudiation, feared that they had lost their easy access to offices and governmental patronage. The continued demands of some Southern Democrats for the immediate annexation of Texas aggravated their already serious problems with an increasingly antislavery constituency. Here, then, was one crack in the foundation of the party, the disaffection of the Northeastern Democrats, that would contribute powerfully to the party's final division along sectional lines.

Events following the election of 1844 placed additional strains on party loyalty. Polk's defeat of Henry Clay weakened the Whigs and led to the abandonment of their remaining political principles. On the Democratic side, the Polk administration soon delivered a series of hammer blows to party unity. Although he ran on a platform proclaiming the "reoccupation" of Oregon, Polk surrendered claims to almost half of that territory. Democrats in the Old Northwest felt betrayed. Almost simultaneously Polk's provocative policy on the Texas frontier ignited a war with Mexico that many Northerners saw as part of the slaveocracy's plot to augment Southern power.

The worst was yet to come. A major objective of Polk's administration was a reduced tariff, aimed at eventual free trade with England, a better market for cotton and other commodities, and lower costs for the planter and farmer. The tariff passed in the summer of 1846 attracted numerous Northwestern supporters, who would later claim that they had thereby concluded a bargain with the South: votes for a low tariff in exchange for generous appropriations for internal improvements and support for cheap or even free public lands. But after voting for the tariff, they saw Polk veto the internal improvements bill and Southern congressman defeat the land bill. At the same time, tariff reduction had alienated protectionists throughout the North. More and more Northerners drew what seemed to them an obvious conclusion. The repudiation of Van Buren, Texas annexation, Oregon's partition, the Mexican War, a low tariff, no internal improvements, no cheap land — clearly, Southern policies meant the sacrifice of Northern political, territorial, and economic ambitions. Said the editor of a Chicago paper:

> The North can and will no longer be hoodwinked. If no measures for protection and improvement of anything North or West are to be suffered by our Southern masters, if we are to be downtrodden, and all our cherished interests crushed by them, a signal revolution will inevitably ensue. The same spirit and energy that forced emancipation for the whole country from Great Britain will throw off the Southern yoke. The North and West will look to and take care of their own interests henceforth. They will . . . see . . . that the power to oppress shall not again be entrusted to men who have shown themselves to be slaveholders, but not Americans. . . . The fiat has gone forth — Southern rule is at an end. (From A. O. Craven, *Edmund Ruffin, Southerner.*)

In this gloomy setting the issue of territorial slavery took the center of the stage. The connection between extending slavery and Southern power seemed obvious. For example, the votes of recently admitted Texas provided the margin necessary to pass the Tariff of 1846 in the Senate. Therefore there should be no more slave territory, no more slave states. On August 8, 1846, Representative David Wilmot of Pennsylvania attached to an appropriations bill his famous amendment to exclude slavery from any soil acquired from Mexico.

Party lines disappeared; Southerners of all political persuasions united to repel this attempt to reduce further their already declining strength. The attack on slavery as an institution unworthy of national protection frightened them. The Northern majority in the House passed Wilmot's Proviso; the Senate, more conservative and still equally divided between the sections, did not. In this way the intractable problem of territorial slavery was injected into national politics, never to be entirely removed until it gave way to the even graver crisis of disunion. Its significance can be understood only in the context of the events just sketched, which had illuminated so vividly the sharp clash of interests between North and South. Each section feared subjugation by the other. The South saw itself as the weaker party, which it was; the North believed that the South, already wielding disproportionate influence, was determined to weight the balance of power in its favor. By the late 1840s the idea of a Slave Power conspiracy had gained wider credence, and the conspiracy's primary objective appeared to be the extension of slavery.

The South, on the other hand, regarded the right to take slaves into the territories as a test. The triumph of exclusion would mean that the North was no longer willing to concede to the South equality within the Union, which was an unwritten yet fundamental part of the original constitutional bargain of 1787. Now weaker in numbers, the South could rely only on strict interpretation of the Constitution to safeguard its interests. If slaveowners were denied the right to take their property into the common territories, then obviously the Constitution was no longer to be relied on for protection. The day might not be far distant when the South would be ground down by superior power.

Slavery, in short, was not only an issue in itself, it had also become the symbol of all differences between the sections; that is why it became such a powerful political force. Many Northerners saw it as a moral question, as right versus wrong. By their nature, moral questions are not subject to compromise. Therefore it became evermore difficult for the political process to get past that issue and deal with the very important economic and political matters that were normally amenable to negotiation, and the settlement of which would have substantially reduced the importance of the slavery controversy. The essence of the Union from its foundation had been compromise; without compromise the Union was in danger.

The Mexican War ended early in 1848. The cession of California and the Southwest to the United States, plus the impending presidential election, kept Wilmot's Proviso very much alive. The Democratic platform took no position on territorial slavery, al-

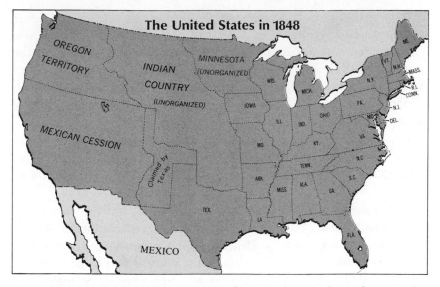

The United States in 1848

OREGON TERRITORY

MINNESOTA (UNORGANIZED)

INDIAN COUNTRY (UNORGANIZED)

MEXICAN CESSION

Claimed by Texas

MEXICO

ME. VT. N.H. MASS. R.I. CONN. N.Y. N.J. PA. DEL. MD. VA. N.C. S.C. GA. FLA. ALA. MISS. LA. TEX. ARK. TENN. KY. MO. ILL. IND. OHIO MICH. WIS. IOWA

though its nominee, Lewis Cass of Michigan, endorsed "popular sovereignty." This expedient would allow the settlers to decide local questions, including slavery, without interference from Congress, and for a few years this middle course was acceptable to many Democrats from both sections. The Whigs finessed the issue by ignoring it and nominating Zachary Taylor, a Louisiana planter and Jackson-type military hero. In the South the Whigs stressed Taylor's Southern identity, and in the North they emphasized his alleged willingness (which Taylor neither affirmed nor denied) to accept the Wilmot Proviso.

There was a party that faced the territorial question squarely: the new Free Soil party, built around the embittered Van Buren faction of the New York Democracy and the old Liberty party. The Free Soilers met first at Utica and then at Buffalo, bracketing the district of the Finney revivals. They sang hymns and nominated Van Buren. Their platform called for resisting the aggressions of the Slave Power and excluding slavery from the territories. It also dealt with more mundane matters: free Federal land, Federal funding of internal improvements and, by clear implication, a higher tariff. Hardheaded economic objectives were now coupled with the moral issue of slavery. Here began the forging of a wholly Northern party that would no longer seek to compromise sectional differences.

The Free Soil ticket attracted about 10 percent of the popular vote in 1848; it almost certainly threw New York to Taylor, and with New York went the presidency. For the first time a purely Northern, anti-Southern party had apparently tipped the scales in a presidential election.

THE COMPROMISE OF 1850

The election of 1848 was a clear warning that the two major parties probably could not survive a protracted conflict over slavery. Many believed that the Union could not survive the destruction of intersectional parties. Consequently, slavery had to be banished from national politics if the Union was to be saved. At least three matters required prompt attention: the territories, extradition of slaves who escaped to the North, and the status of slavery in the District of Columbia, which had been a prime concern of the great petition campaign of the 1830s.

The territorial puzzle was a complex one. In 1787 the Confederation Congress had barred slavery from the Old Northwest, and in the Missouri Compromise of 1820 the Federal Congress had done the same for the Louisiana Purchase north of 36° 30'. Now the antislavery faction (including numerous Northern Democrats and Whigs as well as Free Soilers) wished to complete the process and ban slavery from the Mexican Cession. On the other hand, many moderates from both sections favored some form of popular sovereignty. A significant number of Southerners, led by Calhoun, maintained that Congress could not constitutionally outlaw slavery and, if necessary, was duty-bound to protect the property rights of slaveowners in the territories. For the most part this group was willing to compromise by extending the Missouri Compromise line to the Pacific.

Congress attempted to deal with the Mexican Cession while the presidential campaign was in progress. In July the Senate voted to create territorial governments for California and New Mexico, which then embraced all of the Mexican Cession, denying them authority to establish or forbid slavery; questions on that subject could be appealed to the Supreme Court. A territory of Oregon would likewise be created, excluding slavery indirectly by applying to Oregon the provisions of the Northwest Ordinance and by validating antislavery laws already passed by the Oregonians' extralegal squatter government. The Senate plan was defeated in the House mainly by Northern votes, although the division was as much partisan as sectional, with Whigs in opposition. Oregon was finally organized without slavery, but California and New Mexico remained in limbo.

Senator Stephen A. Douglas tried again after Congress reconvened in December. He proposed to admit the entire Mexican Cession as the state of California, reserving the right to create additional states from the eastern portion. In this way the Illinois Democrat hoped to circumvent the difficult constitutional question. Later he offered an alternative plan to admit California proper, saying nothing about New Mexico. Neither this nor any other project advanced during the 1848-1849 session commanded majority support. In the meantime Calhoun and the Southern Democrats published an address detailing the aggressive behavior of the antislavery forces and warning their constituents that they must meet these attacks firmly. Southern Whigs refused to sign the address. They feared absorption into the opposition party, disliked antagonizing the incoming Whig president, who opposed Calhoun's views, and hoped that when sectional interests were at stake, Taylor would be loyal to his heritage.

Many soon wished they had signed, because in his brief and noncommittal inaugural address Taylor said nothing about the territories. Instead, he secretly instructed military officers in New Mexico and California to assist the settlers in forming state governments, thus skipping the territorial stage. Californians had completed this work by the time Congress met in December 1849, and the New Mexicans followed suit a few months later. When Congress got wind of these activities, Taylor explained that his strategy would relieve Congress from the necessity of dealing with the territorial question. Furthermore, Texas and New Mexico were engaged in a potentially explosive boundary dispute, and if New

Mexico were a state, the Supreme Court would have jurisdiction over the case.

Taylor's program was intolerable to many Southerners, who believed it was indistinguishable from the Wilmot Proviso. California had already voted against slavery; if admitted immediately as a state, the sectional balance in the Senate would shift permanently in favor of the North. Calhoun's warning of a year ago now seemed distressingly believable. The possibility of secession could no longer be lightly dismissed. A convention of Southern states, inspired by Calhoun and summoned by Mississippi, was scheduled to meet at Nashville in June. Events had begun to take on a momentum of their own that, if not somehow deflected, would lead inexorably to national disaster.

At this grim juncture of affairs, Henry Clay, once more in the Senate, stepped forward to resume his accustomed role as peacemaker. His solution was all-inclusive, as he explained to the Senate early in February 1850. California would be admitted immediately as a free state. Its inhabitants had decided against slavery anyway, so the South would lose nothing. New Mexico and Deseret (Utah), comprising the rest of the Mexican Cession, would be organized as territories without forbidding slavery. The North would be making no concession here, because slavery was barred by the environment. The Texas-New Mexico boundary dispute would be equitably resolved by having Texas surrender its claims in exchange for Federal assumption of the Texas Republic's debt. There would be a new, effective fugitive slave law, since the extradition of runaways was a plain constitutional duty. The slave trade would be abolished in the District of Columbia, and no vital Southern interest would be injured thereby. Finally, Congress would renounce any intention to interfere with the interstate slave trade, which abolitionists had long wished to outlaw as one way of undermining slavery in the upper South. This would be a concession to the South. A month later the other Whig patriarch, Daniel Webster, endorsed Clay's plan in his famous "Seventh of March" speech, showing that he could rise above principle in the interests of national harmony. The Massachusetts senator had long been a towering political landmark, and his speech naturally received wide attention. Even if Webster did not change any votes on the spot, his conciliatory attitude certainly allayed Southern fears to some degree and so advanced the cause of compromise.

Three days before Webster's address, a fatally ill Calhoun had offered his valedictory to the nation in a speech read by a colleague. Calhoun scornfully rejected Taylor's Trojan horse of California statehood and dismissed Clay's resolutions as mere symptomatic treatment. Nor did he believe in the efficacy of impassioned patriotic rhetoric. "The cry of 'Union, union, the glorious union!' can no more prevent disunion than the cry of 'Health, health, glorious health!' on the part of the physician can save a patient lying dangerously ill. . . . " He addressed his analysis to the causes, not the symptoms of the disease. The equality of political power once enjoyed by the South had been overturned by discriminatory economic policies and by excluding the South from most of the public domain. Simultaneously the growing Northern majority had begun to construe the Constitution so as to magnify Federal power and belittle states' rights, the ultimate safeguard for the Southern minority. For years the North had denounced the South — its institutions, morals, and way of life; Northern hostility appeared to intensify as Southern strength diminished. Little wonder, said Calhoun, that his section had begun to ask if it could remain much longer in the union with safety and honor. If disunion was to be averted, the North must cease its attacks and agree to a constitutional amendment that enabled the South to protect itself from the Northern majority.

The Great Triumvirate was followed by a prominent antislavery Whig from New York, William H. Seward. He was one of a new breed of politicians to whom compromise on the slavery question was contemptible, men who would in a few years construct a sectional anti-Southern party that would win the presidency in 1860. Seward denounced any compromise of the territorial question. Not only did the Constitution bar the extension of slavery, he said, but a law higher than the Constitution had already banned it from that vast area. Moreover, the abolition of slavery everywhere was both inevitable and imminent. Nor could the South escape its fate by seceding, because the perpetuity of the Union had been ordained by the laws of nature. Seward, in effect, told the South that his section, representing an aggressive industrial and commercial capitalism, was the wave of the future, and that the South's archaic society was doomed to early extinction.

Seward was right, of course, and there is perhaps no more tragic event in all of American history than the failure of the South to accept the inevitability of adjusting to the main currents of the modern world. Had the South made those changes gradually and voluntarily, much that was valuable in the Southern tradition might have been saved; instead, everything was swept away by the withering blast of war. However, before condemning antebellum Southerners as stupid or blindly stubborn, it may be well to point out that the situation of the United States in the late twentieth century is not unlike that of the South in the 1850s: a minority defending a social and economic system that is supported by a dwindling portion of the human race.

In Congress during the winter of 1849-1850 tempers were higher than ever before. The House, where a handful of Free Soilers held the balance of power between Democrats and Whigs, had taken three weeks and 62 ballots to choose a speaker, to say nothing of protracted contests over minor offices down to and including the doorkeeper. Extremist opinion challenged the soothing influences of Clay and Webster, and although Calhoun died at the end of March, his doctrinaire spirit still animated his disciples. With Seward at his elbow, Taylor stubbornly held to his original plan, while the impending convention at Nashville was a continual reminder that the South might well unite to oppose the President. The scattered population of New Mexico had drawn up a free-state constitution and thus won Northern support in their boundary quarrel with Texas. Southerners, for the same reason, sided with Texas. An armed collision there involving volunteers from other states seemed a real possibility. In Congress several of Clay's proposals were combined into one "Omnibus Bill," thereby uniting the opposition from both sections. All things considered, the prospects for compromise were indeed bleak.

Then early in June the tide began to turn. The proceedings of the Nashville Convention showed that the South was not yet as united or as militant as many had feared. Only nine states sent delegates, and they were willing to accept as minimum terms extension of the 36° 30' line to the Pacific. The next month the most formidable obstacle to compromise was eliminated when President Taylor died suddenly. Taylor's successor, Millard Fillmore, belonged to the conservative branch of the New York Whigs and was personally hostile to Seward. The new president used all the prestige and patronage at his command to promote the compromise. The Omnibus Bill was defeated, but this was the necessary prelude to passing the compromise measures separately, a tactic that secured the votes of either Northern or Southern extremists, depending on which bill was pending. These, added to the votes of the procompromise moderates, made a majority for every measure. When Clay left Washington for a rest late in July, Stephen A. Douglas became field general for the compromise and did more than any other member of Congress to convert resolutions into laws.

Pressure by businessmen alarmed at the threat of disunion probably changed some votes. Others may have been secured by promises of railroad land grants or higher tariffs. The adjustment of the Texas-New Mexico imbroglio was partly the work of speculators who had bought up Texas Republic bonds at 25 cents on the dollar. Their lobbyists swarmed over the floor of Congress with arguments that some might have found hard to resist.

By September 17 it was all over. California had been admitted as a free state. The territories of New Mexico and Utah had been created without the Wilmot Proviso and with the promise that when the time came, they would be admitted as states with or without slavery. The law was ambiguously phrased, but seemed to mean that the territorial legislatures could either permit or prohibit slavery. Cases involving slavery could be appealed directly to the Supreme Court. Texas receded to the east in exchange for a promise of Federal assumption of $10 million of its debt. The slave trade was abolished legally if not actually in the District of Columbia.

The compromise passed, but the outcome might easily have been quite different. Its defeat would almost certainly have been followed by secession; many saw that. What they did not see was that postponement of disunion was fatal to the dream of Southern independence. Northern conquest of the South in the early 1850s probably would have been impossible. By the early 1860s that was no longer true.

Southern reaction to the compromise ranged from the diehard

disunionism of the fire-eaters to a grudging if relieved acquiescence by the majority. The latter made clear their intention to hold the North to both the letter and the spirit of every measure. Acceptance of compromise, however qualified, brought with it a strong conservative reaction throughout the South. The unknown perils of secession had been averted. The cotton crop was good, prices were the highest in a decade, and prosperity bred complacency. The South had bought a few years of peace at a price yet to be disclosed. The compromise was accepted more readily in the North, which had not felt as threatened or as alarmed as the South. There also prosperity played its usual role as a moderating influence, and the business community strongly endorsed the compromise as a permanent settlement. Approval was not universal; abolitionists and free soilers were irreconcilable. Even among those who acquiesced there was not so much enthusiasm as a willingness to let sleeping dogs lie.

The apparent success of the compromise should not obscure a very ominous development — that is, the serious internal damage suffered by the two major political parties. During the preceding four years, sectional allegiance had repeatedly shattered long-standing party loyalties. Although the ties of party interest reasserted themselves when the crisis was over, the American political community carried a heavy burden of personal enmity and suspicion that, when added to conflicting interests in the nation at large, would finally destroy intersectional parties. Calhoun had been right; Clay's medicine treated only the symptoms, not the disease.

Chapter II

The Compromise Breached

KNOW-NOTHINGS, JINGOES, AND UNCLE TOM

Both major parties sought to banish the slavery issue after 1850. Politicians long habituated to that heady wine sought frantically for a substitute, and some embraced strange and unattractive causes. Heavy immigration in the 1840s had caused apprehension and resentment among native Americans, especially in the Northeast. A majority of these newcomers were Catholics, and in those states where Calvinist churches were strongest, hatred of Rome rivaled repugnance for slavery. Antiforeign sentiment was institutionalized in various organizations, such as the "Supreme Order of the Star Spangled Banner." Nativism had already affected elections in pivotal states such as New York and Pennsylvania. Now in the 1850s it emerged as a full-fledged party, the American party, better known as the Know-Nothings, and would enter the presidential contest in 1856. The Know-Nothings also attracted voters not especially interested in nativism who were looking for a political home. Most of these recruits were formerly Whigs, refugees from a party that was disintegrating rapidly after the deaths of Clay and Webster in 1852. The American party disappeared after 1856, having been destroyed by the force of sectionalism. Then Northern Know-Nothings joined the new Republican party, which came to be geographically mottled with a selective nativism favoring Protestant immigrants, mainly Germans and Scandinavians, but spurning Catholics, especially the Irish.

Another phenomenon of the 1850s was the Young America movement, whose devotees specialized in a tubthumping jingoistic liberalism. They whooped it up for unlikely causes such as Hungarian nationalism and, in fact, for the liberation of all the peoples behind what might be called the "Hapsburg Curtain," to say nothing of their demands to annex Ireland and Sicily, and their grandiose dreams of expansion in the Western Hemisphere. Louis Kossuth, leader of the unsuccessful Hungarian revolution of 1848, was welcomed to the United States with extraordinary enthusiasm; other Hungarian rebels were offered asylum, such as their descendants would be in 1956. The Young Americans were Democrats, and their program was to some extent a response to the Whiggish Know-Nothings.

These exotic diversions formed a crust beneath which the fires of sectionalism smouldered and occasionally broke forth. Next to the territorial laws the most conspicuous part of the 1850 settlement was the Fugitive Slave Act, which is an excellent example of the illusory (and elusive) character of political issues associated with slavery. To begin with, very few slaves escaped into the free states, although some Southerners believed the number was large. The census of 1860 reported 803 runaway slaves out of a slave population of nearly 4 million. Many were quickly recaptured, others melted into the large free black population in the South, and some voluntarily returned to their masters. Even allowing for twice the number of runaways reported by the census, only a few slaves could have reached the North. The relative and absolute growth of the free black population in the North and in Canada points to the same conclusion, as does research into the number of fugitives apprehended during the 1850s.

The law's notoriety was not based on hordes of fugitives or numerous recaptures, but on the propaganda efforts of abolitionists who saw enormous potentialities in the issue. Properly publicized, they contended, even a few attempts to drag helpless blacks into bondage would be worth more than tons of tracts and petitions. As one of them said, "If Ohio is ever abolitionized, it will be by the fugitive slaves from Kentucky; their flight through the State, is the best lecture. . . . "

Although fugitive slave cases no doubt stirred the hearts of anti-slavery Northerners, hostility to the law, especially in the early 1850s, should not be exaggerated. The congressional debates in 1850 were quite tame, and had it wished the Northern majority in Congress could have defeated the bill. Neither in 1856 nor in 1860 did the Republican platform call for its repeal. Abraham Lincoln, in fact, was painfully anxious that it not be made an issue in 1860. In the early 1850s opposition came mainly from abolitionist and free soil strongholds, and by the summer of 1851 even this agitation had subsided. Objection to the law revived when the Missouri Compromise was repealed in 1854, yet it was most intense in those states farthest from the South and least likely to see any fugitives. The famed personal liberty laws enacted by some states were usually intended to prevent kidnapping, not to nullify the act of 1850. All these facts suggest that the issue was largely symbolic and that it was used effectively for political purposes.

The extradition of runaways was even more of a symbolic issue in the South. The Constitution guaranteed the right of recapture; much of the North seemed to be flouting this requirement. It was argued that concession on a single point, no matter how insignificant, would jeopardize the immediate substantive issue and the whole constitutional structure on which the South depended for protection. Even though few slaves successfully escaped to the North, Southerners were convinced that the right of recapture had to be vindicated, just as the right to hold slaves in the territories had to be upheld even though few slaveowners contemplated going there. Demand for a stringent law was greater in the Deep South, from which few slaves escaped, than in the border states, which suffered most of the loss, indicating that pecuniary considerations were not important. Of course, should Northern hostility ever succeed in seriously undermining the security of property in slaves, the South stood to suffer enormous material loss. Insecurity would drive down the price of slaves; that, in turn, would depress all property values. Needless to say, the South would leave the Union before that could happen.

The Fugitive Slave Act of 1850 provided for the appointment of commissioners to enforce the law, allowed them to require the assistance of local citizens, prescribed fine and imprisonment for anyone helping or attempting to rescue a runaway, excluded as evidence the alleged fugitive's testimony, did not provide for a jury trial, and authorized the commissioners to collect a $10 fee for each prisoner remanded to a claimant and $5 for each one released. The law's critics objected most strenuously to the lack of a jury trial and the exclusion of the prisoner's testimony, claiming that the door had been opened to the kidnapping of free blacks. Extravagant fears of incursions by Southern man-stealers were clearly farfetched. With 250,000 free blacks in the slave states, it is difficult to see why kidnappers would have gone to the trouble and expense of invading the North to conduct their nefarious business.

Southerners replied to the demand for a jury trial by arguing that the Founding Fathers saw the rendition of fugitives essentially as an extradition proceeding. Both subjects were dealt with in the same article and section of the Constitution (IV, 2), and both were included in the Federal act of February 12, 1793, which is almost invariably identified only as the first fugitive slave act. The status of the alleged slave, the argument continued, like that of the alleged criminal, was determined according to the laws of the state from which the slave had fled. As for the exclusion of the fugitive's testimony, that was entirely consistent with the practice in the South and in several Northern states that prohibited Negro testimony in cases to which whites were a party. For that matter, defendants in criminal cases had no right to testify in their own defense either in Federal courts or state courts. Charges that the fee differential was a bribe to find for the claimant were answered by citing the additional paperwork involved in such cases, and by pointing out that $5 was a sum altogether too paltry to serve as a bribe.

Conflict between Wisconsin's personal liberty law and the 1850 act led to a Supreme Court decision (*Ableman* v. *Booth,* 1859) upholding the constitutionality of the Federal law. But to men and women who believed slavery was wrong, law and logic were beside the point. No amount of constitution-studded argumentation could justify delivering the pathetic fugitive into the hands of the slave-catcher. And by denying the runaway a jury trial and the right to testify on his own behalf, the Fugitive Slave Act became yet another symbol of the Slave Power's continuing assault on civil liberties and free government. It was, moreover, the primary inspiration for the most famous novel of the Civil War era, *Uncle Tom's Cabin,* by Harriet Beecher Stowe.

Mrs. Stowe's fundamental concern was morals, not slavery. She did not blame the South alone for slavery; instead, she endeavored to show that the whole nation was at fault, and that individual slaveowners, however humane, could not overcome the inherent cruelty of the system. Such subtleties were lost on the average reader. This was a gullible and unsophisticated age when, as Barnum said, "a sucker was born every minute." Sympathetic Northerners who read the story came away with one supreme picture indelibly imprinted on their memories: the death of Uncle Tom at the hands of the archvillain, Simon Legree. Here was a melodramatic and, to many of that generation, intensely believable portrayal of the South and slavery. Their perceptions sharpened by 30 years of pamphlets, tracts, revivals, and speeches, Northerners at last saw the Slave Power personified. Now they had what every people must have before it can fight a war with gusto, an image of the enemy. A familiar anecdote has President Lincoln saying, when he met Mrs. Stowe, "So here is the little lady who made this big war!" She has been compared to Thomas Paine, who helped to prepare the mind of the Revolutionary generation for the war with England. Actually, Mrs. Stowe's generation was already prepared, as the extraordinary popularity of her novel proves. She merely helped to stimulate and shape existing emotions: indignation in the North, resentment in the South.

THE SECTIONAL DRIFT

The 1850s witnessed economic and demographic trends far more dangerous to the union than the Fugitive Slave Act or *Uncle Tom's Cabin.* Political alliances, whether domestic or international, are based on what is seen as a community of cultural ideals and economic interests. For many years Southerners had regarded the Old Northwest as their natural ally. As early as the 1780s Thomas Jefferson promoted the idea of close commercial ties with that section as the basis for an agrarian alliance, a concept later championed by John C. Calhoun. During much of the antebellum period, the South was the major purchaser of Northwestern crops and, via the Mississippi, the main avenue to overseas markets. Many Southerners participated in the early settlement of Illinois, Indiana, and Ohio.

Then came the construction of the Erie Canal in the 1820s, initiating a shift in the Northwest's orientation that accelerated rapidly with the completion of direct rail connections to the Northeast in the 1850s. During that decade an ever larger percentage of Northwestern crops found markets in the Northeast or through its ports. Simultaneously the economy of the Northwest was becoming more diversified, more like that of the Northeast. The same was true of its people. The tide of immigration from New England and the middle states, reinforced by Germans in large numbers, reduced the settlers of Southern origin to a shrinking fraction of the population and widened the cultural and ideological gap between the Northwest and the South. Even though the South still had many friends there, the trend was unmistakable; a political realignment was developing that would deprive the South of at least some of its Northern allies.

As the Northern sections drew closer together, the South's sense of alienation and resentment grew keener. Attempts were made in the 1850s to end what many saw as a colonial dependence on the North, develop direct trade with Europe, cut out the expensive Northern middleman, encourage manufacturing, and put the South on the road to economic self-sufficiency. Some slight progress was made in manufacturing; otherwise little was accomplished. Resources, expertise, and a sense of urgency all were insufficient to bring about such a sweeping change in the South's commercial relationships.

Some Southerners, resenting the incessant criticism that poured across the Mason-Dixon line, also wished to sever social and cultural ties with the North. Already dissension over slavery had split the Methodists and Baptists in the 1840s and would do likewise to the Presbyterians in 1857. Why not complete the process? Stop visiting summer resorts such as Saratoga; patronize instead the mountain springs of Virginia. Stop sending young men to Yankee colleges where they were exposed to abolitionism, free-thinking, and other heresies. Educate them at home; if necessary, build Southern universities to keep alive the pure flame of truth, an idea that eventually led to the founding of the University of the South at Sewanee, Tennessee. Stop buying textbooks written and printed in the North; let Southerners write their own, imbued with their own moral and constitutional principles. These efforts had little success, and the section remained culturally dependent on the North. When the South's psychological declaration of independence did finally come, it resulted from the pressure of direful events instead of from a deliberate choice.

In 1852 the Democratic party nominated Franklin Pierce of New Hampshire, one of those men whose enemies called them "dough-faces," that is, Northerners who acted like Southerners politically. The platform pledged allegiance to the Compromise of 1850; otherwise it merely restated the party's customary dogmas about a small, frugal, and inactive central government. Meanwhile the Whig party continued its swift decline. Clay was dying of tuberculosis; his death in July preceded by only a few months that of an embittered Daniel Webster, who went to his grave believing he had been rejected by his own people. The Whigs turned to the strategy that had given them their only presidential successes, the nomination of a military hero. Unfortunately for them, General Winfield Scott did not have the frontier glamor of a Harrison or a Taylor, and they were badly divided by the slavery question and weakened by the nativist infestation. Southern members correctly regarded Scott's candidacy as a stalking-horse for antislavery forces and began to drift out of the party.

The Free Soil faction ran its second and last race in 1852, nominating John P. Hale of New Hampshire and adopting the Wilmot Proviso as its platform. Compromise had made the slavery issue temporarily less appealing. Some prominent Free Soilers of 1848, including Martin Van Buren himself, returned to the Democratic fold — for the moment, at least. Hale received little more than half the votes polled by Van Buren four years earlier. Pierce won handily in the electoral college, but attracted not quite 51 percent of the popular vote. The protection of that slender majority depended on the continued disarray of the opposition, which in turn depended largely on keeping slavery out of national politics.

SLAVERY AND MANIFEST DESTINY

The expansionist "Young Americans" saw the election of Pierce as a triumph for their principles, and they were pleased when the new president immediately announced that he was not intimidated by the possibility of further territorial acquisitions. Although he did not openly avow it, Pierce had for his main foreign policy objective the purchase or at least the liberation of Cuba, one of the last remnants of Spain's once mighty New World empire. In April 1854 Secretary of State William L. Marcy directed the American minister to Madrid, Pierre Soulé, to offer $130 million for Cuba, and if the offer were rejected, to seek to "detach" the island from Spain. He suggested a conference between Soulé, James Buchanan, minister to Great Britain, and John Y. Mason, minister to France. They met first at Ostend, then moved to Aix-la-Chappelle because of the unwelcome publicity they were receiving. There they composed a secret dispatch to the State Department advising that if Spain refused to sell Cuba, and if Cuba became a threat to the internal peace or existence of the United States, it should be wrested from Spain. The acquisition of Cuba would improve relations with Spain, promote a more prosperous commerce, facilitate the suppression of the African slave trade, protect the main route to the Pacific Ocean by way of Central America, and forestall the "Africanization" of Cuba, thus preventing it from becoming another "St. Domingo, with all its attendant horrors to the white race" and threats "to our neighboring shores."

This secret dispatch was delivered to Washington by special messenger in November 1854. The Pierce administration rejected its advice for several reasons; one was the fall election losses caused by the Kansas-Nebraska act, to be discussed later. Despite the dispatch's confidentiality, distorted rumors seeped into the newspapers hinting of an ultimatum to Spain: sell Cuba or we will take it by force. Congress asked to see the dispatch. Marcy supplied it and related correspondence, although he deleted his remarks about detaching Cuba from Spain. The wrath of the antiadministration forces, now taking shape as the Republican party, was heaped on what they called the "Ostend Manifesto." They saw the insatiable Slave Power conspirators once again after land to be exploited by slave labor and more slave states to bolster their already formidable political influence. Filibustering forays against Cuba and Central America, the Gadsden Purchase, and renewed efforts to buy Cuba in 1859 were later represented as parts of the same plot. Like domestic affairs, the foreign policy of the 1850s was refracted through the prism of antislavery politics; the evil purpose of the slaveocracy was the all-sufficient explanation for what was done or attempted.

The expansionism of the 1850s, far from being a slaveholder's conspiracy, was actually an extension of what had been going on for generations and would continue for generations to come. The colonials had more than once invaded New France. At the end of the Seven Years' War, Benjamin Franklin urged the British to take Canada and expatiated on the advantages of having Mexico and Cuba. During and after the Revolution, Americans regarded the annexation of Canada as being merely a matter of time. As for Cuba, Jefferson, Madison, Gallatin, John Quincy Adams (who announced that the whole of North America rightfully belonged to the United States), Clay, Polk, Douglas, and others were anxious to bring that island within the American orbit. Fear of foreign intentions figured prominently in American designs on Cuba, as it had in the acquisition of the Louisiana Territory, Texas, and the Pacific coast. The possession of California and part of Oregon gave new strategic and commercial significance to a possible interocean canal. For this and other reasons American hegemony in Central America and the West Indies was regarded as natural and inevitable. Hegemony was finally achieved, not, however, in the 1850s when the South was allegedly directing the nation's diplomacy, but 40 years later when the Slave Power was just a bad memory. The process began in 1898 under a Republican president from Ohio, and within a decade or so the United States presided over a network of island possessions, leaseholds, naval bases, protectorates, and client states that stretched from Panama to Puerto Rico.

The point is that expansionism was not a sectional phenomenon in the 1850s. The slavery question entered the picture because it served as a rallying cry for rival political organizations. The question was not whether or not to expand, but instead which party or section would reap the profits and the patronage, the commercial and political benefits. Politicians who were out of power naturally did not yearn to see their competitors preside over the creation of this glittering empire.

THE BIRTH OF THE REPUBLICAN PARTY

When Pierce was inaugurated, four states bordered the west bank of the Mississippi: Louisiana, admitted in 1812, Missouri (1821), Arkansas (1836), and Iowa (1846). Population pressure was greatest in the latitude of Missouri and Iowa. West of those states lay an area called Nebraska or the Platte, extending from the Canadian frontier to what is now the northern border of Oklahoma. It had no formal government; most of its inhabitants were Indians. Federal authority consisted of a few military posts and Indian agents.

Interest in Nebraska grew steadily in the 1840s and early 1850s. There was the usual frontier desire to cultivate virgin soil and to profit from the business and political opportunities offered by a newly opened territory. And after the acquisition of California and Oregon, with their deep-water ports, many Americans began to dream of untold wealth to be gained by tapping the fabled markets of the Far East. Connect the Atlantic and Pacific by railroad and the United States would become a great commercial thoroughfare, the corridor through which all trade between Europe and Asia would pass. It would become the short route to the Indies, fulfilling Columbus's dream. America would be the middleman for the world, which, as Seward and others predicted, it would make over in its own image. There would be a new golden age, a Pax Americana to rival the Pax Romana of antiquity, and it would all be exceedingly profitable.

Where would this railroad, this new "Enterprise of the Indies," be built? Would its eastern terminus be in the North or in the South? The Southern route had a distinct edge. It presented fewer engineering problems, especially after the Gadsden Purchase of 1853. More important, it would run entirely through states or organized territory (Louisiana, Texas, New Mexico Territory, California), areas with populations to profit from, support, and protect the railroad, with land that was open to settlement. Northwesterners feared that the Pierce administration, influenced by formidable Southerners such as Secretary of War Jefferson Davis, would adopt the Southern route. The best way to enhance the claims of a Northern route would be to provide a territorial government for Nebraska, opening it for settlement and making possible Federal land grants to help finance the railroad. This immediately raised the question of slavery.

Nebraska lay north of the line of 36° 30′, from which slavery had been barred by the Missouri Compromise of 1820. Some Southerners had always stigmatized that compromise as an unwise concurrence in the exercise of a power not delegated to the Federal government. There were now in Congress powerful Southerners, still loyal to the dead Calhoun, who thought to restore their section's equality of rights in the territories by repealing the 1820 prohibition. They also wished to use the question as a test of party loyalty. Pierce had tried to heal the Democracy's wounds by bestowing favors on erstwhile Free Soilers who claimed to be good Democrats in 1852. Now they could prove their fidelity by supporting the application to Nebraska of the principle of congressional noninterference adopted in 1850.

Among Northern Democrats, the Nebraska question was of particular importance to Stephen A. Douglas of Illinois. He had worked for the organization of Nebraska ever since coming to Congress in 1843. It was a matter affecting his own political career and the future of the Democracy in his section. It was the essential prelude to the coming of age of the great American heartland, which was fated, said Douglas, to rule the national destiny. As far as slavery was concerned, Douglas told a correspondent late in 1853, all would "be willing to sanction and affirm the principle established by the compromise measures of 1850." Indeed, his only alternative would have been to espouse the doctrine of exclusion, that is, to join the Sewardites, Free Soilers, and their sympathizers in the Democratic party. So for Douglas as well as for the Calhoun faction, the test of party allegiance was to be congressional noninterference, or popular sovereignty. As it happened, when applied to Nebraska that meant repeal of the exclusion clause of 1820, because without repeal or something equivalent to it, the necessary Southern votes could not be had. The stage was now set for the reappearance of the fatal question.

In December 1853 Douglas, chairman of the Senate's Committee of Territories, received a Nebraska territorial bill. It contained no reference to slavery and hence presented Douglas with a knotty tactical problem. The slightest tinkering with the Missouri Compromise was anathema to the antislavery faction; anything less than outright repeal was considered with suspicion by certain influential Southerners. In this tight spot Douglas argued that the Compromise of 1850 had substituted popular sovereignty for exclusion and had, at least by implication, made the Missouri Compromise obsolete. The point was, he said, not to introduce or forbid slavery, but to uphold self-rule for the actual inhabitants of the territories.

During the early months of 1854 the bill underwent many changes in wording and substance, among the latter being the creation of two territories: Kansas, lying west of Missouri, and Nebraska, adjacent to Iowa. A reluctant Douglas was driven in the direction of outright repeal, although in its final form the bill still hedged somewhat. It declared the 1820 prohibition to be "inoperative and void" because it was inconsistent with the 1850 compromise, and affirmed that the intention of the bill was "not to legislate slavery into any Territory or State, nor to exclude it therefrom, but to leave the people thereof perfectly free to form and regulate their domestic institutions in their own way."

Northern opponents sounded the alarm even before the bill became law. In the celebrated "Appeal of the Independent Democrats," Salmon P. Chase of Ohio, Charles Sumner of Massachusetts, and other antislavery leaders denounced the bill as "an atrocious plot" to fill the territories with slaves, thus excluding white settlers from the free states and forever blocking a homestead law and a Pacific railroad. They called on God and all "Christians and Christian ministers" to aid them in their struggle against the Slave Power. Their appeal found a quick response. Repeal of the Missouri Compromise touched a raw nerve in the North and set off a reaction far beyond anything Douglas had anticipated. Old Free Soilers, Liberty party members, abolitionists, disgruntled Democrats, and homeless Whigs began to coalesce as a new, wholly Northern party to oppose the South and its allies. As Douglas put it, the movement was "a crucible into which [was] poured Abolitionism, Maine liquor-lawism, and what there was left of northern Whiggism, and then the Protestant feeling against the Catholic and the native feeling against the foreigner." The Republican party had been born. In odd contrast to this furor, Southerners outside of Congress generally were little interested in the Nebraska question at first, but as the volume of Northern denunciation swelled, the usual defensive reaction took place.

What was really at stake? The economic grievances that underlay hostility toward the South have already been described; they were as important as ever. While the Kansas-Nebraska bill was still under consideration, the House of Representatives passed a homestead bill (for whites only), Northerners voting 74 to 3 in favor, Southerners 41 to 33 against. The Senate amended it to death. And, in August 1854, Pierce took a leaf from Polk's book and vetoed a rivers and harbors bill.

The "Appeal of the Independent Democrats" had stressed just such economic matters. It had also indirectly summoned up Northern hostility toward blacks. Throughout the antebellum North, blacks were discriminated against by law or custom, or both. They were barred from better jobs, segregated in public schools and facilities, confined to ghettos, disfranchised, excluded from some states by law, and regarded as forever inferior to whites in every way. Some Northerners opposed slavery in the territories not only because blacks were slaves, but because slaves were blacks. Abraham Lincoln condemned slavery as well as the Kansas-Nebraska Act, but at the same time declared that he had no disposition to interfere with slavery in the South, that he as well as the mass of Northern whites opposed political and social equality for free blacks, and that "we want them [the territories] for the homes of free white people."

Racial prejudice helps to explain why many Republicans preferred containment to abolition. Confining slavery would not merely limit Southern political power; it would keep the blacks, as slaves, in the South. Conversely, abolition would increase Southern political strength by enlarging the basis of representation and eventually would allow the ex-slaves to move into the North if they wished. Certainly there were many Northerners, like Lincoln, who were opposed to slavery in principle, but the form their opposition took illustrates how the marriage of ideals and self-interest can make the pursuit of righteousness so rewarding. When emancipation did finally come in the 1860s, it came for reasons no more and no less idealistic than the reasons for opposing the Kansas-Nebraska Act in the 1850s.

THE PRACTICAL USES OF ANTISLAVERY

Nebraska was safely within the Northern sphere of influence, but a political battle quickly developed in Kansas between settlers from the South, mainly Missouri, and those from the free states. Eli Thayer of Massachusetts founded the New England Emigrant Aid Society to promote a Northern settlement in Kansas and save it from the Slave Power. This sort of thing was a shock to Missourians, who for years had looked forward to the opening of an area they had come to regard as peculiarly theirs to exploit. Now it appeared that the North was about to snatch this prize from them, and they rushed into Kansas to protect their interests. The antislavery press depicted the ensuing contest as one between upright, hardworking, Godly, freedom-loving Northerners on the one hand, and on the other, degenerate, brutal, ignorant "border ruffians," "hirelings picked from the drunken spew and vomit of an uneasy civilization," as Senator Sumner phrased it.

Matters were not so simple. For one thing, the New England Emigrant Aid Society, whose main business was real estate speculation in Kansas, was part of a more general impulse centered in the Northeast that looked toward redeeming the unregenerate South by a Northern migration. As early as 1845, when Congress passed the joint resolution annexing Texas, Edward Everett Hale published a pamphlet entitled "How to Conquer Texas before Texas Conquers Us," proposing a Northern settlement to save that state from the slaveocracy. In the 1850s Frederick Law Olmsted, famous for his travel accounts of the South, described in *A Journey Through Texas* the brilliant future of that vast empire, if only it were flooded with an enlightened population that would raise huge crops of cotton with free labor. Olmsted lobbied for his idea at home as well as with the English textile industry. The interest he aroused in the Northeast helped to promote an invasion of Texas in 1863.

Texas and Kansas were not the only targets. In the late 1850s Eli Thayer turned his attention to Virginia and other parts of the upper and border South, once again combining redemption with real estate speculation. He told Southerners that resistance to this colonizing venture would be useless. "We shall not be intimidated. . . . If half of us were shot or hung, the rest would press on toward the shining dollars even though they should rush 'Into the jaws of death.' " When the war came, volunteers were enlisted and expeditions sent out composed of soldier-settlers to seize the rebels' lands, and Northerners continued to come south after the war in search of wealth and offices.

The troubles in Kansas should be seen within the context of this domestic imperialism, as a microcosm of the sectional conflict, with the issue of slavery covering a multitude of ambitions. Mark Twain, himself an early settler in Nevada, once observed that territorial governors were politicians who took the job only because they expected to come back East as U.S. senators. To be among the first inhabitants could mean not only an accelerated political career, but favors from one's friends in the territorial government or in Washington. For example, one prominent antislavery congressman wrote to a protégé about the opportunities in the Colorado territory, "The gold mines and the Pacific R. R. will enable the Surveyor General . . . to make a fortune of 50 to 100,000 dollars in the four years. . . . " He had promised to congressional colleagues a share in the surveyor's subordinate offices; this was necessary to buy the influence required to secure the appointment. For himself, all he asked was to be "a full partner in all land speculation and town sights [sic]."

The territorial governor appointed the Indian agent, who licensed the traders, creating an apparatus often used to defraud the helpless aborigines of the money voted them by Congress. The legislature's choice of location for the capital or even for a county seat could mean instant profits for the local landowners. The latter were not disposed to leave such decisions to chance, and they cultivated the lawmaker's goodwill in the usual manner. One whose taste did not run to town-lot speculation might secure, for example, a toll road franchise or an appointive sinecure. And, of course, the first-comers could preempt land at busy fords or crossroads, or in the rich river bottoms in case they intended to add farming to their more speculative activities. All things considered, the chance to go from rags to riches never seemed brighter than on the newly opened frontier, but it was necessary to get there first with the most men and control the government.

Therefore the Missouri "border ruffians" rushed across the line and organized a territorial government for Kansas. The new legislature met at Shawnee Mission and passed oppressive laws requiring settlers to acknowledge the legality of slavery, thus hoisting the political battleflag of that day. Northern settlers denounced the Missourians' government as "bogus," established their own government at Topeka, drew up a constitution, claimed to have created a functioning state government, and asked to be admitted to the Union. This extralegal Topeka government outlawed slavery and simultaneously barred free blacks from Kansas. Since there were never more than 200 slaves in Kansas, it seems unlikely that the institution would ever have taken root in Kansas, even if there had been no opposition to it.

It has never been established that violence in "bleeding Kansas" greatly exceeded the average for the frontier. Much of the blood was transmuted printer's ink; the antislavery press entertained its readers with tales of "sacks" and "wars" and "battles," with the peace-loving free-staters as victims of the border ruffians. There was, of course, bloodshed, although most of it had nothing to do with slavery. Disputes over property lines were a fruitful cause of quarrels; trouble, it was said, arrived with the surveyor. Horse-stealing, claim-jumping, and miscellaneous mayhem accounted for much of the disorder. These customary activities were aggravated by the presence of rival governments and led to incidents such as the "sack of Lawrence," a Northern settlement, by a posse of the pro-Southern government. The sack, which became a *cause célebre* in the North, consisted of demolishing newspaper presses, wrecking a hotel, and burning a house. The damage was done after the hotel's proprietor, in an ill-considered spasm of hospitality, served free drinks to the posse. In retaliation for the sack of Lawrence, a strange, remorseless zealot named John Brown perpetrated a grisly massacre at Pottawatomie Creek. On the night of May 24, 1856, Brown, five of his sons, and two other men descended stealthily on the little settlement at Dutch Henry's Crossing, dragged five men and boys from their cabins, murdered them in cold blood, and mutilated the bodies. Then they stole a horse, saddles, guns, and ammunition and slipped away. The victims owned no slaves, but they were associated with the Missouri faction. They had, said Brown, "committed murder in their hearts," and their execution had been ordained by God from all eternity. The killings terrified Southern homesteaders, as Brown intended, and many fled from the territory. Brown's actions also gave great impetus to the violence that would provide Republicans with their potent battle cry of "bleeding Kansas" in the election of 1856.

Meanwhile an event in Washington had further aroused the antislavery community. Charles Sumner, earnest, erudite, and self-righteous, treated the Senate to a vituperative speech entitled "The Crime Against Kansas," containing vulgar and offensive personal remarks about some of his colleagues. On May 22, two days after the speech was delivered, Representative Preston Brooks of South Carolina entered the Senate chamber. He was a kinsman of one of Sumner's targets and had come to avenge the family's honor. He proceeded to cane Sumner as he sat at his desk. "Bully" Brooks' disgraceful behavior proved to many that Simon Legree was real. Sumner's physical injuries were probably superficial, but his psychic wounds were deep. He retired temporarily from public life to recuperate, and Massachusetts left his desk unoccupied as a mute witness to the slaveocrat's brutality. "If health ever returns," vowed Sumner later, "I will repay to slavery and the whole crew of its supporters every wound, . . . ache, pain, trouble, grief which I have suffered." And so, as historians desperate for a joke too often have observed, the new Republican party was able to enter its first presidential campaign with two dramatic issues: "Bleeding Kansas" and "Bleeding Sumner."

Federal elections in antebellum days were not uniformly scheduled. There was almost always a campaign in progress somewhere for congressional seats, to say nothing of state offices. Intense electioneering kept the voters in a constant state of excitement. The grand climax came every four years with the election of a president, when the public's pent-up passions found their greatest outlet. As issues became more sectional, these periodic eruptions steadily weakened the bonds of union. The election of 1856 is a case in point. Resurrection of the slavery question rescued national politics from the lassitude of the early 1850s and brought about the realignment of parties that had been threatening for a decade. The new Republican party embodied the ideology of "free labor." This was the creed of an aggressive, expanding, entrepreneurial capitalism that regarded itself as the vanguard of civilization, as the very antithesis of the regressive, illiberal, slave-labor South. The free-labor ideology was the positive side of antislaveryism, and it embraced the same collection of concrete interests. As Eric Foner has said, "the fundamental achievement of the Republican party before the Civil War [was] the creation and articulation of an ideology which blended personal and sectional interest with morality so perfectly that it became the most potent force in the nation."

Republican strategy in 1856 was to alarm the North. The Slave Power was in control of the government. It was actively spreading slavery. After the territories had succumbed, the free states would be next. Unless the champions of human freedom united, the nation would fall permanently under the control of a little oligarchy of slave barons who would then destroy civil and constitutional liberties. Republicans called on the voters "to deliver the Constitution and the Union from the subjugation which threatens both." The party platform dealt mainly with territorial slavery. The brief economic sections urged construction of a Pacific railroad and Federal subsidies for other internal improvements, leaving untouched matters such as the tariff, land legislation, and financial policy. The Republicans chose as their leader a political neophyte, John C. Frémont, who had won a colorful reputation exploring the Far West. He had married the daughter of Thomas Hart Benton, enemy of Calhoun and anti-Nebraska Democrat from Missouri.

These qualifications, such as they were, comprised his only claim to high office.

The Democrats passed over Douglas, whose popularity had suffered because of his part in repealing the Missouri Compromise, and picked an elder statesman, James Buchanan. As minister to Great Britain during the uproar of 1854, he had been largely out of harm's way; on Pierre Soulé had fallen most of the blame for the Ostend Manifesto. The party platform supported popular sovereignty without clearly defining it, and as usual, endorsed a small, frugal and inactive Federal government.

A third candidate in the field was ex-president Millard Fillmore, nominee of both the Know-Nothings and the Whig remnant. The Know-Nothing platform was a nativist document that also decried the repeal of the Missouri Compromise. The Whigs merely warned against the dangers of sectionalism; otherwise they had no program.

While Republicans tried to frighten voters with the Slave Power conspiracy, Democrats tried to frighten them by depicting their opponents as dangerous radicals, as abolitionists and Negrophiles whose triumph would endanger the Union. There was plenty of ammunition in Republican speeches. The Democrats quoted Joshua Giddings, Republican congressman from Ohio, who said he looked forward to the day "when there will be a servile insurrection in the South, when the black man . . . shall . . . wage a war of extermination against his master; when the torch of the incendiary [shall] light up the towns of the South." They told how a prominent Republican orator at Boston's famous Faneuil Hall said, "Remembering that he was a slaveholder, I spit on George Washington." They pointed to Horace Greeley, editor of the powerful *New York Tribune,* who seriously suggested disunion. The nation was being prepared for the final crisis by the politics of hate and fear.

Republican strategists, who counted heavily on the struggle over Kansas, were taken aback in the summer of 1856 when Senator Robert Toombs of Georgia offered a plan to pacify Kansas by cleaning up the political process. A special presidential commission would conduct an impartial census to identify all bona fide voters, who would then elect a constitutional convention. The convention would draw up a constitution with or without slavery, as the people wished, and Kansas would enter the union without further delay. All that Southerners wanted, said Toombs, was a fair vote. Republicans were hard-pressed to oppose so reasonable a plan, one that met all their complaints about bogus legislatures and crooked elections. When they objected that an election would not be fair because so many free-state people had supposedly fled from Kansas, the bill was amended to allow time for the refugees to return. Then they said that President Pierce could not be trusted to appoint an impartial commission. Finally the Republican majority in the House killed the Toombs plan, and with it the last best hope of a quick end to the difficulties in Kansas. Douglas denounced them savagely. "All these gentlemen want is to get up murder and bloodshed in Kansas for political effect. They do not mean that there shall be peace until after the presidential election. . . . Their capital for the presidential election is blood."

Buchanan won, but his victory was cold comfort for the Democrats. He received less than half the popular vote (46 percent); Frémont got 33 percent, an astonishing total for the first presidential contest of a new party, and Fillmore got 20 percent. More important than these percentages was the geographical distribution of the votes. Republican strength was concentrated north of the 41st parallel and corresponded closely with the areas heavily colonized by New Englanders: New York; the northern sections of Ohio, Indiana, and Illinois; Michigan, Wisconsin, and Iowa. Republicans were especially strong in the areas most influenced by the revivals and antislavery crusade of the 1830s. And the 1850s saw a revival of revivalism. It moved from the countryside, where Finney and Weld had labored, into the cities, reached a fever pitch little more than a year after Frémont's campaign, and in the opinion of some contemporaries cleared the way for the Republican victory of 1860. An election map also shows that in most areas Republican strength coincided with the rapidly developing rail network that was binding the Northeast and Northwest together.

Thus the new alliance that had appeared in the upper North was a complex mixture of cultural, religious, commercial, and industrial affinities. It had won all but five non-Southern states: Illinois (which it carried at the state level), Pennsylvania, Indiana, New Jersey, and California. If Frémont had carried Pennsylvania plus either Indiana

or Illinois, he would have won the election without a single Southern vote. Conversely, the Democrats could not have won without
the South. Division of the major parties along sectional lines took
a giant step forward in 1856.

Chapter III

Right Versus Rights

DRED SCOTT'S CASE

With the political process underway in Kansas, the time had come when the Democrats had to decide exactly what popular sovereignty meant. Could settlers exclude slavery during the territorial stage, or must they wait until they adopted a state constitution and applied for admission to the Union? Most Northern Democrats took the former view, Southern Democrats the latter, but for the last 10 years they had tacitly agreed to allow this awkward question to lie dormant. The territorial legislation of 1850 and 1854 had not required it to be answered explicitly. Now it could no longer be sidestepped. President Buchanan grasped the nettle in his inaugural address.

> A difference of opinion has arisen in regard to the point of time when the people of a territory shall decide this question for themselves. This is, happily, a matter of little practical importance. Besides, it is a judicial question, which legitimately belongs to the Supreme Court of the United States, before whom it is now pending, and will, it is understood, be speedily and finally settled. To their decision, in common with all good citizens, I shall cheerfully submit.

Buchanan admitted that in his personal opinion slavery could not be acted on until a constitution was adopted.

On March 6, 1857, just two days after Buchanan's speech, the Supreme Court handed down its decision in the case of *Dred Scott* v. *Sanford*. Scott, a slave, had sued for his freedom on the grounds that he had resided in a free state (Illinois) and in territory made free by the Missouri Compromise. His case came into Federal court by virtue of the diverse citizenship clause of the Constitution (III, 2), the defendant being a citizen of New York, and Scott claiming to be a citizen of Missouri.

There were nine different opinions in the Supreme Court decision, seven against Scott's claim to be free, two for it. The opinion of Chief Justice Roger B. Taney was declared to be the opinion of the court. There were three main points to be decided: (1) was Scott a citizen and hence entitled to bring suit in a Federal court? (2) had he been freed by his sojourn in Illinois, or (3) in Louisiana territory north of 36° 30′? Taney answered all three in the negative. As to the first, Taney argued that only those persons, and their descendants, who were citizens at the time the Constitution was adopted were citizens of the United States. He marshaled much evience to show that Negroes were not citizens at that time. Nor could native-born Negroes be made citizens by legislative act. The Constitution "took from the States all power by any subsequent legislation" to make anyone a citizen of the United States. The conferral of citizenship by a state for state purposes did not confer citizenship within the meaning of the Constitution. On the other hand, the jurisdiction of Congress was limited to naturalizing the foreign-born. Therefore native-born Negroes, such as Scott, could not be U.S. citizens and could not sue in a Federal court. As to Scott's claim to be a free man, Taney said that despite his stay in Illinois his status was determined by the laws of the state to which he had returned, and according to the law of Missouri he was still a slave. On the third and most controversial point, Taney maintained that Federal authority over land acquired since the Constitution was ratified flowed exclusively from the treaty-making and war-making powers. New territory could be acquired only for the purpose of adding new states to the Union, and Congress' power was limited to preparing it for statehood. In doing so it could not act in a manner inconsistent with the letter and spirit of the Constitution. It could not, for example, abridge freedom of speech in a territory, or pass a law establishing a religion. Nor could it, said Taney, deprive any person of life, liberty, or property without due process of law. To take away the slaveowner's property merely because he carried it into a territory could scarcely "be dignified with the name of due process of law." And Congress, remarked the Chief Justice in passing, could not delegate to a territorial government a power that it did not itself possess.

The Dred Scott case was interesting for several reasons not connected with the sectional controversy. Not since *Marbury* v. *Madison* (1803) had the Supreme Court struck down a law of Congress. Second, the Scott decision for the first time brought into prominence at the highest judicial level the concept of dual citizenship and the substantive interpretation of the due process clause. The latter doctrine held that there are some rights the government may not curtail even by legislation. It would be amplified by the Fourteenth Amendment and construed by conservative judges after the Civil War so as to block state regulation of corporations. It should also be pointed out that in the 1850s the modern role of the Supreme Court as the final arbiter of constitutional disputes, the enunciator of the "law of the land," was not widely accepted. Many agreed with Andrew Jackson, who had said that "the opinion of the judges has no more authority over Congress than the opinion of Congress has over the judges." Ironically, the heirs of Jefferson and Jackson, whose fathers had denounced the centralizing influence of the Marshall court, now spoke in hushed and reverential tones about the Scott decision, while the spiritual descendants of Hamilton and Marshall cried out against judicial tyranny.

At the time, of course, the part of the Dred Scott case that attracted everyone's attention was Taney's ruling that neither Congress nor a territorial government could ban slavery. Taney had virtually told the Republicans that even if they won control of the Federal government, they could not execute their pledge to outlaw slavery in the territories. It appeared to them that he and other members of the court's majority were part of the Slave Power plot. Buchanan's reference to the decision two days in advance was seen by some Republicans as proof of corrupt collusion between court and president. The Supreme Court, said Seward, "can reverse its spurious judgment. . . . Let the court recede. Whether it recedes or not, we [the Republicans] shall reorganize the court and thus reform its political sentiments and practices, and bring them into harmony with the Constitution and with the laws of nature." Who knew, asked Abraham Lincoln, when the court might decide that slaveholders could not be deprived of their property even if they took chattels into states now free. "There is such a thing as THE SLAVE POWER," said a Cincinnati newspaper. "It has marched over and annihilated the boundaries of the States. We are now one great homogeneous slaveholding community."

The decision was not the result of a plot. One justice told Buchanan before the inauguration that most of the court leaned toward passing on the constitutionality of the Missouri Compromise, that is, on Congress' power over slavery in the territories. One of those still not committed to address that matter was Justice Grier from Buchanan's state of Pennsylvania. The President wrote Grier and urged on him the necessity of deciding this vexed question once and for all. There may have been impropriety in this, but no conspiracy. Spurred by the determination of two Northern members to uphold explicitly the Missouri Compromise, most of the justices had come to believe that the country expected them to confront the issue. A judicial solution had received wide support from the backers of the abortive compromise of 1848; in this tradition the territorial acts of 1850 mandated direct appeal to the Supreme Court. The idea was to render the issue harmless by getting it out of politics and into the courts. That might have worked in 1848; by 1857 it was too late. Too much had happened, and the Dred Scott decision only exacerbated an already dangerous situation.

KANSAS PACIFIED

A solid substratum of economics always underlies the jagged landscape of the slavery controversy. Just before Buchanan began his unhappy term of office, President Pierce signed into law the lowest tariff since 1816. Despairing for the time being of getting higher protection for their products, Northeastern textile interests had settled for the next best thing — reduced protection for raw materials. Southern leadership played a conspicuous part in the enactment of the new law. Its consequences fell with special severity on Pennsylvania's iron industry and Northwestern wool growers. The tariff once more entered politics, and the Republicans soon would bring forward a program to capitalize on the dissatisfaction created by the 1857 law.

The tariff was only the beginning of the bad economic news. A financial panic began in the summer of 1857. It had nothing to do with the new import duties or any other domestic policy; instead it stemmed from tight credit in England and the withdrawal of capital from the United States. Although the banking industry quickly recovered, other sectors of the economy did not. There had been some major business failures, among them the Illinois Central and the Michigan Central railroads, and hard times lingered on in the Northwest. Low prices for commodities such as wheat persisted until the Civil War, the sale of public lands dropped off sharply, railroad construction slowed, and money was scarce. The speculative nature of the Northwest's economy, with card-castles of credit resting on railroads not yet built and on land not yet cleared, guaranteed a day of reckoning; the Panic of 1857 merely set the date.

These complexities were often beyond the ken of the farmer who lost his land because of low prices, the debt-burdened merchant left with unsalable inventories, the banker who could not collect loans, or the speculator who saw the railroad in which he owned stock go bankrupt. Many blamed a familiar villain as at least partly responsible for their troubles: the Slave Power. The lower tariff was a direct result of the swelling surplus in the Federal Treasury, and that was the consequence of the Southern fetish, going back to Jefferson, of a pinchpenny government. In Congress, Southerners commanding powerful committees fought and usually defeated river and harbor bills, free homesteads, the Pacific railroad, bounties to New England fisheries, and subsidies to trans-Atlantic shipping companies. What relief was possible as long as they were in power?

These frustrations coincided with the climax of the Kansas controversy. That tumultuous territory was without a governor, having used up three in three years. One of Buchanan's first tasks as president was to find a more durable politician who could make Kansas a state and bury that dangerous problem once and for all. His choice seemed at the time to be a shrewd one, Robert J. Walker, a man of national reputation and a power in the Democratic party during Polk's presidency. Walker was an imperialist in outlook and a speculator by nature, irresistibly attracted to get-rich-quick land deals. He could speak the language of the hustling, acquisitive frontier. According to one leading scholar, Walker and the Buchanan administration planned to obtain for the territory an abnormally large Fedral land grant that could be sold to finance all sorts of moneymaking schemes. A golden poultice would heal the wounds of "Bleeding Kansas." Gratitude would quickly make Kansas a state under Democratic control. The devisers of this strategy did not realize that suspicion and hostility between the contending factions ran so deep as to prevent them from sharing political power and the spoils. Buchanan and Walker agreed that the people of Kansas must be allowed to control their "domestic institutions" by voting on the state constitution, when one was drawn up. Northern Democrats would denounce any other course as a betrayal of popular sovereignty, even though past territorial conventions had invariably promulgated constitutions without a referendum.

The territorial government took a census in the spring of 1857 preparatory to holding elections for a constitutional convention. Many Northern settlers, who gave allegiance to the extralegal Topeka government, drove off or evaded the census takers. If they kept themselves off the census rolls, they did not officially exist and could not be taxed. They had never paid taxes to the "bogus" proslavery government and did not intend to begin. Only taxpayers could vote for delegates to the convention, but the Topeka men subsequently attempted to turn this disfranchisement to their advantage by claiming that the convention was unrepresentative and hence contrary to popular sovereignty. They could then continue to press for acceptance of their own Topeka constitution and state government. But if actual Northern settlers were missing from the rolls, the names of nonexistent Southerners often took their places.

Walker managed to antagonize the proslavery element without winning over the free-state people. He announced in his inaugural address that the constitution would have to be submitted to the voters. As for slavery, the environment excluded it. Why, then, agitate the question? Get on with the work of developing Kansas, he said, dangling before his audience the great Federal land grant. Walker later asked the free-staters to vote in the next election for territorial offices, which they could do without being taxpayers, and in the constitutional referendum, which he was working to bring about.

Delegates to the constitutional convention were chosen in a clean election on June 15. Because Northern settlers did not participate, Southerners overwhelmingly controlled the convention. This much-maligned group met at Lecompton and quickly drew up a state constitution. By a narrow margin they voted to present two versions of the constitution that were identical except for slavery. One recognized the institution fully. The other omitted the article establishing slavery, but protected the rights of those who owned slaves then in Kansas. The referendum took place on December 21. Free-state settlers refused to participate, and the vote was 6226 to 569 for the Lecompton constitution "with slavery."

The abstention of the Northerners has always been a puzzle. Two months before these same people had taken part in the elections for territorial offices. They had won a majority in the legislature after Walker overturned several fraudulent elections, and had sent a Republican delegate to Congress. They could have voted for the "no-slavery" version of Lecompton with every expectation of winning. There were never more than about 200 slaves in the territory, and the no-slavery version of Lecompton would surely have amounted to gradual emancipation, the policy Northern states had pursued when eliminating slavery. Free-staters could also have called another convention after Kansas had become a state and abolished slavery altogether. As was pointed out at the time, a clause in the Lecompton constitution that seemed to defer any amendments until 1864 did not take precedence over the sovereign will of the people in convention assembled.

Slavery, then, could not have been the only issue. Some claimed that the free-staters desired to keep the controversy alive for the benefit of the Republican party. Another and perhaps more persuasive explanation may be found by comparing the Lecompton constitution with the free-state constitutions of 1855 and 1859. Sharp practical and philosophical differences in matters of incorporation laws, taxation, internal improvements, banking, and eligibility for public office help to explain why the free-state faction insisted on a chance to vote against the whole of Lecompton. The legislature, now controlled by free-staters, scheduled another referendum, this time giving the voters an opportunity to reject both versions of the constitution. When it was held early in January 1858, the proslavery faction abstained on the grounds that the constitution had already been approved and sent to Washington for action. The result was a resounding defeat for Lecompton — 10,266 to 162. On the same day elections were held for state offices, in case Congress should admit Kansas under the Lecompton constitution. The free-state party again carried the day, and Lecompton supporters faced a dismal prospect. Should Congress accept the constitution, Kansas would enter the Union as a slave state with Republicans in control at every level. Some now began to call on Congress to reject their handiwork. Better to be a territory under the friendly tutelage of a Democratic administration at Washington than a sovereign state under the Republicans, slavery or no slavery. As a territory they would at least be favored by the patronage of a Democratic governor; as a state they would be out in the cold.

In January 1858 the Lecompton constitution was presented to Congress as having been duly approved by the convention and the voters; it was accompanied by a request that Kansas be admitted as a state and given an extraordinarily large grant of public lands. Senator Stephen A. Douglas, chief protagonist of popular sovereignty, leader of the Northwestern Democracy, now came to the crossroads of his career. All eyes had turned to the senator when news of Lecompton had arrived late in 1857. His reaction was one of outrage. For one thing, Douglas had no great fondness for Buchanan, who had beaten him in the Democratic convention of 1856 and had slighted Douglas's friends in distributing the patronage. Now, probably at the behest of his Southern advisers, he seemed to be trying to destroy Douglas politically by forcing him either to side with the proslavery faction in Kansas or break off with the administration. Douglas had not forgotten 1854, when he had so grossly underestimated the hostile reaction that the Kansas-Nebraska Act would provoke. With the Republican party on the rise in his state and section, Douglas could not afford the least appearance of surrendering to the South. He was, after all, up for reelection in 1858.

Therefore Douglas promptly denounced the Lecompton constitution as a travesty on popular sovereignty. The convention had acted illegally, he said, did not represent the people, and had not given the voters a chance to reject the constitution altogether. By taking this stand Douglas hoped to rally the party to his leadership and attract the support of those independents and Democrats who were drifting toward the Republicans. In the 1840s the Democracy's center of balance had shifted from the Northeast to the South. Douglas was trying to move it to the Northwest. However, the ties of party were now so weak that instead of shifting its balance, the party would split along sectional lines.

At the time such a fracture did not seem inevitable. Buchanan wished the Lecompton constitution had been fully submitted to the voters, but instead of prolonging the agony he was willing to make the best of what he had and get Kansas out of Congress before it wrecked the party. He recommended admission under Lecompton. Douglas was immovable; he insisted on a new referendum. Buchanan retaliated by purging Douglas men from Federal offices in Illinois, to no avail: Douglas voted with the Republican minority in the Senate against admission. In the House enough anti-Lecompton Democrats deserted the administration to defeat Lecompton. The House voted to resubmit the constitution to the people.

Administration Democrats were desperate to achieve a compromise before the party was racked to pieces. Over solid Republican opposition and by a narrow margin in the House, they succeeded in sending the two Kansas bills to a conference committee. Here Representative William H. English, a moderate Democrat from Indiana, concocted the last compromise on slavery ever to pass Congress. It tried to satisfy the Douglas Democrats, who said that Lecompton violated popular sovereignty, and the Southerners, who claimed that the opposition's real object was to keep another slave state from entering the Union — a dangerous precedent and a blow to Southern pride. English's bill accommodated these seemingly irreconcilable positions by concentrating on the land grant. Instead of the 23,500,000 acres asked for by the Lecompton convention, his bill offered Kansas the usual grant of 3,500,000 acres. Kansans would be given another chance to vote. If they agreed to the small grant, they would enter the Union immediately as a state under the Lecompton constitution. If they refused, they would have to wait until the population of Kansas reached the ratio of representation in the House (93,560) before they could again apply for admission. This pacified some Southerners because the issue was land, not slavery, and partially mollified some of the anti-Lecompton Democrats because the Kansans would be given a chance to vote down Lecompton in any form.

The English bill was not primarily intended to coerce or bribe Kansas into accepting Lecompton. Its purpose was to end the destructive civil war within the Democratic party, which partially explains the Republicans' dogged opposition. Using every kind of argument, inducement, and threat in its political arsenal, the Buchanan administration broke the ranks of the wavering anti-Lecompton Democrats in the House. The Senate was safe, although Douglas, after some indecision, voted nay. The English bill became law on May 4, 1858. Three months later the Kansans defeated Lecompton again by a vote of 11,300 to 1788, most of the proslavery minority again abstaining. Kansas was at last disposed of, but not before great damage had been done.

LINCOLN AND DOUGLAS

With the sudden end of the Kansas battle, politicians were like soldiers after a prolonged artillery barrage — dazed, disoriented, and deafened by the silence. After the dust had settled, the Democrats realized that their partial reunion in support of the English bill had only saved face; the party's divisions were deeper than ever. The travail of the Democrats had caused both congratulations and confusion among the Republicans. The latter had watched in puzzled surprise as Douglas opened his heavy guns on Lecompton and the Buchanan administration. They found themselves fighting side by side with the author of the hated Kansas-Nebraska Act. The man whom Senator Sumner had once compared to a "noisome, squat, and nameless animal" was, like the bewitched frog-prince, magically transformed — but into exactly what they could not tell. Douglas found himself courted and praised by Republican titans such as Seward, Greeley, and Benjamin Wade of Ohio, to name only a few. Some believed he was ready to be baptized into the true faith.

Although Douglas's Republican admirers were found mainly among certain Eastern leaders instead of among the rank and file, their attitude was nevertheless the symptom of a potentially grave danger to the party. The Kansas question had been settled and slavery defeated on the basis of popular sovereignty, Douglas's principle. Did this mean that no positive legislation against slavery was needed? Did it mean that the danger was over? Some came close to saying just that when they praised Douglas and the victory in Kansas. Others went even further. As early as February 1858, Seward had said that the battle was already over, that there were then 16 free states and 15 slave states, and before the year was out the count would be 19 to 15. Colleagues took him to task for this incautious prophecy. After all, the alleged danger of slavery expansion had called the party into being. If the danger was over, the Republicans might follow the Free Soilers into oblivion. Yet mere silence could not conceal what had happened in Kansas, and Republicans began to wonder how the party could justify its continued existence.

The man most threatened by the admiration for Douglas provided the answer. Abraham Lincoln had not held public office since the late 1840s, when he represented Illinois in the House of Representatives. He had labored patiently in the political vineyard, missing election to the Senate by a hair's breadth in 1855, moving with the tide out of the dying Whig party and into the new Republican movement, campaigning for Frémont in 1856. Now it was time for his reward, Douglas's Senate seat. But if the party adopted Douglas, or if Greeley's influential *Tribune* persuaded enough Illinois Republicans not to oppose Douglas, Lincoln's career would be at a dead end. Therefore it was essential for Lincoln to deny flatly that Douglas was almost a Republican or deserved Republican support, to reaffirm the difference between exclusion and popular sovereignty, and to proclaim that the Slave Power plot was more dangerous than ever. As events showed, this was the correct prescription for the whole party, not only for Lincoln and the Illinois Republicans.

The nomination of a senatorial candidate by a state convention was unprecedented, yet in 1858 Illinois Republicans did just that. They declared Lincoln to be their only choice and in this way deliberately rebuked the Easterners who had been urging that Douglas not be opposed for the Senate. On June 16, following his nomination, Lincoln delivered the famous "House Divided" speech. Its thesis was simply and succinctly stated.

> "A house divided against itself cannot stand."
> I believe that this government cannot endure, permanently half *slave* and half *free*.
> I do not expect the Union to be *dissolved* — I do not expect the house to *fall* — but I *do* expect it will cease to be divided.
> It will become *all* one thing, or *all* the other.
> Either the *opponents* of slavery, will arrest the further spread of it, and place it where the public mind shall rest in the belief that it is in the course of ultimate extinction; or its *advocates* will push it forward, till it shall become alike lawful in *all* the States, *old* as well as *new* — *North* as well as *South*.

Lincoln found it "impossible not to believe" that Democrats such as Douglas, Chief Justice Taney, and Presidents Pierce and Buchanan had not been part of a deliberate scheme to extend slavery. Their target thus far had been the territories, but the next decision of the Taney court might well declare that states could not prohibit slavery. Staunch Republicans were needed to meet this threat, men who believed that slavery was wrong and must be stopped in its tracks, not Douglasites, with their amoral popular sovereignty.

In the grueling campaign that followed, Lincoln and Douglas faced each other in seven set debates; both men gave scores of other speeches as well. Douglas tried to paint Lincoln as a radical, citing the "House Divided" thesis and accusing him of favoring complete equality between whites and blacks. Lincoln denied both charges. He had no inclination, he said, to interfere with slavery in the Southern states, and he thought the Fugitive Slave Act should be enforced. He believed in white supremacy and opposed racial intermarriage, social equality, and letting blacks vote, hold office, or serve on juries. Lincoln counterattacked by hammering away at the moral issue: he and the Republicans believed slavery was wrong and should be confined, whereas Douglas did not care about slavery one way or the other, only about his principle of popular sovereignty. He also forced Douglas to broadcast his view (which he had stated previously) that the people of a territory could legally exclude slavery despite the Dred Scott decision. This "Freeport

Doctrine" increased the "Little Giant's" growing unpopularity in the South.

The contest was close. Lincoln probably had somewhat more popular support than Douglas, but the election produced a Douglas majority in the legislature, which returned him to the Senate. Yet Lincoln had won more than a moral victory. Now he was mentioned as a possible presidential candidate, something he had probably barely considered before. Illinois in 1858 turned out to be a dress rehearsal for the national drama of 1860.

ALARM BELLS IN THE NIGHT

Buchanan Democrats fared poorly in the congressional elections of 1858, just as Pierce Democrats had done after the Kansas-Nebraska Act in 1854, although their defeat was perhaps not as sweeping nor the Kansas issue as dominant as once believed. Nevertheless, the loss of 18 House seats, and with them the majority, and the great decline in Pennsylvania's Democratic vote were serious matters for the party. In the New York campaign Seward took a lesson from Lincoln, calling the Democrats tools of the Slave Power who would, if not stopped, reopen the African slave trade and spread the peculiar institution over the whole land. There was, he said, an "irrepressible conflict" that would end with the country being all slave or all free. Seward's rhetoric sounded more radical than Lincoln's, and Seward's words were given the weight due the leading figure of his party. Even some of the senator's friends thought he had gone too far; Southern reaction can easily be imagined.

Compared with the "House Divided" and the "Irrepressible Conflict," Douglas's Freeport Doctrine appeared to be moderation itself. But because of his apostasy on the Kansas question, there was a growing bitterness against Douglas on the part of administration Democrats. When Congress met in December 1858, they removed Douglas from the chairmanship of the Committee on Territories, a valuable position politically and one that he had held for a decade. Some fellow Democrats snubbed or verbally attacked Douglas. Although personal resentments were partly to blame for these actions, they sprang mainly from a determination to reduce Douglas's influence in the party. His enemies were resolved either to bring him to heel or force him to defend publicly his heretical doctrines. For a long time Douglas refused to be provoked; then he finally found it necessary to restate and defend his Freeport Doctrine: the people of a territory could exclude slavery by unfriendly legislation. Later on, in a much publicized *Harper's* article, Douglas tried to root his doctrine more firmly in the Constitution. This ill-timed publication alienated many of his Southern defenders, and pronouncements of excommunication rang out from the Chesapeake to the Gulf. The doctrinal lines were now drawn. The minimum position of Douglas men was nonintervention by Congress; the minimum position of the states' rights faction, now stronger than ever in the Deep South, was the constitutional duty of Congress to protect the rights of slaveowners if the territorial government failed to do so. The manner in which the dispute was settled would decide whether Douglas or someone acceptable to the South would be the candidate in 1860, and which faction would be dominant in party councils.

Ultimately the stakes in this game were far higher than a fairly routine intraparty struggle for supremacy. The syllogism was simple and chilling. If Douglas could not unite the party, no one could. If the party split in 1860, the Republicans would win. If the Republicans won, another sectional crisis might mean secession by one or more Southern states.

The danger is more obvious in retrospect than it was at the time. Attempts to read the public mind are bound to be uncertain and tentative at best. Yet the impression is inescapable that, as the summer of 1859 passed, neither Douglas's rebellion, the alarming speeches of Seward and Lincoln, Republican successes at the polls, nor all of them together had sufficed to produce in any Southern state a majority determined to secede should the Republicans win in 1860. More than that would be required. Excitement over Kansas had disappeared. Territorial slavery was now an abstraction only tenuously connected with the real world. However important the contestants, the debates between Douglas and the Southern rights champions aroused little public interest. Times were good. The cotton crop of 1858 was the second largest in history, and prices were high. New crops and scientific farming techniques were restoring the soil of the older states. The value of manufactures, although small, had nearly doubled in the decade. Railroad construction proceeded at a startling pace, connecting the Atlantic seaboard with the Mississippi, while hundreds of steamboats navigated that great highway and its tributaries. In short, the section's healthy and dynamic economy helped to counterbalance the anxiety aroused by the slave controversy. The South had lived with the latter for some time now and still had prospered. A conservative mood prevailed, just as it had after the Compromise of 1850. Then came John Brown's raid on Harper's Ferry.

John Brown was not a remarkable man; in ordinary times he would have been interesting mainly in a clinical sense. The first 55 years of his life were a story of failure, incompetence, and shady dealings. His chief characteristics were physical courage, self-righteousness, mendacity, and an unlimited capacity for self-delusion. For years historians have debated the question of Brown's sanity. Affidavits presented at his trial in 1859 stated that Brown and many of his blood relatives were insane, and a conservative count of the latter brings the total to three aunts, two uncles, a sister, a brother, two sons, a niece, and five first cousins. Brown conceded that a broad streak of insanity ran through his mother's family, but indignantly repulsed any suggestion that he was similarly afflicted. Scholarly admirers of Brown have impeached the affidavits as false statements designed to save his life. One would think that the affidavits were superfluous, that the midnight murders and mutilations at Pottwatomie Creek, the fantastic invasion of the South, and all the other weird incidents in Brown's life would be sufficient to settle the question. Perhaps as revealing as anything else is a poignant remark by one of the Harper's Ferry raiders. As the day for the great attack approached, he said, "Capt. Brown was all activity, though I could not help thinking that at times he appeared somewhat puzzled."

The real question is not Brown's sanity, but instead how such a man could have shaken the Union to its foundations. The mind of the American people, not Brown's mind, is the proper object of investigation.

For months after the Pottawatomie massacre (May 1856), Brown and his followers, now fugitives from justice, lived by cattle rustling, robbery, and so forth, activities occasionally punctuated by gunfights with their pursuers. All this was reported by part of the Northern press as a gallant battle between freedom and slavery, with Brown as the hero. In October he started east, pausing in Ohio to get a character reference from Governor Salmon P. Chase; he already had one from Charles Robinson, "governor" of the Topeka regime. Upon his arrival in Massachusetts, Brown was warmly welcomed by Ralph Waldo Emerson, Henry Thoreau, Theodore Parker, and other leading New England intellectuals, as well as by prominent men of business. Here Brown met the men who would later finance his invasion of the South. The youngest was Franklin Sanborn, protégé of Emerson and intimate of the Concord literary set. Another was Dr. Samuel Gridley Howe, militant abolitionist and humanitarian, whose wife later wrote the "Battle Hymn of the Republic." There was also George L. Stearns, who believed Brown to be another George Washington. Gerrit Smith was a New York philanthropist, former member of Congress, and an ardent crusader against virtually all fleshly pleasures. There were two men of the cloth. One was Theodore Parker, renowned Unitarian minister, graduate of Harvard Divinity School, and reputed master of 20 languages. The other was Thomas Wentworth Higginson, who said he was always "ready to invest in treason," and who realized that "the delicate balance of the zealot's mind" was "somewhat disturbed." Higginson had the courage of his convictions, and during the Civil War led a regiment of black troops against the Confederacy.

These men, who came to be known as the "Secret Six," knew what Brown planned to do, although they asked not to be told exactly when and where he would strike. Then they would be able to parry awkward questions without actually lying. They must have realized that if Brown succeeded in raising a slave insurrection, there would surely be an indiscriminate slaughter of men, women, and children, whether or not they owned slaves, for they had before them the familiar examples of Santo Domingo and Nat Turner.

John Brown planned to invade the South, raise the slaves, and set up an abolitionist republic. He and his disciples ratified a constitution for this new nation that provided, among other things, for the division of property taken from Southerners. In the summer of 1859 Brown established his headquarters in a Maryland farmhouse, where he accumulated hundreds of firearms and pikes to arm the slaves, relying on funds supplied by the Secret Six. Brown's primary objective was the Federal arsenal at Harper's Ferry, Virginia, where more weapons would be secured. Brown and his "army" of 18 men entered the town on the night of October 16. The raid was an utter fiasco. Awakened by alarm bells in the night, men poured into Harper's Ferry and trapped the invaders, and a contingent of marines from Washington, D.C., quickly captured the survivors, including the wounded Brown. No slaves attempted to join the revolution.

Papers found at the Maryland farmhouse soon revealed the role played by the Secret Six. Of the five then in the country, three fled to Canada; Gerrit Smith proclaimed his insanity and retired to an asylum. Only Higgison stood his ground. With the identity of Brown's backers known to all, the raid could not be dismissed as the isolated act of a lunatic. The exalted standing of the Secret Six shocked Southerners, and subsequent events heightened their apprehensions. One prominent figure after another joined in a paean of praise for Brown. In his famous "Plea for Captain John Brown," Thoreau said: "Some eighteen hundred years ago Christ was crucified; this morning, perchance, Captain Brown was hung. These are the two ends of a chain which is not without its links. He is not Old Brown any longer; he is an angel of light. . . . " Theodore Parker named him a saint and predicted with apparent relish a slave rebellion that would race through the South, to be extinguished only with "the white man's blood." Louisa May Alcott, author of *Little Women,* dubbed Brown "St. John the Just." To Emerson he was a "Saint . . . whose martyrdom . . . will make the gallows as glorious as the cross." To list Brown's admirers is almost to call the roll of New England's literary giants — Longfellow, Channing, Lowell, and so on.

At first Northern opinion generally was not favorable to Brown. Republicans felt obliged to disown him because of Democratic charges that Brown's infamous scheme was the logical outcome of their policies. However, as the weeks passed, as Brown lay wounded in his prison cell sending out a stream of eloquent, self-serving letters, a curious and disquieting change manifested itself. There was an increasing tendency to overlook Brown's bloody deeds and to praise him as an antislavery hero. For example, John A. Andrew, soon to be governor of Massachusetts, said, "I know only that whether the enterprise was one or the other, John Brown himself is right." "The method is nothing," said Thoreau, "the spirit is all." Even so pragmatic a politician as Seward wrote his wife that the courageous monomaniac rose "morally above his prosecutors so much that you almost forget his criminality."

Brown, convicted of murder and of treason against the state of Virginia, was executed by hanging on December 2. Throughout his ordeal he had displayed a fortitude that won praise even from Southerners. All across the North bells tolled, guns boomed, and people gathered to mourn his passing. Grief for Brown was accompanied by anger toward the South. Joshua Giddings observed that he found "the hatred of slavery greatly intensified by the fate of Brown, and men are ready to march to Virginia and dispose of her despotism at once." As C. Vann Woodward has so aptly remarked, it was not long before men from the North were marching to Virginia, singing a song called "John Brown's Body." Faced by this reaction, Southerners drew together in a spirit of defensive unity. On the matter of invasion and race war there was no division between slaveholders and nonslaveholders; all were potential victims, all equally threatened. The election of 1860 began to take on a grimmer significance. What would happen to the South if the government should fall into the hands of people who compared John Brown with Jesus Christ? More Southerners than ever before were willing to contemplate the possibility of secession and, if necessary, war. If Northerners saw Simon Legree as the personification of the Slave Power, Southerners saw John Brown as the symbol of Northern intentions. Fear swept the South. State legislatures reorganized and rearmed their militias. Northerners were suspected and sometimes persecuted, and native Southerners had to watch their words. It is easy to call this fear paranoia, and perhaps reactions sometimes went beyond normal limits, but subsequent events satisfied Southerners that they had not greatly overestimated their peril.

More remarkable than the fear and anger engendered by John

Brown was the persistence of conservative sentiment in both sections of the country. In spite of the inflammatory events of a generation, a majority of citizens appeared to be more bewildered than hostile. That bewilderment, however, would play into the hands of an angry and purposeful minority.

THE ELECTION OF 1860

The John Brown affair could not have been better timed to do maximum damage to the political process. Even as Brown mounted the gallows, preparations were under way to select delegates to the national nominating conventions. There could now be no doubt, if any had ever existed, that the presidential campaign would revolve around the slavery issue. The bitterness with which that question was debated derived in no small degree from the continuing sectional estrangement over economic policies. The effects of the 1857 panic lingered on in the Northwest, where people blamed the Southern-dominated Buchanan administration for refusing any relief whatever. In the congressional session of 1858-1859, Vice-President John C. Breckinridge, a Kentuckian, defeated a homestead bill by casting his tie-breaking vote in the Senate. Buchanan vetoed an internal improvements bill that would have funded projects in the Northwest, as well as a bill to establish Federal land grant colleges which had been passed over Southern opposition. A Pacific railroad, the project dearest to the hearts of Northwestern promoters, fell victim to the perennial quarrel over the location of its eastern terminus. Upward revision of the tariff got nowhere.

The story was much the same in the session of 1859-1860. Buchanan again vetoed a homestead bill. A higher tariff passed the House, only to suffer defeat in the Senate, with Southerners providing most of the negative votes. River and harbor appropriations and the transcontinental railroad again failed to pass. The full meaning of the slavery issue cannot be appreciated unless these repeated blows to Northern ambitions are taken into account. Even though a majority of Northerners had no direct material stake in the tariff, or dredging out rivers, or a Pacific railroad, an influential minority

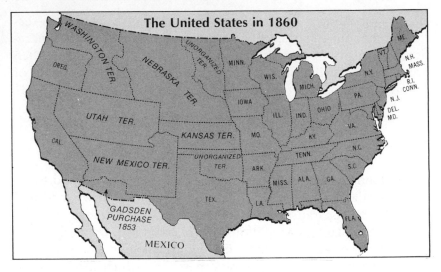

did; with the help of their political allies, they convinced the majority that their prosperity depended on such projects. In this way the political influence of economic issues was mightily magnified; there is no surer way to win votes than to inculcate a sense of grievance. If it is true that there would have been no Civil War without slavery, it is equally true that slavery would never have come to dominate national politics without a conflict of economic interests between the sections.

By 1860 there were three distinct policies on slavery in the territories: exclusion by act of Congress, protection by act of Congress, and nonintervention by Congress. Then there were those who would banish slavery from the political arena. Each of these positions would be represented by a presidential candidate.

The Democratic convention met at Charleston, South Carolina, on April 23. Several Deep South delegations came with instructions to walk out unless the platform demanded a Federal slave code for the territories. This the Douglas men could not accept. When they lost the battle over the platform, the Deep South delegates seceded from the convention. Although a majority of those remaining were for Douglas, they did not have the necessary two-thirds to nominate him and so they adjourned to meet at Baltimore in June. Some of the seceding delegates attempted to rejoin the party at the Baltimore convention, but many were denied their seats, and there was another secession, this time including the upper South. The rump convention then nominated Douglas, and the seceders nominated Breckinridge. The Douglas platform omitted any mention of a slave code, although it made a limited concession to the Southern Rights men by proposing to refer all such conundrums to the Supreme Court. The Breckinridge platform called for a territorial slave code. At the moment the party divided on this question, there were in all the vast western territories only 20 slaveholders and 46 slaves.

While the Democrats were committing hara-kiri, the Republicans met in Chicago. It was, writes Allan Nevins, a "convention unlike any thus far known in national history. It was greater in size, in enthusiasm, in noise, in wire-pulling, in self-righteousness, in lust for office, and in its blend of mass hysteria with idealistic fervor." The party's task was plain. The Democrats had won four Northern states in 1856 — Pennsylvania, New Jersey, Indiana, and Illinois. The Republicans would have to add to their column either the last three or Pennsylvania and one other. Republicanism was more conservative in these states than in those farther north, which had voted for Frémont in the last election and now favored Seward. Even in these states the New Yorker's reputation for radicalism was something of a handicap; so was his close association with Thurlow Weed, Republican boss of New York and a reputed dabbler in corrupt schemes. Seward's candidacy was further weakened by the many enemies he had accumulated during his long career.

These factors helped Abraham Lincoln to emerge from the ranks of a half-dozen other candidates as Seward's strongest challenger. He was popular in Illinois, one of the states carried by the Democrats in 1856. He was supposedly more conservative than Seward. Because of his comparative obscurity, he had made fewer enemies than the New Yorker. He had kept clear of nativism, offending neither the foreign-born nor the Know-Nothings, whereas Seward had championed the cause of the immigrant. Finally, the convention met in Lincoln's own state; his backers made sure that many of the 10,000 spectators roared, shouted, and cheered for their favorite son. They also tried to win delegates by offering cabinet seats to Caleb Smith of Indiana and Simon Cameron, head of the venal Republican machine in Pennsylvania. Both accepted, although these states very probably would have gone to Lincoln anyway.

Lincoln pulled almost even with Seward on the second ballot. He won on the third, and Thurlow Weed wept. The platform announced that freedom was the natural condition of the territories; where necessary, slavery would be excluded by law. It condemned secession as treason. It came out for a Pacific railroad (as did both Democratic platforms) and a homestead law. The glibly ambiguous tariff plank could be, and was, interpreted according to local necessities either as a low revenue tariff or a high protective tariff. Soon after the convention, protectionists were reassured when House Republicans passed a bill containing higher rates. The platform denounced the Lecompton constitution, dead since the summer of 1858, the African slave trade, outlawed since 1808, and corruption. After some hesitation, the convention decided to endorse the Declaration of Independence. The platform was a seamless garment. The sharpest eye could not see where antislavery left off and the pursuit of profits began.

One reason that Lincoln's conservative image appealed to Republican strategists was the fourth candidate in the race, John Bell, an elderly Tennessee Whig. He had been nominated about a week before Lincoln by the Constitutional Union party. This was a concoction distilled from the debris of the Whig and Know-Nothing organizations. The platform deprecated sectionalism and stood four-square on the Constitution, the Union, and enforcement of the law. No specific proposals dimmed the luster of these noble sentiments, which appealed especially to the orphaned followers of Clay and Webster. The nomination of Seward would doubtless have driven more conservatives to Bell, whereas Lincoln was himself an old Clay man who could appeal to the Kentuckian's aging disciples. Thus, all unwittingly, the most conservative part of the electorate helped to nominate the Republican who was most likely to win and whose victory would precipitate secession. The Old Whigs, it seemed, could do nothing right.

With the conspicuous exception of Douglas himself, most Democratic leaders soon realized that neither Breckinridge nor Douglas could obtain an electoral majority. A few hoped that no candidate would get a majority, throwing the election into the House of Representatives where each state would have one vote. The strategic location of Lincoln's strength became ever more apparent. Eleventh-hour attempts by his opponents to fuse their tickets in various states accomplished nothing. They saw their doom sealed in October, when the Republicans easily won elections for state offices in Pennsylvania and Indiana. In fact, with the exception of New Jersey, where he got four out of seven votes, Lincoln swept the free states. He received not a single electoral vote from the South. Douglas carried only Missouri, and Bell took Tennessee, Kentucky and, by a hair's breadth, Virginia. Breckinridge carried the rest of the South. The electoral and popular totals were as follows: Lincoln, 180 and 1,866,352; Douglas, 12 and 1,375,157; Breckinridge, 72 and 849,781; and Bell, 39 and 589,581. A purely Northern candidate had won the presidency with 39.9 percent of the popular vote. Only John Quincy Adams had reached the White House with a smaller percentage. Curiously, if all those who voted for Lincoln's opponents had cast their ballots for a single candidate, Lincoln would still have won in the electoral college. Had the Democrats been united and enthusiastic, it is conceivable that they could have got out a larger vote. On the other hand, the total Democratic vote in 1860 was about 22 percent larger than the party had polled in 1856, so it is more likely that the three non-Republican tickets represented more shades of opinion and might well have attracted a larger total vote than a single candidate could have done.

It is difficult to decide what the American people were trying to say about the crisis of the Union in 1860. The Republicans, trying to calm the citizenry, insisted that Lincoln's election would not trigger secession, which they had denounced in their platform. Douglas unequivocally condemned the idea of disunion, the Constitutional Unionists were against it by definition, and Breckinridge, in his only campaign speech, opposed secession. Clearly the politicians believed that the temper of the majority was distinctly conservative. They were doubtless correct, if "conservative" is applied to those who were alarmed at the possibility of disunion, to say nothing of civil war. However, in the Deep South there was a powerful minority willing to accept the risks of secession, and perhaps an even larger element among the Republicans willing to put down secession by force. Some people at the time understood that this was the real issue, but apparently more did not. Had the question been put to the people explicitly, the result of the election surely would have been different; Lincoln and Breckinridge certainly would have received fewer votes. Probably no candidate would have received an electoral majority, sending the election to the House, where the chances for a peaceful solution would have been better. Perhaps what the people were trying to say in 1860 is less important than what they would have said had they been asked the right questions.

Chapter IV

The Final Crisis

NO COMPROMISE

Congress assembled on December 3. By that time seven Deep South legislatures from South Carolina to Texas had ordered the election of state conventions to prepare for whatever action the crisis might require. South Carolina's secession, which occurred on December 20, was a certainty from the beginning. The other states waited to see what Congress and the Republicans would do. In his annual message Buchanan stated that although the Constitution did not permit secession, neither did it empower the Federal government to keep a state in the Union by armed force. Even if it did, a Union kept together with bayonets would be worse than none at all. Buchanan recommended calming Southern fears by amending the Constitution to recognize expressly the right to hold slaves under state law, protect the same right in the territories, and enforce the fugitive slave clause more effectively. Amendments would reassure the South by putting these guarantees beyond the reach of a transitory majority, such as the Republicans, which otherwise might repeal a compromise that consisted merely of statutes, or reverse Supreme Court decisions by "reforming" the Court.

Each house established a committee to consider compromise proposals. The Senate Committee of Thirteen, by far the more important because of its membership, was eminently representative. Of eight non-Republicans, two came from the Deep South (Robert Toombs of Georgia and Jefferson Davis of Mississippi), two from the border slave states, and three from the North, one of whom was Douglas. Seward was one of the five Republicans. The committee adopted the rule of dual majorities: to succeed, any proposal had to be accepted by at least three Republicans and five others, recognizing the fact that no compromise amendment could be ratified without the support of the Republican party. Proposals sent to the states by a congressional majority composed of the Democrats and a handful of Republicans would merely raise false hopes and confuse the people.

The principal plan to come before the Senate committee was presented by one of its own members, John J. Crittenden, a Kentucky Whig. It consisted of six unamendable amendments that would recognize and protect slavery in the territories south of 36° 30′; deny to Congress any power to interfere with the interstate slave trade or to abolish slavery on governmental installations in the South or, except by consent and with compensation, in the District of Columbia; compel Congress to compensate owners who lost slaves in the North through illegal interference with the Fugitive Slave Law; make perpetual the fugitive slave and three-fifths ratio clauses of the Constitution; and deny to Congress any power to interfere with slavery in the states. Crittenden's proposal came to a vote in committee on December 22. All the Democrats supported it; all the Republicans were immovably opposed. Therefore Davis and Toombs invoked the rule of dual majorities, voted nay, and the Crittenden Compromise lost seven to six. Republican resistance to the compromise was part of a consistent policy pursued throughout the crucial session of 1860-1861.

Crittenden tried to salvage his plan by recommending to the full Senate that it be submitted to the people in a referendum. It probably would have received a large majority in the North as well as in the South, but a majority of the Republicans voted nay. Despite its victory in 1860, their party was still in a precarious position. It was a minority, and it contained internal differences that had been submerged only by the need to oppose a common enemy, the South. Make peace with that enemy and the party might well come unglued. It needed time to strengthen and unify itself through its newly won control of the executive patronage. Therefore to compromise on the issue that symbolized everything the party stood for would be as suicidal for the Republicans as refusing to compromise had been for the Democrats at the Charleston convention.

No one realized this more clearly than Lincoln. Wielding all the immense influence of a president-elect of a new party with unprecedented patronage at his disposal, he wrote letter after letter during those fateful December days, telling party leaders to resist any compromise on territorial slavery. For example, on December 10 he wrote to an Illinois senator, "Let there be no compromise on the question of *extending* slavery. If there be, all our labor is lost, and ere long, must be done again. Have none of it. Stand firm. The tug has to come & better now, than any time hereafter." He was, he told Thurlow Weed, "inflexible on the territorial question," a message that Weed was supposed to pass along to a forthcoming meeting of Republican governors.

These events had a heavy impact on the Deep South conventions that met in January. The delegates' attitudes ranged across the political spectrum from Southern nationalism to unconditional Unionism. Both extremes were small minorities. More numerous were those who had been willing to give compromise one last chance, and who now, compromise having failed, advocated immediate secession. The largest group of conservatives were the cooperationists, so called because they wished to delay secession until the South was sufficiently united to act as a unit. They believed that a united South would have a better chance of bargaining within the Union, or of surviving outside it. Finally, there were those delegates who believed that secession should be resorted to only if the Republican administration took hostile action against the South.

Opponents of immediate secession were quite strong in several Deep South conventions, but they were gravely handicapped by their inability to cite any evidence that the Republican leadership was willing to compromise. In contrast, advocates of immediate secession could point to a great deal of Republican enmity and intransigence. Republican acceptance of the Crittenden Compromise would almost certainly have defeated secession in every state except South Carolina; even there, lack of Southern support would surely have produced a conservative reaction, as it had in 1833. Instead of agreeing to concessions, however, the Republicans held fast "as with a chain of steel," to use Lincoln's words. Some of them, notably Seward, spoke vaguely of possible future adjustments, which Southerners interpreted correctly as strategems intended to prevent any more states from seceding until Lincoln took office.

The immediate secessionists insisted that further delay would only play into the hands of the South's avowed enemies. For months Republican paramilitary organizations such as the Wide Awakes had been parading and drilling all across the North. Why wait any longer? They had their way. State after state enacted ordinances of secession; by February 1 South Carolina had been followed by Mississippi, Alabama, Georgia, Florida, Louisiana, and Texas. Once the decision had been made, most former opponents of secession wholeheartedly supported Southern independence.

Delegates from the seceded states met at Montgomery, Alabama, early in February, quickly drew up a provisional Constitution for the Confederate States of America, and organized themselves as the provisional Congress; they chose Jefferson Davis of Mississippi to be president of the new nation and Alexander H. Stephens of Georgia to be vice-president, pending regular elections. In his inaugural address on February 19, Davis repeatedly expressed an earnest hope for peace, a hope that the North "shall permit us peaceably to pursue our separate political career." But, he continued, "if this be denied to us, and the integrity of our territory and jurisdiction be assailed, it will but remain for us, with firm resolve, to appeal to arms and invoke the blessings of Providence on a just cause."

WHY SECESSION?

> Yes, call us rebels, 'tis the name
> Our patriot fathers bore

So began a poem written in the spring of 1861. There were others like it in theme, and they provide a valuable clue to the fundamental causes of secession.

Some historians have blamed secession on a carefully contrived conspiracy by a small minority of disunionists, an opinion popular in the North for many years. Others have said that a growing slave population, soil exhaustion, and the ambition of most Southerners to become planters generated a need for more slave territory that could not be satisfied while the South remained in the Union. Still others have explained secession as a rational response to an irrational estimate of the South's peril. Attempts have been made to discover the connection between secessionism and slaveowning, density of the black population, wealth, past political affiliations, geography, and so forth. Although these studies have presented useful information and fresh viewpoints, they have perhaps made the subject appear more complicated than it is. The reasons for seceding were not at all obscure to Southerners at the time. Many saw themselves fighting a second War for Independence. For example, the South Carolina convention made an explicit comparison between 1776 and 1861 and charged that the Northern majority, by arrogating more and more power to the central government, had imposed the same unjust burdens on Southern commerce as the British had attempted to levy on the colonies. "No man can, for a moment, believe that our ancestors intended to establish over their posterity, exactly the same sort of Government they had overthrown." Not content with draining off Southern wealth by unfair and unconstitutional laws, now, through the agency of the Republican party, they were in a position to carry out their announced purpose of overthrowing the basis of the South's economy and society: slavery. The incoming president had announced that it was the policy of his party to guarantee slavery's "ultimate extinction." The North would have the power to remake the Supreme Court so that it could not prevent Republican usurpations. There can be, said the Carolinians, "but one end by the submission of the South to the rule of a sectional antislavery government at Washington; and that end, directly or indirectly, must be — the emancipation of the slaves of the South."

Southerners discounted assurances that the incoming president would not interfere with slavery in the states. Whatever Lincoln's intentions might be, he was, they believed, a prisoner of the movement that had elevated him to the presidency. Thus everything pointed to the destruction of slavery. At best abolition posed seemingly insoluble problems of race relations; at worst — the memory of John Brown was still fresh — it promised the horrors of a race war. Moreover, so much Southern wealth was invested in the 4 million slaves that abolition would mean an economic catastrophe for the entire section.

The Confederate Constitution throws considerable light on the reasons for secession. Southerners had claimed all along that there was nothing wrong with the Federal Constitution; the problem was the North's interpretation of that document. Consequently the changes that they introduced into their own charter of government reflect the nature of their grievances against the North and what they hoped to accomplish by seceding. In their main outlines, and leaving aside reforms intended to make government more honest and efficient, these changes fall under three headings: the nature of the Union, economic policies, and slavery.

For many years there were those who argued that the phrase "we the people" in the preamble to the Federal Constitution meant that the government had been ordained by the people generally, instead of by the people of each state acting as a separate sovereign community. To settle that question, the Confederate preamble inserted the clause "each state acting in its sovereign and independent character." In a similar vein legislative powers were "delegated" not "granted," the latter term smacking too much of an irrevocable transfer of sovereign powers. The amending process could originate only with the states, not, as in the Federal Constitution, with Congress as well, and there were several other minor provisions tending to magnify the status and authority of the states. The right of secession was not mentioned only because it was taken to be self-evident.

As to economic issues, protective tariffs were prohibited, but now, with no hostile Northern majority to fear, export tariffs were allowed if passed by a two-thirds vote. There was no conveniently elastic phrase about levying taxes "for the general welfare," but instead only for necessary revenue and to carry on the government. National expenditures for internal improvements were severely restricted. In fact, all expenditures were made more difficult. With certain limited exceptions, Congress could appropriate money only upon a request by the president based on the estimate of a department head, unless by a two-thirds vote.

The Constitution outlawed the African slave trade and required

Congress to pass legislation that would "effectually" enforce that provision. There was nothing to prevent any state from abolishing slavery or to keep nonslaveholding states from joining the Confederacy. On the other hand, the rights of slaveowners in any territories that might be acquired were upheld, as was the right to travel with such property through any future free states. The plain word "slave" was used in place of the circumlocution "persons held to service."

These innovations can be summarized as an attempt to protect the rights of the states, to limit the power of the central government by reducing taxes and expenditures, to prevent legislation on behalf of special interests, and to recognize unequivocally the institution of slavery. All things considered, the Confederate Constitution is a revealing document.

But secession cannot be explained only by citing dissatisfaction with Northern economic objectives, or fears of an economic collapse, or even of a race war. Underlying the Southern movement for independence was an abiding passion to be free from outside control and interference. This is a phenomenon with deep roots in Anglo-American history.

An English scholar has argued that the social, political, and ideological pattern of the Old South was firmly impressed on seventeenth-century Virginia by the early colonists, a great many of whom came from the county of Kent. The Kentish gentry were a classic example of the English squirearchy. Among this class, the basic social unit was an extended family with a recognized head or patriarch whose authority was acknowledged by family members within and outside the immediate household, and whose word was law to his often numerous servants and retainers. Like the gentry everywhere, they governed the county and enforced the authority of the central government at the local level. Moreover, the Kentish gentry were conspicuous for their unusual influence in the realm at large and were very proud of that distinction. Their other salient characteristics included an intense interest in political theory, political institutions, and history. Above all, they were dedicated to their pride of place and their unchallenged domination of local affairs.

This social ethos was carried lock, stock, and barrel to the first English settlements in Tidewater Virginia and from there was spread across the South. The social ideal of the section became the planter-patriarch, with his extended family of blood relations and his numerous black servants. The spirit of proud independence that this ethos contained was reinforced by the plantation system and by the frontier conditions that prevailed in much of the section for many years. It gave birth to various forms of Southern political philosophy, all of which in one way or another emphasized states' rights or state sovereignty.

So Southern belief in a Northern determination to transform the United States into a consolidated nation, where the majority must always rule a central government endowed with large, indefinite implied powers, loomed as a grave threat to many Southerners' most cherished ideals of society, of government, of life itself. When secessionists insisted that they left the Union to preserve states' rights, they meant exactly that. In the last analysis, they seceded for an idea, the idea that they would not meekly submit to Northern rule. If they were rebels, so be it. After all, it was the name their "patriot fathers bore."

FORT SUMTER

There were a few forlorn attempts at compromise in Congress during the early weeks of 1861. As in December, not a single proposal received a majority of Republican votes. Lincoln's influence was decisive in preventing the Crittenden plan from reaching the floor of Congress until early March, when the government of the Confederate States had been in existence for almost a month and the question was academic. Even then, not a single Republican in either house voted aye.

Another anticlimax was the Washington Peace Convention, called by the state of Virginia in belated effort to prevent disaster. The Deep South had seceded by the time the convention met on February 4, and it sent no delegates. Seven of the eight Southern states still in the Union were represented, as were a dozen Northern states. Some of the latter sent delegates expressly to oppose compromise. After much acrimony the convention finally recommended a constitutional amendment resembling the Crittenden plan in some respects, but not as sweeping or as favorable to the South. The Senate voted it down, and the House never considered it. Nevertheless, by coming at this particular time, the convention had the effect of raising false hopes of conciliation. One student of the subject believes that it helped to keep the border states from seceding. It doubtless had a moderating influence on the February elections for state conventions in the upper South, although the final outcome turned many disillusioned conservatives into enthusiastic secessionists.

As hopes for compromise faded and Lincoln's inauguration drew near, the old issues dividing the sections gave way to one overriding question: Would the North agree to a peaceful separation, or would it put down the Confederacy by armed conquest? Only by the latter could the Federal government enforce its authority in the seceded states. When compared to the power of today's mighty, omnipresent government, that authority was quite limited; it was confined to military installations, custom houses, mints, arsenals, navy yards, post offices, and Federal courts. When South Carolina left the Union, Federal civil officers, as loyal Carolinians, resigned. Federal power was thus extinguished except for a garrison of troops at Fort Moultrie, part of the defenses of Charleston Harbor. Early in December, anticipating secession, South Carolina congressmen discussed the situation at Charleston with the President, and they thought Buchanan agreed not to disturb the military status quo in the harbor. Later in the month, South Carolina sent commissioners to Washington to negotiate settlement of all questions arising from secession, such as the state's share of the national debt, payment for Federal property, and, above all, removal of the garrison from Charleston Harbor. Scarcely had the commissioners arrived when, on December 26, they learned by telegraph that the commander at Fort Moultrie, Major Robert Anderson, had spiked his guns and secretly moved his men under cover of darkness to Fort Sumter. Moultrie was on the mainland, facing the water, and was indefensible on the land side; Sumter was a larger fortification in the mouth of the harbor and better able to resist attack. Anderson's actions seemed clearly to indicate that the Federal government had no intention of evacuating the garrison and was preparing for hostilities. Therefore state troops promptly occupied Fort Moultrie and

Castle Pinckney, a small vacant post in the harbor. The commissioners accused Buchanan of breaking faith, and after a torrid exchange of letters with the President, the angry Carolinians went home.

In conjunction with the practical defeat of the Crittenden plan on December 22, events at Charleston were taken by many Southerners to mean that there would be no compromise and no recognition of secession by the Federal government. The popular response in the Deep South was to demand the immediate seizure of Federal property there. State officials intervened and took possession of the various buildings and installations. Soon Federal authority existed only where there were military garrisons: Fort Sumter, Fort Pickens in the harbor at Pensacola, and two remote forts in the Florida Keys. Of these, Sumter was by far the most important, both militarily and symbolically. Day after day it flew the Stars and Stripes in the birthplace and citadel of secessionism. Early in January, in the wake of his quarrel with the South Carolina commissioners, Buchanan dispatched the *Star of the West* to Fort Sumter with supplies and reinforcements. When the ship was driven off by South Carolina batteries, passions were aroused in the North as well as the South; but although the flag had been fired on, Buchanan issued no call to arms, and the crisis passed. The expedition riveted the nation's attention on Fort Sumter as never before: it now embodied the one great question of the day. Its evacuation would be understood as *de facto* recognition of Confederate independence, a resolute effort to hold it as a decision to preserve the Union by whatever means necessary.

Buchanan avoided any further provocative acts, and the question of union or disunion, of peace or war, was passed on to his successor, Abraham Lincoln. There are times when an individual can influence or even direct events of historic importance, and it was Lincoln's fate to be such an individual at such a time. As president and commander-in-chief, he could assert the full range of Federal authority in the seceded states by military means, or he could relinquish the last vestiges of that authority by eventually abandoning Fort Sumter and Fort Pickens. There were many indications as to what Lincoln would do when the fatal moment arrived. Years before, during the 1856 campaign, he had told Southerners that if they tried to secede, "*we won't let you.* With the purse and sword, the army and navy and treasury in our hands and at our command, *you couldn't do it."* Late in 1859 he said the South would be treated as Virginia had treated John Brown if it tried to leave the Union. A year later, in December 1860, when Lincoln heard rumors that Buchanan might surrender the forts, he stated privately that if so he would retake the forts after his inauguration. And in the first draft of his inaugural address he wrote, "All the power at my disposal will be used to reclaim the public property and places that have fallen. . . . " This was too forthright for Secretary of State Seward, and it was softened to read that the President would "hold, occupy, and possess the property and places belonging to the government. . . . " Lincoln no doubt quickly saw the tactical wisdom of this ambiguous phraseology. He would need time to take full control of the executive branch; it would not do to risk precipitating a crisis before he was prepared to deal with it.

Meanwhile a Confederate commission had arrived in Washington to arrange a peaceful settlement of the problems arising from secession. Their major objective, leaving aside diplomatic recognition, was to secure the evacuation of Fort Sumter. They were taken aback by Lincoln's inaugural address, which to them sounded like a war message. It seemed as if their mission might be over before it began, but at this critical moment Seward intervened. Still accustomed to think of himself as the leader of his party, Seward intended to use his position as Secretary of State to dominate the Lincoln administration. His policy in the secession crisis was to delay, temporize, and avoid a collision. He believed that given time a conservative reaction would occur in the Deep South and permit a peaceful reconstruction of the Union under his expert guidance. Seward hoped the Confederate commissioners, by serving as an authoritative means of communication with their government, could be manipulated so as to control Southern policy. Through various prominent intermediaries, he led the commissioners to believe that he was the guiding force in the Lincoln administration. They should not be alarmed at the inaugural; there would be no war. He persuaded them to defer any embarrassing demands for recognition in exchange for the evacuation of Fort Sumter within a few days. During most of March and the first week in April, Seward repeatedly promised that the fort would be given up. Lincoln almost certainly knew, in a general way, what Seward was telling the Confederates, although he took care to know nothing specifically or officially.

While the befuddled Confederates were kept dangling, the astute Lincoln gained priceless time to mature his own plans. The Sumter garrison would run out of food on April 15. Having decided to hold Sumter, Lincoln had to pick the best possible moment between March 4 and April 15 to act. This was more a political than a military problem, hence one that Lincoln was admirably equipped to handle. On March 15 he polled his cabinet on supplying the fort; most of them advised against it. Obviously the time was not yet ripe. However, pressure for decisive action accumulated rapidly during the latter part of March, and when Lincoln put the same question to the cabinet on the 29th, he got the answer he was waiting for. The cabinet fully expected that an expedition to Sumter would mean war, and there is ample reason to think the President shared their belief. Nevertheless, he ordered a relief expedition to be prepared. If not resisted, it would merely resupply the fort; if opposed, it would land reinforcements as well.

The Confederate commissioners soon heard rumors of a powerful flotilla secretly being readied for a descent on the Southern coast, but Seward continued to assure them that Sumter would be given up. On April 7, in response to their latest anxious enquiries, Seward told his go-between: "Faith as to Sumter fully kept; wait and see. . . . " It was a short wait. The very next day a clerk from the State Department handed Governor Francis Pickens of South Carolina an unsigned, unauthenticated memorandum saying that Sumter would be supplied, peacefully if possible, by force if necessary.

Lincoln had seized the initiative. If the Confederates allowed the fort to be provisioned, Lincoln would be hailed in the North for calling their bluff, and many Southerners, and perhaps foreign governments, would find it difficult to take the Confederacy's claim to nationhood seriously. If the Confederates fired on the ships or the fort, Lincoln could claim that they had started the war and call the North to arms.

The situation seemed even more threatening than that from the standpoint of the Confederate government at Montgomery. Messages had come in telling of a formidable expedition that would not stop at provisioning Sumter, but would invade the mainland. Could the Confederates afford to believe the suspiciously unofficial promise given to Governor Pickens that the only object was to send food to the garrison? In light of Seward's tactics to date, President Jefferson Davis decided not to risk accepting as truth what might be merely the last in a long series of lies. He concluded that Lincoln had decided to conquer the Confederacy by force of arms rather than acknowledge its existence. If war was inevitable, he thought it would be foolish to allow a reputedly powerful fleet to steam unopposed into Charleston Harbor and possibly administer a crippling wound to the new nation. Davis decided the fleet must be resisted. When Major Anderson refused to surrender or to remain neutral in the forthcoming engagement, Davis ordered Fort Sumter to be attacked; the Confederates could not afford to fight the fort and the ships simultaneously. The bombardment opened at 4:30 A.M., April 12. The fleet, which arrived at about the same time, was unable to render any assistance. After a gallant though bloodless resistance, Sumter surrendered on the afternoon of April 13. Two days later Lincoln called on the states for 75,000 troops to put down "combinations too powerful to be suppressed by the ordinary course of judicial proceedings," thus in effect declaring war on the Confederacy.

Northern response to the President's summons was enthusiastic, and Lincoln was well pleased with the success of his strategy. On May 1 he wrote G. V. Fox, who had organized the relief expedition, saying: "You and I both anticipated that the cause of the country would be advanced by making the attempt to provision Fort Sumter, even if it should fail; and it is no small consolation now to feel that our anticipation is justified by the result." Two months later Lincoln told his old friend O. H. Browning, who recorded the conversation in his diary, that "he himself conceived the idea, and proposed sending supplies without an attempt to reinforce [,] giving notice of the fact to Gov[.] Pickens of S. C. The plan succeeded. They attacked Sumter — it fell, and thus, did more service than it otherwise could."

"I WOULD SAVE THE UNION . . . "

At first glance one might think the North would have welcomed secession. Now Southerners could no longer block homestead laws, a Pacific railroad, river and harbor improvements, or higher tariffs. There would no longer be the slightest threat of slavery spreading into free territories and states. In short, secession cleared the way for enactment of the entire Republican platform. Yet Northerners were willing to fight to keep the South from leaving. When asked why, the usual answer was that "the Union must be preserved." But what did "the Union" signify? Was the preservation of a certain type of political apparatus an end in itself? Was the South to be coerced in the name of an abstraction? For many Northerners — no one can say how many — the answer was surely "yes." The sanctity of the Union had long been part of the nation's patriotic creed, going back to the War for Independence and reinforced by innumerable orations, Fourth of July celebrations, and other such observances. The peroration of Webster's second reply to Hayne rang down through the years: "Liberty and Union, now and forever, one and inseparable." Many still remembered how Andrew Jackson had looked Calhoun straight in the eye and proposed the toast, "Our Federal union: it must be preserved." It was to this spirit that Lincoln, coached by Seward, appealed in the last sentence of his inaugural address. "The mystic chords of memory, stre[t]ching from every battlefield, and patriot grave, to every living heart and hearthstone, all over this broad land, will yet swell the chorus of the Union, when again touched, as surely they will be, by the better angels of our nature." Furthermore, ever since the Nullification Crisis, threats of disunion had come to be associated with the machinations of the Slave Power. Except for some of the more radical abolitionists, opposition to disunion was inseparable from opposition to slavery.

So for many in the North the preservation of the Union was an end in itself. They did not rush to the colors to get a higher tariff or a Pacific railroad, however much they may have favored those measures, but to protect the sacred Union against the assaults of a pack of sinful, brutal, tyrannical, overbearing, slave-driving Simon Legrees. A fervent evangelical desire to trample out the vintage where the grapes of wrath were stored permeated the popular enthusiasm for putting down secession. Yet the cause of the Union could sanctify some very practical purposes. Various weighty Northern interests regarded secession as a deadly threat. The withdrawal of Southerners from Congress had allowed the Republicans to raise the tariff in March. Duties on goods entering the United States were now higher than on those imported by the Confederacy. Northern manufacturers faced the loss of their Southern market to cheap foreign goods. Merchants who enjoyed a lucrative position as middlemen between the South and the rest of the world feared the deflection of trans-Atlantic commerce to the low-tariff Confederacy. Southern dreams of direct trade with Europe were on the verge of realization; Confederate independence had already ended the North's time-honored monopoly of coastwise shipping. Merchants and bankers who had lent money in the South were afraid they might not be able to collect their debts. Propertied persons generally expected that secession, if not suppressed, would mean the collapse of government and private investments and a sharp decline in property values. Already there was a panic in the making; business had slowed during the winter of 1860-1861, and stock prices had dropped sharply. These and other considerations led Northern businessmen to favor concessions that would keep the South in the Union. But when compromise failed and the Confederacy was born, many of them joined with Republican militants and called for stern action to put down secession and save them from ruin.

Fear of the economic consequences of secession extended far beyond the business community. There was widespread concern in the Northwest that free navigation of the Mississippi might end, leaving that section in bondage to Eastern railroads and cutting off important Southern markets for Northwestern meat and grain. Some predicted that these considerations might even induce the Northwest to secede and join the Confederacy. And everywhere the growing number of unemployed waited impatiently for some action that would revive business and create jobs.

All these anxieties translated into heavier and heavier political pressure on the party in power. Lincoln allowed that pressure to build up as long as he could, given Major Anderson's shrinking food supply. Then came the cabinet meeting of March 29 and the decision to relieve Fort Sumter. Lincoln thereby extricated himself and his party from a dangerous dilemma. Moderate Republicans, like Northern Democrats, had been shocked when, contrary to their leaders' assurances, Lincoln's election had been followed by secession. And although they wanted to preserve the Union, they were far from reconciled to the possibility of a civil war. By contrast, the radical Republicans were not dismayed at the thought of bloodshed; in fact, some seemed to relish the idea. This wing of the party urged Lincoln to get tough with the South. Lincoln found his way out of this predicament by "the giving of bread to the few brave and hungry men" of Fort Sumter, an ostensibly conservative action that he had every reason to believe would provoke the Confederates into firing the first shot. Moderates could not blame Lincoln for a war the South seemingly had begun, and the militants could not blame him for not acting decisively. The Republicans united behind the President's policy; many Democrats joined them, at least so far as preserving the Union was concerned. Lincoln had rallied his party and consolidated his leadership of it. No wonder he told Browning that when Sumter fell, it "did more service than it otherwise could."

On July 4, 1861, the day after his talk with Browning, Lincoln sent a message to Congress describing and justifying his actions since taking office. As to facts it was disingenuous and inaccurate, but given the circumstances Lincoln should not be judged with undue harshness on that account. The message is important because it contains Lincoln's own explanation of what was at stake. When faced with a choice between disunion and war, he said, he regretfully chose war because it was both his duty and desire to preserve the institutions of popular government in the United States.

> And this issue embraces more than the fate of these United States. It presents to the whole family of man, the question, whether a constitutional republic, or a democracy — a government of the people, by the same people — can, or cannot, maintain its territorial integrity, against its own domestic foes. . . . It forces us to ask: "Is there, in all republics, this inherent, and fatal weakness?" "Must a government, of necessity, be too *strong* for the liberties of its own people, or too *weak* to maintain its own existence?"

He characterized the war as "essentially a People's contest."

On the side of the Union, it is a struggle for maintaining in the world, that form, and substance of government, whose leading object is, to elevate the condition of men — to lift artificial weights from all shoulders — to clear the paths of laudable pursuit for all — to afford all, an unfettered start, and a fair chance, in the race of life . . . this is the leading object of the government for whose existence we contend.

Was Lincoln using high-sounding ideals to cloak shady methods and selfish ends? Probably Lincoln indulged in this kind of all-too-human hypocrisy less than most politicians. Of course, one may doubt if Lincoln really believed that free government would have perished from the earth had he decided to leave the Confederacy alone; even if he did not, this is the kind of harmless hyperbole that politicians customarily employ. Leaving aside such utterances, Lincoln was certainly a man of ideals, but they apparently did not extend beyond what he believed to be politically possible. His reach did not exceed his grasp. For him political imperatives were moral imperatives. Lincoln's behavior in the Sumter crisis and throughout his career cannot best be understood by seeing him as a Machiavelli on the one hand or a paragon of moral grandeur on the other. He is much easier to fathom if seen as an intensely ambitious man who thought, acted, and moralized almost entirely within the confines of a political universe. As his old antagonist Douglas once remarked, "he [is] preeminently a man of the atmosphere that surrounds him."

SECESSION COMPLETED

Lincoln's call for troops awakened upper South conservatives from their dream of peace. For them it was the knell of the Union that Jefferson had heard from afar when slavery made its political debut 40 years before. However devoted to the Union, however repelled by secession, they could scarcely comprehend an act that was to them so full of effrontery or folly or both as a command to march against their Southern brothers. "You have chosen to inaugurate civil war," replied Governor John Letcher of Virginia, "and having done so, we will meet it in a spirit as determined as the Administration has exhibited toward the South." John Ellis of North Carolina, who found it difficult to believe that the dispatch he had received was genuine, told Lincoln that if it was, he would get no troops from North Carolina to enforce "this wicked violation of the laws of the country." Governor Isham Harris flung back, "Tennessee will not furnish a single man for coercion, but fifty thousand, if necessary, for the defense of our rights and those of our Southern brethern." Arkansas' governor replied in like spirit.

The Virginia Convention, which had defeated a secession ordinance as recently as April 4, voted on April 17 to leave the Union. Almost all the opposition came from the northwestern counties that would later break off from the state to form West Virginia. The people ratified the convention's actions on May 23 by a five to one majority. The Arkansas convention reassembled on May 10 and seceded the same day. North Carolina hurriedly elected a convention, which took the state out of the Union by a unanimous vote. Tennessee dispensed with a convention and submitted the question directly to the voters, who returned a more than two to one verdict for secession.

It was a different story in the border states. Delaware scarcely needs to be mentioned. It was small and exposed, with no chance to leave the Union even had it been so inclined. In Maryland secessionist sentiment was quite strong, but Governor Thomas Hicks, a Unionist, refused to call a special session of the legislature until after the war had begun. He knew that if he did, the election of a convention would follow, and a convention might vote to secede. On April 19 there was a bloody collision between a pro-Southern crowd and a Massachusetts regiment passing through Baltimore. The railroad leading to Washington was cut, and for a time the Northern capital was all but cut off. In this alarming situation, Lincoln could afford to take no chances; should Maryland secede, the seat of government would be in the Confederacy. Numerous citizens, including the mayor of Baltimore and 19 members of the legislature, were seized by soldiers and thrown into prison. Soon the state was under tight military control.

The large and populous state of Kentucky could not be so treated. If some hasty act should provoke it into joining the Confederacy, the latter might be too strong to subdue. Opinion in the state was sharply divided, although the prevailing desire was to remain neutral, and for nearly five months both sides respected Kentucky's wishes and kept their troops out of the state. Then in early September, hearing rumors that the Federals were about to cross the Ohio, the Confederates seized the strategic town of Columbus. The Federals responded by occupying Paducah. Other troops came in, and soon a military frontier ran the length of the state from Columbus on the Mississippi to Cumberland Gap in the mountains. In November delegates representing 65 counties declared the state to be out of the Union, an action not recognized by the state government or by most of the people. Although Kentucky was received into the Confederacy, its membership was little more than nominal. By the end of February 1862, it had been almost entirely occupied by Union troops, an occupation that was uninterrupted save by occasional Confederate raids. Disgust with the excesses of Northern rule eventually led many Kentuckians to wish they had joined the Confederacy.

Divisions within Missouri led to a civil war and the establishment of rival state governments. The pro-Southern regime was inducted into the Confederacy late in 1861, but Southern forces in the state were decisively beaten before the war was a year old, and Missouri was firmly in Union hands.

The Confederates had some success in wooing the tribes of Indian Territory away from their dependence on the Washington government. They not only signed treaties of alliance with them, but opened the door to future statehood, a concession unparalleled in the long and dismal history of Indian affairs. Most Confederate Indians remained close to home and fought against tribes loyal to the Union, although a few units took part in more conventional campaigns.

For a brief time there was a Confederate Territory of Arizona, created by the inhabitants of southern New Mexico as a result of local political rivalries. This experiment lasted less than a year before it was crushed by Union expeditions from California and Colorado.

Chapter V

Armies, Strategy, and Politics

COMPARATIVE RESOURCES

Historians have often speculated as to why the South lost the war. A simple catalog of resources suggests that the question should be, "How did the South hold out so long?" The most obvious Northern advantage was in population. Making due allowance for divided sentiment in the border slave states and elsewhere, total population in the North came to 22 million, in the Confederacy to 9.4 million. The actual discrepancy was much larger because the Confederacy did not use blacks as soldiers: the North had 3.67 times the white population of the Confederacy. It also drew on its own blacks and those of the border states and, as Federal armies advanced, on those of the Confederacy as well. A majority of the 180,000 Negroes who served the Union were enrolled in occupied parts of the Confederacy. About 45,000 additional white recruits came from Unionist areas in the South such as East Tennessee. Finally, Northern agents abroad succeeded in recruiting perhaps 300,000 men, although one estimate goes as high as 400,000 to 500,000. All things considered, the North could draw on four times as many men of military age as the Confederacy could. It used about 44 percent of that manpower pool; at least 2 million men served substantial terms in the Union army. The Confederacy fielded 75 percent, approximately 850,000 men who served longer terms on the average than their adversaries did. On the field of battle the Union very occasionally found itself outnumbered; usually it enjoyed a heavy numerical advantage, sometimes ranging as high as four to one. In the eastern theater of operations the average ratio for major engagements was about 11 to 6, less in the early months, much greater in the last year of the war.

These statistics show that the South poured a far larger percentage of its human resources into the crucible of battle and therefore suffered far heavier proportional losses. Based on incomplete Confederate records, it appears that there were about 100,000 battle-caused deaths, 200,000 deaths from disease, and 230,000 surviving wounded, a total of 530,000 or 62 percent of those who served. These are casualties on an Old World scale and remain without parallel in American history. Union dead came to 360,000 (about two-thirds from disease), and the surviving wounded to at least 275,000, a total of 635,000, or 31 percent of those who served. Because a much smaller percentage of Northern manpower was used, the ratio of casualties to the total white male population was about one-fourth that in the South.

The North's huge preponderance of material resources was even more overwhelming than its numerical superiority. Its manufacturing output in 1860 was 10 times that of the South, and the difference in quality and versatility was almost as striking. Northern iron foundries, shipyards, and machine shops could produce far better tools and weapons, such as superior artillery and ammunition, turreted ironclad warships with efficient engines, and repeating rifles using metallic cartridges. The North had two and a half times the railroad mileage of the South and was able to lay track and build rolling stock as the war continued. Southern railroads steadily deteriorated; almost no railroad iron was rolled, and not a single car or locomotive was manufactured. Accessible supplies of necessary raw materials such as coal, iron ore, and copper were plentiful in the North, scarce in the South.

When Fort Sumter fell, Federal arsenals contained 530,000 small arms, mostly outdated smoothbores; of these, less than one-third were in the 11 Confederate states. Although the Union army and navy, 16,000 men and 50 ships, were wholly insufficient for the task at hand, the Confederacy began its career with no army and no navy whatever. The North possessed an established, functioning government with which to mobilize its resources; the South had to build its national government from the ground up. Most of the banks, specie, and currency were in the North, which led to acute financial difficulties for the Confederates.

The catalog of Northern advantages could be extended almost indefinitely. The main effect was to give to the Union a margin of error that the South did not enjoy. The former could afford to make large mistakes and still win; the latter depended for survival on fighting a nearly letter-perfect war. The only edge the South possessed was generals with more talent and common soldiers who fought harder on the average than their opponents. Together they were able to prolong the contest beyond what might have been expected, but in the end they could not withstand the weight of men and matériel thrown against them year after year.

CALL TO THE COLORS: THE UNION

Never had the nation seen armies of the size raised during the Civil War. The grand total in the Mexican War had not exceeded 112,000 men; the largest field army numbered 11,000. These figures can be compared to more than 2 million Union enlistments and Union field armies of more than 100,000 men.

The building of this vast force was a haphazard process. Lincoln did not call Congress into special session until the war was 11 weeks old, thereby delaying essential military legislation by precisely that period of time. As mentioned before, the President called on the states to supply 75,000 militia immediately after Fort Sumter surrendered, and on May 3, without legal sanction, he authorized the enlistment of 82,000 additional soldiers and seamen, promising to seek Congressional approval later. In his July 4 message to the special session, Lincoln asked for 400,000 more volunteers. All this occurred before any battle had been fought; Lincoln obviously could not have expected a quick, easy victory.

There were three types of army service: volunteer, regular, and state militia. Militia supplied most of the men for the Revolution and the War of 1812, volunteers for the Mexican and Civil Wars, although after 1862 for many the alternative to volunteering was the draft. Raising volunteer troops was very much of a state affair. The Federal government gave each state a quota of men to furnish and relied on state officials to enlist and organize the troops. According to the act of July 22, 1861, the governors chose regimental officers up to and including colonel. Instantly military commissions became a fruitful source of patronage. Instead of sending recruits to fill out the depleted ranks of veteran regiments, new regiments were created so as to multiply the number of offices. The President nominated candidates for the rank of general, and he came under heavy pressure from governors and congressmen who pleaded the cause of political associates from their respective states. One entry in the diary of Illinois' Senator Browning offers a glimpse of the way things were done. "At night went to Trumbulls rooms to meet the Illinois delegation and agree upon the Brig: Genl for our state. Pope and Hurlbut being already appointed we thought we would be entitled to seven more." Officers' promotions as well as their appointments often depended more on political claims than military ability.

Lincoln had political reasons of his own for selecting general officers, and the results were sometimes astonishing. For instance, between the relief of George B. McClellan in November 1862 and the appointment of Ulysses S. Grant as lieutenant general in March 1864, the ranking field generals in the Union army were Nathaniel P. Banks and Benjamin F. Butler. Both were Massachusetts politicians, devoid of military training, whose martial accomplishments had ranged from disasters to fiascos. In 1863, about a year after he had come to Washington to be general in chief, Henry Halleck wrote Grant, "I sincerely wish I was with you again in the West. I am utterly sick of this political Hell." And a year later he told William T. Sherman, " . . . It seems a little better than murder to give important commands to men such as Banks, Butler, McClernand, Sigel, and Lew. Wallace, and yet it seems impossible to prevent it." The common soldier paid with blood for the bungling of these misfits. It is usually said that such was the price Lincoln had to pay to attract support for the Union cause, an explanation that, if true, sheds much light on the nature of Northern politics. If false, it raises interesting questions about the President's judgment or priorities.

The burst of volunteering during the early months of the war did not outlast the realization that the war was not after all to be a one-battle affair with little risk and much glory. An element of compulsion was required. In July 1862 Congress empowered Lincoln to call on the states for 300,000 nine-month militia and if necessary to fill up the quotas by conscription. This law was not satisfactory, and so Congress, stimulated by a series of major defeats in Virginia, passed the Enrollment Act of March 3, 1863. All men between 20 and 45 years of age were to be enrolled. The physically unfit, convicted felons, aliens, certain government officials, and men who were the sole support of aged parents or of orphaned children were excused from service. Those not exempted could escape by hiring a substitute or by paying a commutation fee of $300, which amounted to a year's wages for many Northern workers. Commutation was defended — by the President and others — as necessary to keep down the price of substitutes, since no one would hire a substitute for more than $300 if he could use that amount to purchase his exemption. This ingenious argument finessed the charge that the substitute clause itself discriminated against the poor. Congress bowed to public protests and eliminated commutation in July 1864. Substitution survived, and the price of substitutes greatly increased. With their options narrowed, some hard-pressed eligibles took out draft insurance, a wartime creation of commercial inventiveness by which the insuring company undertook to supply a substitute should the policyholder be called up. Some sunshine patriots would grasp at any straw. In Philadelphia several hundred innocents answered an advertisement promising an infallible escape from the draft for $1. They received for their money a dazzlingly simple solution: "Enlist."

Threat of conscription brought into being a new kind of businessman, the substitute and bounty broker. For a fee, the man anxious to avoid military duty and the exempt man willing to serve as substitute for a price would be brought together. Far more extensive was the business of bounty brokerage. Communities unable to produce their quotas of volunteers faced the prospect of having their unwilling young men drafted, so they offered bounties to induce others to volunteer. Rich towns naturally had a great advantage over poor ones in attracting recruits. Rallies were held to raise bounty money, real estate taxes were increased, bonds were issued, and often the services of the broker were required. The latter "bought" prospective recruits for a comparatively small sum and sold them to desperate towns, often at enormous prices. The broker might acquire gangs of men by the use of lies, drugs, beatings, and kidnappings. Brokers swarmed about army recruiting offices and physically prevented men who wanted to join up from doing so until they paid over a portion of the bounty. They secured the release of men from jails and poorhouses on condition that they enlist. They "doctored" physical wrecks and doddering oldsters so that they would pass the medical examination. They sent runners into Canada for recruits who promptly returned home after signing up and getting their cut of the bounty money.

Thousands of men engaged in the practice of enlisting, collecting their bounties, deserting, enlisting again, and so on; these were the "bounty jumpers." One industrious individual reportedly enlisted 100 times. Another claimed to have made $20,000 by joining up 15 times; he may well have done so, because the combination of Federal, state, and local bounties could come to more than $1000 per enlistment. Occasionally bounty jumpers were executed for desertion, but the main risk in the profession seems to have been leaping from moving trains.

The total amount paid in bounties has been estimated at $750 million, or nearly one-fourth of all Northern wartime expenditures. Commutation was paid by 86,724 men, and substitutes were hired by 117,986. To these must be added roughly 250,000 deserters (estimates range from 197,000 to 278,000) and 200,000 others who absconded after being drafted but before being sworn in, bringing the total who escaped service by one means or another to nearly 655,000. Even this figure does not tell the full story; an unknown number fled to escape enrollment by draft officials.

The main effect of the draft was to stimulate volunteering by compelling the individual either to join up and collect a large bounty, be conscripted and get little or no bounty, or run away. The draft was used four times under the Enrollment Act of 1863. Of 776,829 men called up, 21 percent failed to report, 11 percent were dismissed for unknown reasons, 41 percent were exempted, and 27 percent were held to service, of whom 42 percent commuted and 35 percent furnished substitutes. Only 46,347 were actually enlisted — 6 percent of those originally called. Ineffectual though it was, the draft sometimes met with violent resistance. Opponents accused the system of discriminating in favor of the wealthy and the Republicans, both because more Democrats were poor and because the provost marshal's bureaucracy was allegedly a Republican political machine and saw to it that Democrats had a better chance of being drafted. The biggest draft riot occurred in New York City in July 1863, but there were similar outbreaks in other towns and cities.

The history and statistics of Union recruiting show that approximately one-third of the men in blue joined up without compulsion or extraordinary inducements. The others seemingly did so to collect bounties and escape the draft, were drafted or, especially in the case of aliens and blacks, were often tricked or coerced into enlisting. All things considered, it is easy to understand why the North, with four times the South's military manpower, was scarcely able to achieve a two to one battlefield superiority.

MANAGING THE WAR: LINCOLN AND THE HIGH COMMAND

The North's objective was nothing less than total victory — to extinguish the Confederacy as an independent nation. Given the South's huge area and its people's determination to resist, this would have been a formidable undertaking in any circumstances. It was especially so because the government was woefully unready to prosecute a major war. Simon Cameron, secretary of war, was a machine politician who held his office because he helped put Pennsylvania in Lincoln's column in 1860. The regular army and the War Department bureaus were small, there was no general staff to coordinate strategic planning, and General-in-Chief Winfield Scott, who had conquered Mexico in brilliant style, now was old — older than the Constitution — portly, and physically feeble.

Scott was too acutely aware of the North's unpreparedness and of the high quality of military leadership available to the Confederacy to believe that a quick victory was possible. His strategic plan called for a blockade of the Southern coast and a powerful expeditionary force to take possession of the Mississippi River. In this way the heart of the Confederacy would be cut off from the outside world. Slow suffocation would encourage the growth of loyalist sentiment that would eventually lead the errant states back into the Union. But popular clamor and Republican politics called for stronger medicine. Horace Greeley, who "dipped his pen of infallibility into his ink of omniscience with as little distrust as a child plays with matches," cried "On to Richmond" in the *New York Tribune*. Lincoln ordered an advance, and the Union army was routed at the First Battle of Manassas (July 21, 1861).

The next day Lincoln summoned George B. McClellan, who had won some small successes in western Virginia, to take command of the force that would soon be known as the Army of the Potomac. During the next several months, McClellan whipped his green regiments into shape, instilling in them discipline and high morale, forging an instrument that would outlast a shocking succession of defeats. The elderly Scott soon retired; McClellan replaced him as general-in-chief on November 1. In January 1862 Cameron gave way to Edwin M. Stanton, who remained in charge of the War Department until he was dismissed by President Andrew Johnson after the war. Like his predecessor, Stanton knew nothing of military matters. The customary portrait of this strange individual reveals a distinctly unpleasant man who would, as General Grant once observed, rather disappoint than oblige. He was rude and quick-tempered, a bully to those in his power, obsequious to those he feared, vindictive to opponents, and a skilled hypocrite. Stanton's perceptions were warped by his abnormal suspiciousness, his judgment of others often dictated by personal or political bias. He is usually given credit for throwing himself wholeheartedly into his work, enlarging and reforming the War Department bureaucracy, and fighting favoritism and corruption in the awarding of government contracts. His net value to the Union war effort is difficult to estimate.

A new factor injected into military affairs in the fall of 1861 was Congress' Joint Committee on the Conduct of the War, created in the wake of the minor disaster at Ball's Bluff, Virginia (October 21, 1861). Republican militants, or Radicals, dominated the committee. In the view of one distinguished historian, "It investigated the principal military campaigns, worked to undermine Democratic and conservative officers, interfered boldly with the plans of commanders, and bullied Lincoln into accepting the radical program." The committee was determined that the war would be fought along partisan political lines so as to guarantee not only military victory over the Confederacy, but Republican ascendancy in the nation at large. Stanton was its willing ally, working secretly with the members and giving them whatever War Department documents they required. The committee grilled various generals and occasionally uncovered wrongdoing or incompetence; otherwise, it was perhaps not as influential or destructive as once thought.

General-in-Chief McClellan soon showed himself to be not only a superb organizer, but also an ambitious, egotistical, and arrogant young man who was reluctant to take the offensive and was forever demanding more men, more supplies, and more time. Growing resentment at his inertia was compounded among Republicans by the fact that he was a Democrat, as were his most trusted associates. Insinuations circulated about alleged Confederate sympathizers and even traitors in the army, men who really did not want to win the war. The real problem for the Republicans was the mere presence of Democrats in high command. If Democratic generals lost the war, the Republican party would take the blame; if they triumphed, one of them would surely be the next president. The solution to this problem was obvious: use Republican generals. Lincoln was willing to support any successful and energetic commander, regardless of party, yet even he soon came to suspect that some of the Democratic generals ranged from the halfhearted to the borderline traitor.

After many urgings, pleadings, and cajolings by the harassed Lincoln, McClellan finally agreed to march against Richmond. He would advance from the east, moving his army down the Chesapeake Bay by water. The President reluctantly agreed to this route; he much preferred the overland approach from Washington. Although he feared to overrule McClellan directly, Lincoln now began to take over direction of military operations in the East. He was not qualified to do so, but having initially deferred to the military experts with few good results, he felt compelled to try his own hand. In this he had the full cooperation of Stanton, who detested

McClellan and undercut him politically while simultaneously assuring the general of his eternal friendship.

The spring and summer of 1862 revealed Lincoln's limitations as a strategist and military administrator. On March 8, without consulting McClellan, the President divided the Army of the Potomac

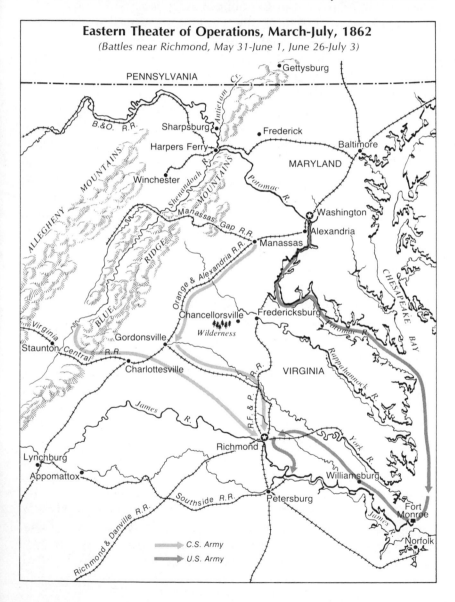

Eastern Theater of Operations, March-July, 1862

(Battles near Richmond, May 31-June 1, June 26-July 3)

into four corps; to lead three of them, he chose generals who had preferred the overland route to McClellan's plan. Three days later he relieved McClellan as general-in-chief, leaving him in command of the Army of the Potomac alone; "Little Mac" learned of his demotion by reading the newspapers. Within the next few weeks Lincoln divided Union forces in the Eastern Theater into seven independent commands, detached one entire corps from the army McClellan expected to use against Richmond, and withheld an infantry division for purely political reasons. Meantime Stanton, assuming that the war would not last more than another year, discontinued recruiting for several months. All of these actions made the cautious McClellan even more wary. He reached the vicinity of Richmond in May and settled down to a siege, his favorite form of warfare. If given proper support, he probably would have captured the city, such was his strength in heavy artillery. However, by fragmenting Union forces, Lincoln gave Robert E. Lee an opportunity to strike them one by one. In the Seven Days' Battle (June-July 1862) Lee lifted the siege of Richmond and drove McClellan into an entrenched camp 20 miles away.

The campaign of Thomas J. ("Stonewall") Jackson in the Shenandoah Valley (May-June 1862) had shown Lincoln the dangers of divided command; late in June he consolidated forces in northern Virginia under the leadership of John Pope, a fellow Illinoisan and a Republican. He had won some reputation on the Mississippi and, more important, had secured the backing of the grittier Republican congressmen with his talk of waging a tough, aggressive war. After McClellan's defeat in the Seven Days' Battle, Lincoln called in another Western Theater general, Henry Halleck, to fill the vacant post of general-in-chief.

By the late summer of 1862 the Union high command was chaos tempered by confusion. Generals in the field were denounced by the secretary of war and other high officials, and yet were not removed. Generals sometimes flouted the chain of command and dealt directly with the President or with influential congressmen, while Lincoln and Stanton bypassed each other as well as Halleck and dealt directly with generals in the field. Military affairs were shrouded in a miasma of intrigue, deception, and political maneuvering worthy of an imperial Byzantine court, an atmosphere that would linger for several months.

McClellan's army was shifted back to northern Virginia to reinforce Pope, leaving "Little Mac" to tag along without a command. Lee and Jackson quickly disposed of the bombastic Pope (Second Battle of Manassas, August 30-September 1, 1862) and crossed into Maryland. Lincoln thereupon restored McClellan to command, even though he believed him to have connived at Pope's defeat. McClellan attacked Lee at Sharpsburg (September 17, 1862) and forced him back into Virginia, but did not pursue. By this time Lincoln as well as the militant Republicans had come to fear that McClellan was trying to transform the Army of the Potomac, which loved the general, into a praetorian guard that might overthrow the government or at least put McClellan in the White House. Citing McClellan's failure to checkmate Lee, the President pacified the anti-McClellanites by relieving the general of command. Lincoln minimized the adverse effects among Democrats as well as within the army by waiting to sack McClellan until the fall elections were over and by picking as McClellan's successor one of his friends and a fellow Democrat, Ambrose E. Burnside. This officer had twice declined the command during the previous summer, not believing himself equal to the responsibility. He soon proved the correctness of his estimate by smashing the army against an impregnable Confederate position at Fredericksburg (December 11-13, 1862).

Meanwhile in other theaters political and economic influences were shaping military events in a manner even more obvious than in Virginia. The war's disruption of intersectional commerce had produced a severe depression in the Northwest that threatened to turn the Republicans out of office. In October, Lincoln authorized General John A. McClernand, a prominent Illinois Democrat allied temporarily with the Republicans, to raise troops in the Northwest and clear the Mississippi from the north. Simultaneously a vociferous lobby of exiled Texas Unionists and New England textile magnates hungry for cotton had been bedeviling Lincoln to rescue the Lone Star State and settle it with Northerners who would raise cotton to feed the idle mills. Lincoln chose the Massachusetts political general, Banks, for this task; soon the latter was enlisting eager throngs of soldier-settlers who looked forward to dispossessing

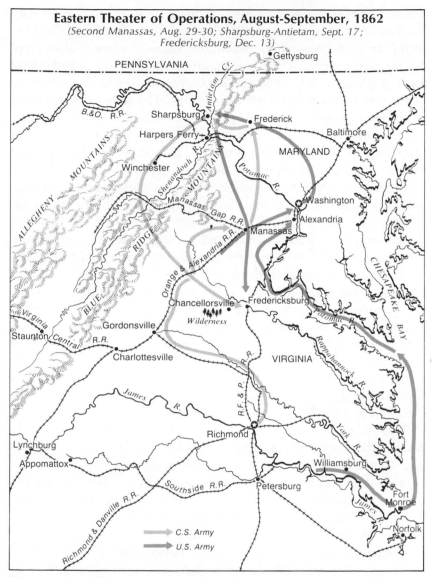

Eastern Theater of Operations, August-September, 1862
(Second Manassas, Aug. 29-30; Sharpsburg-Antietam, Sept. 17;
Fredericksburg, Dec. 13)

Texas rebels of their rich cotton lands. Unfortunately for them, the
1862 fall elections went very badly for the Republicans in the
Northwest. Lincoln decided that opening the Mississippi took pri-
ority over Texas, and so he ordered Banks to sail instead for New
Orleans and clear the river from the south. Banks prudently re-

frained from informing his men of this change of plans until they arrived at New Orleans in December 1862. Then the "Bobbin Boy," as Banks was called, blundered about the lower Mississippi for the next year and a half, tying up thousands of troops and giving further proof of his ineptness. McClernand's expedition was absorbed into the army that took Vicksburg. The general himself was not present on that occasion, having been relieved of command by an exasperated Grant. The Banks and McClernand episodes are classic illustrations of how a surrender to political pressures could beget an incoherent military policy.

In Washington congressional Republicans were mounting a campaign to radicalize the Lincoln administration, including the army. Don Carlos Buell, commanding Union forces in Kentucky and Tennessee, McClellan's friend, and a Democrat, was relieved in October. Fitz John Porter, corps commander, friend of McClellan, and a Democrat, became the scapegoat for Pope's defeat at Second Manassas. He was wrongfully court-martialed and dismissed from the service in disgrace. William B. Franklin, who had the same liabilities as Porter, was blamed for the Fredericksburg debacle and sent to a professional Siberia in Louisiana. Irvin McDowell, army commander in 1861 and corps commander in 1862, found himself denounced in the press and in Congress for treating Southern civilians too kindly. He demanded a court of inquiry, which exonerated him, but Stanton made sure he never again saw service.

This purge reminded the London *Times* of the French Revolution: "The denunciation is precisely the same as those launched against the Girondins by the Mountain in the old French Convention. Disasters in the field have divided the Republican Party, and the zealots impute the reverses . . . to lack of faith in a principle." It must be said, however, that political ambitions and motives were present in the officer corps long before the Republican "zealots" appeared on the scene. A martial reputation had opened the way to the presidency for Washington, Jackson, Harrison, and Taylor. Winfield Scott had run on the Whig ticket in 1852, of course, and McClellan would be the Democratic candidate in 1864. Professional advancement, especially during the Mexican War, was sometimes tinged with political favoritism. Nevertheless, the deliberate politicization of the huge Civil War volunteer army exceeded in extent and degree anything dreamed of before, and the Republicans' attempt to make the army a wing of their party gravely damaged the efficiency of military operations.

Joseph Hooker replaced Burnside as head of the Army of the Potomac on January 25, 1863. "Fighting Joe" was the favorite of

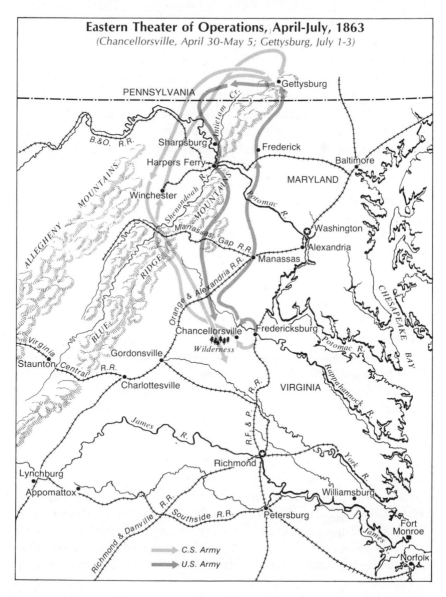

Eastern Theater of Operations, April-July, 1863
(Chancellorsville, April 30-May 5; Gettysburg, July 1-3)

Secretary of the Treasury Salmon P. Chase, who had been assured by Hooker's friends that the general would not challenge Chase for the Republican nomination in 1864. Hooker also enjoyed the backing of the Committee on the Conduct of the War. The decisive consideration with Lincoln was, as the President said, that he was "stronger with the country than any other man." That is, at a time of deep dissatisfaction with the Lincoln administration, Hooker had more political support than any other available candidate.

Hooker's popularity plummeted after his defeat at Chancellorsville by the much smaller force under Lee (April 29-May 6, 1863). When Lee began to move north early in June, Lincoln vetoed Hooker's excellent plans for counterattack. Later interference by Halleck led Hooker to offer his resignation even as he pursued the Confederate invaders. He was instantly obliged. George G. Meade succeeded Hooker and turned back Lee's thrust at Gettysburg (July 1-3, 1863). This was Lee's worst-fought battle, and proved to be the turning point of the war in the East. Meade then, in Lincoln's view, allowed Lee to "escape" to Virginia. During the remainder of 1863, Meade won some minor contests and prevented Lee's weakened and ill-supplied army from undertaking a major offensive.

In the meantime the war in the West had gone much better for the Union. Grant took Fort Henry and Fort Donelson in February 1862, opening the Tennessee and Cumberland rivers to Northern gunboats and throwing the Confederates' main line of defense back into Mississippi. He was inexcusably surprised and nearly obliterated at Shiloh (April 6-7, 1862), but was able to salvage the battle when reinforced by Buell. Grant then fought a confusing although generally successful campaign in Mississippi, and in November began his eight-month struggle to take Vicksburg. That city and Port Hudson fell in July 1863. As New Orleans had surrendered to the Union navy under Farragut in April 1862, the Mississippi was now open from source to mouth. Grant was rewarded with command of the entire Western Theater except for Banks' Gulf Department. In November he and Sherman retrieved William S. Rosecrans' defeat at Chickamauga (September 19-20, 1863) by driving the Confederates off Lookout Mountain and Missionary Ridge and rescuing the Union army at Chattanooga

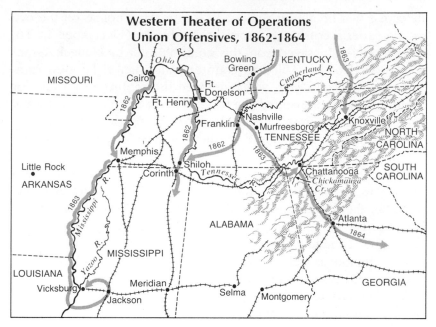

Western Theater of Operations
Union Offensives, 1862-1864

(November 24-25, 1863). Lincoln appointed Grant to the revived rank of lieutenant general and made him general-in-chief of all the Union armies (March 1864). Sherman took command of the Union armies at Chattanooga and prepared to march against the strategic heart of the Confederacy, Atlanta. Although responsible for the direction of all the armies, Grant decided to make his headquarters with the Army of the Potomac. Halleck became chief of staff with headquarters in Washington.

These arrangements have been praised as embodying a modern command system that coordinated the movements of Union forces and thus brought down the Confederacy. Nothing could be further from the truth. Grant quickly took over direction of the Army of the Potomac from Meade, a responsibility that occupied most of his time and attention. Under these conditions he could not act as general-in-chief, and his actions show that he was sorely out of touch with the war at large. For example, when Sherman set out from the ruins of Atlanta on his march to the sea, neither Grant nor anyone in Washington knew whether he was headed for the Atlantic Ocean or the Gulf of Mexico. Grant's grasp of affairs in Tennessee was so defective that he almost removed George H. Thomas on the eve of the latter's crushing victory at Nashville (December 15-16, 1864), only to be saved from this great blunder by Halleck. Grant disapproved of but failed to countermand Banks' bootless campaign up the Red River, which delayed the capture of Mobile for 10 months and augmented the forces facing Sherman in Georgia, and he showed himself unable to face up to that other premier political general, Benjamin F. Butler. Even in Virginia, Grant did not manage the various Union columns effectively.

What brought the Confederacy down was not the sophistication of the Union command system or General Grant's strategic acumen, but the shrewd and skillful campaign by Sherman against the Confederate stronghold of Atlanta. The capture of that city in September 1864 had profound repercussions on Confederate logistics and morale as well as on the fortunes of the Republican party. Subsequent events — the march to the sea, the capture of Richmond, Lee's surrender — were anticlimactic. It is no depreciation of Sherman's achievement to point out parenthetically that his great campaign was made possible by technological resources that were able to support his army in northern Georgia as it dangled at the end of a rail line nearly 400 miles long, or that he enjoyed odds of 10 to 6.

Lincoln's management of the war shows that he was contending for a triple objective: to defeat the Confederacy, ensure the ascendancy of the Republican party, and maintain his leadership of that party. The pursuit of the latter two objectives may have been essential to the accomplishment of the first, or at least Lincoln may have believed such to be the case. The truth of neither hypothesis has been established. Lincoln knew that up to a point the North's material superiority allowed him to put politics first without risking defeat, but he almost miscalculated. In fact, by the late summer of 1864, he feared that the North's will to fight had been nearly exhausted. Grant had lost 100,000 casualties in four months and was apparently no closer to Richmond than McClellan had been two years before. The air of Washington was heavy with the stench of thousands of gangrened wounded lying in military hospitals. Bank's expedition into central Louisiana had failed miserably, and Sherman had been in northern Georgia since early May with little to show for his trouble. In August a despondent Lincoln predicted that he would lose in the presidential election three months hence. Then like a gift from heaven came Sherman's telegram, "Atlanta is ours and fairly won." Lincoln knew he had been saved, the party had been saved, and the Union would be saved. It was a close call.

Chapter VI

The Northern Economy: Policies and Profits

THE SECOND AMERICAN REVOLUTION

The Industrial Revolution reached the United States in the first quarter of the nineteenth century, bringing new means of exploiting the country's natural wealth. Simultaneously there appeared a new class of speculators and entrepreneurs whose first objective was to end what they saw as a monopoly of political and economic opportunity enjoyed by an Eastern elite whose wealth and influence were rooted in the Colonial period. They were determined to break that monopoly by democratizing both business and politics; hence their exaltation of the common people and their champion, Andrew Jackson, and their attacks on that symbol of vested privilege, the Second Bank of the United States. Their ultimate purpose was to control the Federal government and with it the raising and expenditure of tax revenues and the disposal of the riches contained in the vast public lands.

Accidental circumstances had brought this entrepreneurial element into alliance with the agrarian South and its Northern collaborators, making possible the victory of the Jacksonian coalition in 1828. A marriage of convenience, it was wrecked by the South's persistent advocacy of a small, frugal, inactive Federal government. Meanwhile the size and influence of the entrepreneurial interest grew as the country's economy developed. In the 1850s as in the

1820s economic changes brought political changes. The Republican party was created, and the entrepreneurs, having concluded a truce with Eastern capital, had found their new home. Slavery replaced the bank as a symbolic villain, the malign enemy of their hopes and dreams. Their goal now was to expel Southern influence from the Federal government. Southern secession offered a golden opportunity to do just that. As it turned out, the triumph of the entrepreneur, who flourished on easy credit, paper money, small-scale enterprise, and rampant *laissez faire,* was short-lived. By helping to break the power of the South, he hastened the advent of a new era of controlled credit, inflexible currency, giant corporations, and monopoly.

Considerations of this kind led historian Charles A. Beard to call the Civil War the "Second American Revolution," meaning an uprising by the agents of the industrial revolution against the agrarian interest, mainly the South. With the South crushed, industrialization proceeded rapidly at the expense of the agrarians. As Raimondo Luraghi has said of the Civil War, " . . . Nowhere has the industrial revolution ever been achieved except by compelling agriculture to pay for it."

Beard came to professional maturity at the height of the Progressive movement. With his wife he wrote his great synthesis, *The Rise of American Civilization,* during the Republican hegemony of the 1920s. The events of his own time induced a belief that the Republican party was a monolith on economic matters, achieving its ends by manipulative or conspiratorial means. This point of view was applied by Beard and others to their interpretation of the Civil War and Reconstruction. Since Beard's time, however, scholars have discovered that neither the Radicals nor the Republicans generally formed a solid bloc on economic issues. This has produced a tendency among some historians to dismiss the entire Beard thesis out of hand.

The Republican party was not, of course, a sentient, prescient, purposeful entity dedicated to a completely coherent economic program. On the contrary, it was a congeries of interests, with overlapping and sometimes conflicting goals, in the process of evolving a consensus on such matters. And however much Republicans differed among themselves, the vast majority objected far more violently to the policies traditionally espoused by the Democratic party under Southern leadership.

The new dispensation that emerged from the Civil War was not the work of a conspiracy, nor was it an accident. Instead, it was the political and legislative expression, through the medium of the Republican party, of the Industrial Revolution. If that is the main point Beard was trying to make, his thesis as refined and modified is fundamentally sound. The conclusion reached by Robert Sharkey, one of the first to challenge some of Beard's assumptions, seems a fair one: "I have no quarrel with the Beard-Beale concept that the economic play within a play constitutes the hard core of meaning which can be elicited from the drama of Civil War and Reconstruction."

THE NEW DISPENSATION

The Republican platform of 1860 reflected some of the leading economic impulses of the times. Fulfilling that platform was essential to converting a minority party into a permanent majority.

The question of tariff protection had been soft-pedaled in the platform and handled according to local requirements during the campaign, yet the party had committed itself to do something when it capitalized on resentment at the lowering of the tariff in 1857. As mentioned earlier, the bill the Republicans had sponsored since the congressional session of 1859-1860 finally passed in March 1861, following the departure of the free-trade states of the Deep South. Thus a political debt was discharged, especially to Pennsylvania ironmakers and Northwestern wool growers. Then came the war, and the need for money inspired an extensive system of excise taxes on almost every article made in the North. Manufacturers feared the consumer would turn to less expensive foreign goods, demanded protection, and got it with a vengeance. The average rate on dutiable goods climbed from 18.84 percent in the year ending June 30, 1861, to 47.56 percent in 1865 — the highest in history. Excise taxes were repealed after the war, but the tariff remained high. In fact, the average dutiable rate did not drop below 40 percent until 1914, except for 1873 to 1874, when it was 38 percent; after the Wilsonian interlude, the tariff shot back up under Harding, Coolidge, and Hoover. Here, then, was a major victory for which many Northern industrialists had long contended, and which the South had prevented for just as long. It would facilitate a massive transfer of wealth, satisfying the dreariest predictions of John C. Calhoun.

The platform also called for a homestead law and a Pacific railroad. The two were intimately connected. A railroad through the Far West needed a populated country with functioning governments as well as assistance in the form of loans and land grants. The Pacific Railway Act of 1862 chartered the Union Pacific Railway to begin the great push west. It and other lines, either existing or prospective, were given a 400-foot wide right-of-way and 6400 acres of public lands for each mile of track. The land grant was laid off in alternate sections, allowing the railroads to control the development of intervening sections, as well as their own land. In addition, Congress awarded the companies loans of $16,000 to $48,000 per mile of track laid, depending on the difficulty of the terrain, the loans to be secured by a first mortgage. Titles to Indian lands along the right-of-way were extinguished. Thaddeus Stevens, an ironmaker, congressman, and a leading proponent of the Pacific line, inserted a provision in the law requiring all the iron used to be "of American manufacture of the best quality," that is, of the highest price. Generous though these terms appear, they did not satisfy the Union Pacific. In 1864 a compliant Congress, lubricated, some authorities say, by the distribution of $500,000 in bribes, eliminated safeguards to the public's investment, doubled the land grant, and degraded the government's mortgage from first to second, enabling the company to sell first mortgage bonds and paving the way for a speculative takeover that produced the Crédit Mobilier scandal after the war. Between 1862 and 1871 the Federal government gave railroad companies land equal to an area two-thirds the size of Texas. States added yet more land and hundreds of millions of dollars. This was the beginning of a grand giveaway the likes of which the modern world has rarely witnessed. In the postbellum years the public domain was handed over not only to railroads but to other special interests, to the men who became known as the "barons" — of cattle, or timber, or oil.

The Republicans likewise fulfilled their platform pledge to promote internal improvements generally. Although expenditures dropped off during the war for obvious reasons, they picked up soon thereafter. Average annual expenditures for the 10 years ending in 1860 amounted to $370,000; for the 10 years ending 1870, $1,272,300; and in 1880 reached $8,080,000. These "river and harbor bills," so often defeated by Southerners in the antebellum years, were the breath of life to state and local political machines.

While it was lavishing millions of acres on the railroads, in 1862 Congress gave 30,000 acres per congressman to each state containing Federal lands to finance agricultural and mechanical colleges — the "A & M" universities of today. Buchanan had vetoed a less generous bill in 1859. The landless Eastern states were given claims on 7,500,000 acres of the public domain. Scrip representing much of this land soon sold for less than a dollar an acre and fell into the hands of Eastern speculators. The anticipation of this result was undoubtedly one reason why so many Eastern congressmen voted for the bill and so many Westerners opposed it, one of several signs that the war had not erased sectional divisions within the dominant party.

The Homestead Act of 1862 purported to redeem a longstanding pledge by allowing the head of a family to acquire 160 acres of public land by living on and cultivating it for five years. Or the family head could buy it for $1.25 an acre after six months, a provision that opened the door for gigantic frauds by fake settlers in the pay of speculators. Unfortunately, the genuine homesteader found that 160 acres was not enough for a family farm in many parts of the trans-Mississippi West, where rainfall was lighter and crop yields smaller than in the East. Often the farmer had to buy larger tracts from the capitalist. He quickly discovered that vast stretches of vacant land were already owned by railroads, Indians, and speculators. Less than 19 percent of the land put under cultivation between 1860 and 1900 represented homesteads taken up under the 1862 law. The Homestead Act was certainly not without beneficial results — 19 percent comprised half a million farms — but it must be evaluated in the context of a new, exploitative approach to the public domain.

Although Eastern capitalists had partly surmounted their fears that a liberal land policy might drain labor to the West, thereby driving wages up and property values down, support for the Homestead Act was at best lukewarm among Eastern Republicans. A more immediate problem was competing with the army for manpower. The party's platform of 1864 contained a reassuring clause about encouraging immigration, and on July 4, 1864, Lincoln signed the Contract Labor Law. This measure validated contracts in which immigrants pledged up to one year's wages or any land they might acquire as security for loans to pay their passage to the United States. As a further inducement, aliens were exempted from compulsory military service. A commissioner of immigration was appointed to facilitate the anticipated influx. Congress unquestionably had in mind filling up the army as well as relieving the manufacturer. The mayor of New York denounced the new immigration service as a "bait under fraudulent pretenses to enlist foreigners." A London *Times* correspondent reported that within 20 yards of Castle Garden, where as many 10,000 immigrants might arrive in a week, there were two conspicuous recruiting stations advertising large bounties for recruits, with another half dozen nearby. To many friendless, penniless newcomers the offer was irresistible, especially when they were promised automatic citizenship upon being honorably discharged. Trickery was easy and frequent. As one historian observed:

> . . . There was a strange lack of interest on the part of the government in regard to the common charges that immigrants were fraudulently enlisted and that they were led over to these shores in some instances by fair promises, and then through whiskey, bluffs, and threats, just before landing, led to join the army.

The American Emigrant Company was immediately organized to take advantage of the new policy; it sent agents to major European cities and published a sliding scale of charges for interested employers: $10 for skilled workers, $6 for farm laborers, $5 for house servants, and so on. This organization has been described as "a land-jobbing and scab-importing agency consisting of a group of Iowa and Connecticut promoters," and soon after the war became involved in a malodorous scandal involving the purchase of Kansas Indian lands.

The Contract Labor Law was not responsible for bringing in many immigrants — other inducements were sufficient — and it was repealed in 1868, although the contract system continued without government sponsorship for many years thereafter. Congressional policies during the war years are mainly significant as a harbinger of things to come, of the great flood of the New Immigration that began in the late nineteenth century and that would be so beneficial to employers in a time of rapid industrial expansion.

The Republican platform of 1860 had no plank on national financial policy, a potentially divisive subject that had been quiescent since the 1840s. It was, however, not dead but sleeping. As pointed out in an earlier chapter, finances had been bound up with the whole question of the nature of the Union since the 1780s, and it was a question that now required an answer. A national currency and a national banking system were championed on behalf of nationalism versus state sovereignty, Union versus secession, patriotism versus treason. The debate between Hamilton and Jefferson had reached its final stages.

Of the $480 million in circulation when Lincoln was inaugurated, more than 40 percent consisted of notes issued by hundreds of banks chartered under state laws. Some of these notes were almost worthless in terms of gold, others were exchangeable almost at par, and many of them constantly fluctuated in value. They were not receivable in payment of government dues. There was, of course, no longer any central bank and no Federal regulation of state banks.

This chaotic situation was popular with speculators, but it was not adapted to the needs of a government that had to raise large amounts of money in a hurry, and so changes were inevitable. They were accelerated by Secretary of the Treasury Salmon P. Chase, who began by trying to pay for the war by borrowing instead of taxing. His approach frightened the financial community, which did not believe that the government's credit could sustain loans of such magnitude. Their confidence in the government's solvency declined still more in late 1861; military defeats and fear of foreign intervention raised questions about ultimate victory and hence about the value of Federal obligations. To protect themselves in the event of the government's financial collapse, New York banks ceased to redeem their notes in gold. The rest of the Northern banks did likewise, followed by the Federal government. Chase could not sell Federal bonds except at large discounts, which neither he nor Congress was willing to do. Instead, he proposed a national banking system organized so as to induce banks to buy government securities. But the need for money was so urgent that Congress set aside Chase's proposal and passed the Legal Tender Act, authorizing the issuance of paper money, not redeemable in gold, that would be legal tender for all purposes except payment of tariff duties and interest on the national debt. The new notes were popularly called greenbacks. About $480 million in greenbacks was issued between 1862 and 1865, equaling the total amount of money circulating in 1861. They never were at par with gold and reached a low point in the summer of 1864, when $1 in specie was worth almost $3 in greenbacks. Chase continued to promote his banking policy, and eventually he had his way. The National Banking Acts of 1863 and 1864 made the national debt security for a new currency, national bank notes. To join the system a bank had to purchase Federal bonds in the amount of $30,000 or one-third of its capital, whichever was larger. The bonds were held by the Treasury, which issued notes to each bank up to 90 percent of the face value of its bonds. A limit of $300 million was set on total notes issued. The new money was receivable for all government dues and obligations except tariff duties and interest on the debt; otherwise it was legal tender only between national banks themselves. Placing the capstone on the whole system was the immensely important act of March 3, 1865, which drove all state bank notes out of circulation by an annual 10 percent tax. Now it was beyond the power of anyone except the government and the national banks to increase the amount of money in circulation.

The new financial departure significantly affected the nation's balance of economic power. Capital requirements discouraged the formation of banks in small farming communities, and the 1864 law sharply curtailed the amount of loans national banks could extend on real estate, the main collateral available in agricultural areas. These and other features shifted bank funds from agricultural to industrial uses, as did high protective tariffs. " . . . Human ingenuity," writes Robert Sharkey, "would have had difficulty in contriving a more perfect engine for class and sectional exploitation: creditors finally obtaining the upper hand as opposed to debtors, and the developed East holding the whip over the undeveloped West and South."

Like the tariff, financial legislation passed to meet the wartime emergency had been shaped into a tool of special interests, and the stage was set for a battle against the "engine of exploitation" that would polarize national politics for 30 years. By the 1870s the Republicans had taken their stand foursquare on high tariffs and "sound money," while the Democrats were badly split between eastern Gold Democrats and Western inflationists. The latter, joined by some Republicans, first formed the Greenback party, then the Populist party, which succeeded in writing its inflationary panacea into the Democratic platform of 1896. But all such revolts failed, and the movement to democratize national finances came to be as impotent and pathetic as William Jennings Bryan at the "Monkey Trial."

THE PROFITABLE SIDE OF WAR

The Republicans could recruit their ranks by using the war as a bountiful source of patronage as well as by accommodating the various interests that had rallied to their banner. Many people at every social and political level regarded the Union cause primarily as an opportunity to make money or to advance their public careers, or both. The idea — one of great antiquity — that war should be pecuniarily and politically profitable was pervasive, and it coincided with the belief that the South should be punished and made to pay the costs of the war.

Congress passed several acts aimed at extracting profit from punishment. Observers remarked that every lawmaker seemed to have a confiscation bill in his pocket, and the more fervent had scant patience with squeamish members. The object of many was summary confiscation of property belonging to Confederate sympathizers. More cautious Republicans regarded confiscation as a two-edged sword that might set a dangerous precedent; others, including Lincoln, had doubts about its constitutionality. The act finally passed in July 1862 required a judicial determination to precede confiscation. Execution of the law fell to possibly the most conservative member of Lincoln's cabinet, Attorney General Edward Bates. His reluctance to proceed plus legal and practical difficulties limited the value of property actually taken to perhaps less than $2 million.

There was more than one way to skin a cat, however, and while confiscation bills were under consideration, Congress passed a law "for the collection of direct taxes in insurrectionary districts." Commissioners were appointed to follow in the track of Union armies, assessing real estate, setting the tax, and if it was not paid, taking the property and selling it at auction. Since everyone knew that many owners would be absent within Confederate lines, this amounted to confiscation. Those with inside information about the time and place of auctions could pick up valuable real estate for a small sum. One Union general commented on the lack of competitive bidding, with sales being monopolized by "northern sharpers," as a Connecticut private in South Carolina called them. New England capitalists acquired lands along the South Carolina coast under the law, and recently liberated blacks went to work for the new owners. Of course, tax sales were not the only way to wealth. Northern investors acquired much land, especially after the war, by purchasing mortgages and foreclosing on impoverished Southerners.

The proceeds of the Confiscation and Direct Tax laws were small change compared to the bonanza of the Captured and Abandoned Property Act of March 3, 1863. The latter's main concern was cotton, and its execution confirmed Southerners in their belief that the real object of the war was to rob them. Property of a nonwarlike nature taken by Federal forces was regarded as "captured"; property whose owners were absent, presumably within Confederate lines, was considered "abandoned." The Treasury Department was responsible for its collection or administration. This led to a great proliferation of the department's bureaucracy, which was used by Secretary Chase as a political machine to promote his nomination for president in 1864. The full extent of fraud perpetrated by these swarms of agents will never be known. In corrupt collusion with army officers, they got up expeditions whose sole purpose was to capture cotton. The Confederates sometimes made use of their opponents' lust for plunder to control the movements of Federal troops. "See that the Yankees get cotton now and then," wrote General Leonidas Polk while commanding in Mississippi and Alabama, "but not faster than suits our purposes."

Reported gross sales of captured property came to $30 million, over nine-tenths from cotton, but one eyewitness estimated that not a tenth of the proceeds ever reached the Treasury. A conservative estimate is that $100 million in cotton was seized under color of the 1863 law, a sum equal to 40 percent of the value of the 1860 crop. The value of cotton stolen outright is not known.

"Abandoned" property frequently consisted of entire plantations. These were leased to enterprising Northerners who paid ex-slaves low wages to raise cotton. Union army officers often cooperated with the leaseholder by compelling the local blacks to stay on the plantation, and there must have been times when the latter were hard put to distinguish between slavery and freedom.

Some Northerners were impatient of all legal shilly-shally. They demanded that the land of rebels be unceremoniously seized and given to Union veterans; furthermore, if land were substituted for soldiers' pensions, the national debt would be smaller, a subject much discussed in Congress. Organize expeditions of soldier-settlers, ran the argument, and send them south to take what was due them. Eli Thayer of the Emigrant Aid Company suggested Florida as a target, and the House Military Affairs Committee recommended that Lincoln be authorized to accept 30,000 volunteers for that purpose. Edward Atkinson, tirelessly promoting the textile industry, preferred the fertile cotton fields of Texas. Send there enlightened New England warriors, he said, to pluck these lands from their rebel owners, reconstruct Southern society, and raise cotton for the mills of their home section. There would be no labor problem. The ex-slave would have no choice but to work for the new proprietors; the only choice, as Atkinson bluntly said, would be "labor or starvation." If he refused to work, "let him starve and exterminate himself if he will, and so remove the negro question, — still we must raise cotton." The administration eventually dispatched expeditions to both Florida and Texas, where they failed largely for military reasons.

The Union navy was in a good position to acquire movable Rebel goods, particularly cotton. It had mobility, firepower, and cargo space. Under prize law, one-half of all captured enemy property belonged to naval personnel, their shares being prorated according to rank. In coastal waters the age-old practice of collusive captures was often used. To avoid the risk of losing everything, the owner of cotton would get in touch with the commander of a blockading vessel and agree to be captured for a cut of the navy's share. Such subterfuges were unnecessary on inland waters; there Union warships found easy pickings. So assiduous was Admiral David Dixon Porter in this species of warfare that the Confederates awarded him the *nom de guerre,* "Thief of the Mississippi." His reputation for stealing was such that his anxious mother asked him if his cabin was really "full of silver taken from the plantations," as she had heard. Porter's sailors seized wagons and teams, scoured the countryside, and took cotton indiscriminately, stenciling it "C.S.A." to make it liable to condemnation as prize of war. Porter's share of the proceeds from one six-week expedition came to $60,000.

A great deal of cotton was, of course, in Confederate-held territory where it could not readily be seized. This gave rise to an extensive trade through the lines, with the Confederates exchanging cotton for desperately needed supplies of every kind. From the Northern point of view, there were ostensible public reasons for employing unusual means to secure cotton. The more there was on the world market, the less likely it was that Britain and France would intervene to relieve their textile industries. Cotton could also be used as a medium of international exchange, reducing the outflow of gold and hence the strain on Northern finances. These were, in fact, more pretexts than reasons for what went on. The driving force behind the trade was a host of speculators, politicians, army and navy officers, and Treasury agents with an itch to make money. The opportunities were tempting indeed. By mid-1864 the price of cotton had reached the extraordinary price of $1.90 per pound on the New York market. Traders could buy a pound of cotton from the Confederates for bacon that cost 22 cents a pound in New York. If bacon would not do the trick, they offered guns, uniforms, ammunition — anything that Southern armies needed. Major General Edward R. S. Canby, commanding Union forces in New Orleans, said of the traders, "[They] follow in the track of the army, traffic in its blood, and barter the cause for which it is fighting, with all the baseness of Judas Escariot, but without his remorse."

Lincoln was unmercifully dunned by people wanting trade permits. Sometimes he refused, often he did not. Again and again the President's friends and supporters appeared at the military frontier with passes signed by the President allowing them to trade through the lines. Congressmen, past and present, state governors, newspaper editors, well-known businessmen — all were involved. Those not trading themselves peddled their influence with the Treasury Department or the White House. Traders without passes bought their way in and out of Union lines, sometimes paying tolls to generals of high rank. Corruption filtered down and infected every level of the civil and military bureaucracy.

The Confederates relied more and more on their enemies as other sources of supplies dried up. The volume of trade cannot be stated precisely, but it certainly amounted to tens of millions of dollars. It prolonged the war, perhaps by many months. The trade at last became so flagrant that Congress, in an act of July 2, 1864, seemingly took from Lincoln the licensing power it had given him in 1861. In reality, lobbyists managed to insert in the new law a loophole that Lincoln used in late September, only a few weeks before the presidential election, to throw open the floodgates to illicit trade with the South. This enlarged commerce was confined to the friends of the administration, and to friends of friends. Early in 1865 Congress passed a law that would have allowed wider participation, but Lincoln vetoed it. "I suppose the cotton speculators around him were too many for him," commented one disappointed observer.

Fortunes could be made without going south, of course, by dipping into the golden stream that poured from the War Department and the Navy Department. Profitable government contracts were secured by influence, bribes, and kickbacks. During the first year of the war, about a dozen men received the lion's share of Federal contracts; one of them reportedly pocketed $2 million. Some contractors cheated the public treasury by supplying shoddy merchandise. In one lot of 411 horses sold to the army as cavalry mounts, only 76 were fit for service, and 5 were dead on arrival. Sugar sold to the government was "cut" with rye, coffee with sand. Soldiers complained that their meat was sometimes so strong that it could walk by itself, or so full of maggots it could crawl. Textile companies made uniform cloth from what was described as the "refuse and sweepings" of the mills, "pounded, rolled, and glued" to have the appearance of cloth. Shoe manufacturers made soles of wood or even of paper. The first time an unfortunate recruit clad in an outfit of this kind was caught in the rain, he was in danger of seeing his uniform dissolve into a blue fuzz and the bottoms come out of his shoes, leaving the uppers to dangle around his ankles. So fragile were the trousers issued to one regiment in Missouri that for the sake of simple decency the men were compelled to use flour sacks as a sort of apron in the rear. When General Nathaniel Lyon saw a soldier wearing this unmilitary garb, he told him to take it off, immediately perceived his mistake, and ordered the blushing private to put it back on.

The holder of a government contract could make easy money by subletting, a practice Stanton later outlawed. One man, for example, agreed to supply 10,000 head of cattle at eight cents a pound, then sublet the contract for six cents a pound and made a clear profit of $32,000. Sometimes the tables were turned, and the otherwise honest businessman had to bribe army officers to obtain a contract. And even the dead could be made to show a profit. An unscrupulous contractor, paid on a per capita basis to disinter Union dead on the Fredericksburg battlefield, tried to multiply his profits by dividing the remains into as many "bodies" as possible.

Old Edward Bates, from the vantage point of Lincoln's cabinet, remarked in 1864 that "the demoralizing effect of this civil war is plainly visible in every department of life. The abuse of official powers and the thirst for dishonest gain are now so common that they cease to shock." The dreary account of greed and dishonesty seems even darker when contrasted with the thousands of Northerners who sacrificed everything for the Union with no thought of personal gain. The men whose bones were divided by the cynical contractor at Fredericksburg had made 14 successive assaults on the impregnable Confederate position at Marye's Heights. They assuredly did not charge repeatedly into that death trap for the love of money, and yet their sacrifice was often turned to profit by the entrepreneurial element that was so liberally patronized by the Republican party. Edward Bates was only half right when he said that the war had corrupted men. It was a reciprocal process. Men also corrupted the war.

Chapter VII

The Politics of Union

PUTTING DOWN THE DEMOCRATS

The basic Republican war aim was party supremacy within a Northern-dominated Union. This entailed not only strengthening the party by fulfilling the platform, but also breaking the Slave Power by military victory, emancipation, and a political reconstruction of the South. Aside from the war, the most immediate problem that the Republicans faced was fighting off the Northern Democrats and their conservative border state allies.

In the election of 1860 the free states gave Lincoln only 54 percent of their votes; if the border states are included, this figure drops to slightly under 49 percent. The party was obviously in danger of losing control of Congress and, in 1864, of the presidency. Prudence dictated the use of energetic measures, and the appeal to arms put powerful weapons into Republican hands. Part of the Republicans' campaign stock-in-trade before the war had been to stigmatize Northern Democrats as puppets of the Slave Power. Now when Democrats opposed Republican policies or tried to defeat Republicans at the polls, it was easy to depict them as still collaborating with the South. By this line of reasoning, political dissent could properly be treated as dangerous and disloyal conduct. In wartime it was a patriotic duty to suppress disloyalty, that is, to use whatever means were feasible to defeat the Democrats at the polls. Therefore the Lincoln administration and Republican state governments at times resorted to a policy of repression that sometimes provided the margin of victory in crucial elections.

One device was arbitrary arrest by military and civil officers of the Federal government and the states, by local police, or by private vigilante groups. Many arrests were probably made in a sincere attempt to control persons suspected of giving actual aid to the enemy. Others followed a political act that was regarded as disloyal. For example, when some Northerners, like some Southerners, criticized conscription as unconstitutional, they could be arrested for impeding the draft or encouraging soldiers to desert. Finally, there were many arrests for the simple purpose of helping Republicans to win elections.

All this was made possible by Lincoln's suspension of the privilege of the writ of habeas corpus, thus permitting arrest without warrant and indefinite imprisonment without trial. Previously a considerable body of legal and judicial opinion had held that only the legislative branch could suspend the writ; even during the war Congress never clearly agreed that this right was lodged in the executive branch. When military authorities repelled his writ for the release of a prisoner held at Fort McHenry, Chief Justice Taney, in *Ex parte Merryman* (1861), denied the President's right to suspend the writ. Lincoln not only rejected Taney's opinion but he may have considered arresting the Chief Justice himself. Lincoln argued that because the Constitution did not say where the suspending power was located, the emergency justified his assuming it; and in any event it would be better to break a single law than to let "the Government itself go to pieces." Throughout the war Lincoln acted on the premise that he had the power and right to commit unconstitutional acts if he believed the alternative was the breakup of the Union. This made the President's discretion the measure of the law. In March 1863, in the Habeas Corpus Act, Congress stated that the President was "authorized" to suspend the writ, thus leaving unanswered the question of where the power to do so was located, and gave Federal officials immunity from prosecutions arising out of arbitrary arrests. It also ostensibly provided for the release of loyal persons against whom no indictments were found. Provost Marshal General Joseph Holt, who presided over the internal police apparatus, ruled that the law did not cover persons liable to trial by military commission, permitting the protective clause of the act to be circumvented by declaring martial law.

Martial law went much further than the mere suspension of habeas corpus; it permitted not only imprisonment, but punishment by military commissions for offenses unknown to civil law. Lincoln formally took this additional step by executive proclamation on September 24, 1862, two days after his preliminary Emancipation Proclamation. " . . . All persons discouraging volunteer enlistments, resisting militia drafts, or guilty of any disloyal practice, affording aid and comfort to the rebels . . . shall be subject to martial law, and liable to trial and punishment by courts-martial or military commission." A system of provost marshals was established throughout the Northern states to enforce this decree. Military arrest and punishment of civilians in places far removed from the scene of war where civil courts were open was a practice foreign to the experience of that generation and, as carried out by the Lincoln administration, was without precedent or sequel in American history.

Incomplete statistics show that the War Department incarcerated 13,000 persons during the last three years of the war. The number seized by other executive departments or by state and local authorities will probably never be known, but the grand total of arbitrary arrests could not have fallen far short of 20,000. The vast majority of prisoners were never tried, indicating the flimsy quality of the charges, but were imprisoned for varying periods and then released on promise of future "loyal" behavior. As for the use of martial law, that matter was dealt with by the Supreme Court in 1866 (*Ex parte Milligan*). Speaking for the Court, Justice David Davis said that martial law "can never exist where courts are open. . . . It is also confined to the locality of actual war." Otherwise "republican government is a failure, and there is an end to liberty regulated by law." L. P. Milligan, who had been sentenced to death by a military commission in Indiana, was released. Opposition was likewise intimidated by the temporary suppression of about 300 newspapers that expressed the "wrong" sentiments, to say nothing of those attacked by partisan mobs. Military authorities were known to invade sitting courts and disrupt the proceedings, even to arrest the judge on the bench.

There were times when the line between political and military actions was so indistinct as to excuse summary arrests. That was the case in Maryland early in the war (when Merryman was seized); then hostile citizens threatened to cut off access to Washington from the North, and the state seemed on the verge of seceding. Arrests of prominent Marylanders, including a substantial fraction of the legislature, were understandable under the circumstances. For the most part, however, such intervention was not a response to any imminent danger.

An especially effective technique used in the border states was a "loyalty" oath enforced by the army that tended to disfranchise Democrats whether or not they had given aid or comfort to the enemy. Although extreme measures were most common in the border states, they were often used elsewhere too. By extreme measures is meant the arrest of anti-Republican candidates and voters, driving anti-Republican voters from the polls or forcing them to vote the Republican ticket, preventing opposition parties from holding meetings, removing names from ballots, and so forth. These methods were employed in national, state, and local elections. Not only did the army interfere by force, it was used to supply votes. Soldiers whose states did not allow absentee voting were sent home by order of the President to swell the Republican totals. When voting in the field was used, Democratic commissioners carrying ballots to soldiers from their state were on at least one occasion unceremoniously thrown into prison, while Republican agents were offered every assistance. Votes of Democratic soldiers were sometimes discarded as defective, replaced by Republican ballots, or simply not counted.

These means sometimes determined the outcome of elections at every level. In the congressional contest of 1862, when popular sentiment in several states turned against the party in power, military control of elections in the border states saved the Republican majority in the House of Representatives. As for the presidential election of 1864, statistics are suggestive. In those states where soldier votes can be separated from the rest, Lincoln received 56.3 percent of the civilian vote and 77.6 percent of the soldier vote. In the border states party alchemists were strikingly successful in transmuting Democratic dross into Republican gold. There Lincoln's handful of 22,615 votes in 1860 (three-fourths from Missouri) became 164,153 in 1864. Kentucky, for example, gave Lincoln 1364 votes in 1860 and 27,786 four years later. By contrast to these startling increases, votes for Lincoln in the nonborder North increased by only 11.1 percent, including the soldier vote, while the Democratic vote in the same states increased by 10.9 percent. Lincoln's share of the nonborder vote was about 1 percent larger than in 1860. It seems plain that without the use of military force and other extraordinary means in 1864, the Republicans would have been a popular minority in those states and quite possibly would have lost the election. A shift of only 38,111 votes in the right places, less than 1 percent of the 4,015,902 votes cast, would have given the election to McClellan.

The Republican use of political repression was immensely facilitated by the willingness of many Northerners to believe stories of gigantic conspiracies dedicated to helping the Confederacy. The same credulity that had allowed the Republicans to frighten citizens with the Slave Power plot in the 1850s fed on the fear and suspicion that war always breeds. Danger from pro-Confederate subversion was cited to persuade the voters that political power was safe only in Republican hands. For example, just before the all-important elections in the fall of 1864, Judge Advocate General Holt submitted to Stanton a wild, hysterical, and inflammatory report of alleged conspiracies "not paralleled, it is believed, in the world's history." Republican newspapers gave Holt's diatribe front page prominence as the elections reached their climax.

Actually, such secret societies that did exist were little more than conventional political clubs, and the number of people who had any idea of mounting a pro-Confederate uprising was insignificant. The great majority of Northern Democrats wanted to preserve the Union. Like Republicans they joined the army, and their representatives voted appropriations to carry on the war. Many of them, it is true, preferred to restore the Union by negotiation, and few were willing to make abolition a condition of peace. Their leaders certainly foresaw as clearly as the Republicans the consequences for Democrats nationally should the South be crushed by an abolition party. It was to their advantage to bring the South back as undamaged as possible and with full political rights. A favorite slogan of Northern Democrats was "the Constitution as it is, and the Union as it was," a program that would, they hoped, see their party once again a majority in a united nation.

Republicans told Democrats that it was their patriotic duty to sink all party differences and join in putting down treason. Simultaneously they claimed the lion's share of the spoils for themselves. Most Democrats concluded that the Republican brand of patriotism meant political suicide for themselves, and that their opponents were engaged in a partisan war for hegemony over the North as well as the South. Some Democratic leaders converted for a price, but the number of major generalcies and other favors was limited, as was Lincoln's willingness to bestow on former adversaries rewards for which the party faithful clamored. As for the rank and file, any massive defection was precluded by differences on economic, constitutional, social, ethnic, and religious questions that had long separated Democrats from Whigs and then from Republicans.

These were the reasons why the Democrats continued to oppose Lincoln and his party, inducing the latter to use methods that made the war years unique in the history of civil and political liberties in the United States. The Republicans did not of course set up a twentieth-century dictatorship, or even a nineteenth-century despotism. Most Democrats continued to vote; most opposition papers continued to publish. There were no giant concentration camps or wholesale executions. The complete overthrow of constitutional government was not possible, even if it had been attempted, given the size of the Democratic party and the repugnance with which many Republicans would have regarded such a course of action. The Republicans had all they could do to handle the Confederacy, let alone an uprising at home. But they did what they could, and it helped to keep them in office.

SLAVERY AND RACE

The question of emancipation posed a difficult and complex problem for Republicans in general and Lincoln in particular. Official party policy when the war began was to disclaim any right or intention to interfere directly with slavery in states that recognized it. This position grew out of the political circumstances prevailing during the 1850s. Although new conditions supervened, they did not immediately clear the way for emancipation, even though Republican leaders were aware of the great political benefits the destruction of the Slave Power would bring them. For one thing, a decent interval was needed to permit the march of events to justify the party's reversal on such a momentous matter. Prolonged hostilities would take care of that so far as the Republicans themselves were concerned, but there were other and more intractable obstacles. To these Lincoln was keenly sensitive. A premature move toward emancipation might drive the border states into the enemy's embrace; first they must be securely occupied by the Union army. When General Frémont undertook to liberate rebels' slaves in Missouri by military order in August 1861, Lincoln overruled him. He feared, said the President to an old friend, that emancipation now would lose Kentucky, and "to lose Kentucky is nearly the same as to lose the whole game," because it would be followed by Missouri and probably Maryland as well. "These all against us, and the job on our hands is too large for us." A year later the situation of these states was much different.

Lincoln had to think also of the Northerners who objected to emancipation for political or racial or constitutional reasons. The political reasons for the Democrats' opposition has been mentioned. Furthermore, they as well as rank and file Republicans feared an influx of Southern blacks; war had not changed, unless to strengthen, the chronic Negrophobia that overspread the North. In evaluating these factors, the President never forgot the fragility of his working majority. The accession of support his administration received from old opponents because of the attack on Fort Sumter would inevitably dwindle in a prolonged war. One false step on the question of slavery and race and Lincoln might see his majority disappear, and with it all hope of victory. Such was the political minefield through which Lincoln had to lead his party.

Congress sniped away at slavery during the first 15 months of the war, but the resulting legislation was piecemeal, overlapping, and largely ineffectual. In August 1861 it passed a law freeing slaves who were used to aid Confederate armed forces. Little more was done until March 1862, when Congress forbade the army to return fugitive slaves escaping from Confederate-held territory. In April it abolished slavery in the District of Columbia, compensating the owners; in June it emancipated the handful of slaves in the territories; and in July, as part of the Second Confiscation Act, it liberated slaves belonging to persons convicted of treason or of aiding and abetting the rebellion. The legal and practical defects of this last law were so obvious as to raise doubts about the intentions of its supporters.

Meanwhile the President moved cautiously toward emancipation. On March 6, 1862, soon after the capture of Fort Henry and Fort Donelson had driven the Confederates out of Kentucky, and after Missouri and Maryland were firmly under Union control, Lincoln recommended that Congress approve Federal financing for states that voluntarily agreed to emancipate their slaves. Subsequently he used all his persuasive powers to convince border state leaders to take such action; they were immovable. In July he made one last appeal to them. By abolishing slavery, he argued, their states would materially shorten the war by forever ending Confederate hopes of annexing them, and he warned them that they had better accept compensated emancipation instead of waiting until the "friction and abrasion" of war put an end to slavery. He did not insist on immediate emancipation, but "a *decision* at once to emancipate *gradually*. Room in South America for colonization can be obtained cheaply. . . . " Finally he hinted that he might have to take action soon if they did nothing. His revocation the previous May of General David Hunter's order freeing slaves in Georgia, Florida, and South Carolina had given "dissatisfaction, if not offence, to many whose support the country cannot afford to lose. . . . The pressure, in this direction is still upon me, and is increasing. By conceding what I now ask, you can relieve me, and much more, can relieve the country, in this important point."

Still the border state men remained obstinate, and on the next day Lincoln told two members of his cabinet that he had decided to issue a proclamation of emancipation as a military necessity. Probably even more compelling were political considerations. The border states no longer had the option of joining the Confederacy. That factor now weighed less in Lincoln's calculation, and the pressure for abolition weighed relatively more, as he doubtless had expected and hoped it would. Even so, the pros and cons remained almost perfectly balanced in Lincoln's mind. On September 13, just nine days before he issued his preliminary Proclamation of Emancipation, he explained some of the complexities involved to a deputation of Chicagoans. He did not shrink from emancipating the slaves on legal or constitutional grounds; as commander-in-chief he could do what he must to prosecute the war successfully. "Nor do I urge objections of a moral nature, in view of possible consequences of insurrection and massacre at the South." And he believed that emancipation would convince Europe that the North "was incited by something more than ambition. I grant further that it would help *somewhat* in the North. . . . And then unquestionably it would weaken the rebels by drawing off their laborers. . . . " But he did not think arming the blacks would lead to much except their losing their weapons to the enemy, weapons that were already in short supply. There was danger, although he admitted it was lessening steadily, that some border state soldiers might be sufficiently offended by emancipation to desert to the Confederates. And Lincoln expressed reluctance "to issue a document that the whole world will see must necessarily be inoperative, like the Pope's bull against the comet," because it could not reach the slaves it supposedly freed, those within Confederate territory. He concluded by saying that these reservations did not mean he would do nothing; he still held the matter "under advisement." "Whatever shall appear to be God's will I will do." And nine days later, when he presented his preliminary Proclamation to the cabinet, he told them "he had made a vow, a covenant, that if God gave us victory in the approaching battle [Sharpsburg, September 17], he would consider it an indication of Divine will, and that it was his duty to move forward in the cause of emancipation." He is also reported to have said that the Proclamation "had become a civil necessity to prevent the Radicals from openly embarrassing the government [that is, challenging Lincoln's leadership] in the conduct of the war." Of course, if Lee's invasion of the North had not been turned back, a decree of emancipation would only have further divided an already disheartened people.

If God did speak to Lincoln, it was in remarkably guarded terms. The Proclamation issued on September 22 began by announcing that "hereafter, as heretofore," the war would be prosecuted to preserve the Union, and that the President would ask the next session of Congress to compensate any state that adopted immediate or gradual emancipation, and to continue the effort to colonize Negroes outside the United States. Then it declared the President's intention, on January 1, 1863, to proclaim that all slaves within states or parts of states still in rebellion at that time to be free. This was an invitation, which Lincoln could scarcely have expected the South to accept, to save slavery by returning to the Union. The document concluded by citing the Second Confiscation Act and other antislavery legislation, and recommending compensation to slaveowners who could prove their loyalty.

In his annual message to Congress of December 1, 1862, the President pleaded with that body to send the states a series of constitutional amendments that would compensate states voluntarily abolishing slavery by the year 1900, indemnify loyal slaveowners who lost slaves during the war, and finance the voluntary emigration of blacks. Already, he said, he had been negotiating on this subject with various Latin American nations and Liberia. "I cannot make it better known than it already is, that I strongly favor colonization." In the meantime those who feared that "the freed people will swarm forth, and cover the whole land" should remember that blacks were only one-seventh of the population. Besides, they would certainly be willing to remain in the South, working for wages under "their old masters . . . till new homes can be found for them, in congenial climes, and with people of their own blood and race. . . . And in any event, cannot the north decide for itself whether to receive them?" Northern workers had nothing to fear from emancipation. Lincoln said that even without colonization wages would rise at least for a time because the blacks would not do as much work as when they were slaves, and so there would be more work to do, sending wages upward. Later, as the blacks emigrated to those "congenial climes," the supply of labor would decline and wages would rise.

His plan, Lincoln insisted, would hasten the war to a successful conclusion. "Fellow citizens, we cannot escape history. . . . We shall nobly save, or meanly lose, the last, best hope of earth. . . . The way is plain, peaceful, generous, just — a way which, if followed, the world will forever applaud, and God must forever bless."

On December 31 Lincoln signed a contract with a group of promoters, later shown to be corrupt, to colonize free blacks in Haiti. The next day he promulgated the Emancipation Proclamation, basing his authority to act on his powers as commander-in-chief. Exempted from its operation were those portions of the South where rebellion was deemed to have ceased: parts of Louisiana and Virginia, the new state of West Virginia, and Tennessee, where Lincoln had established a Unionist government under Andrew Johnson.

The artistry Lincoln displayed in handling the slavery question speaks for itself. He acted when the short-term advantages and disadvantages were in almost perfect equilibrium; he himself observed later that the Proclamation had done about as much good as harm. However, his policy had unmistakably pointed the nation toward the total abolition of slavery, which would mean, among other things, a great long-term gain for the Republican party.

In public Lincoln consistently justified his Proclamation as a military necessity, and although it addressed itself primarily to political realities, there was indeed a military dimension to it. The war was grinding on. There appeared to be little reason to think it would end soon, especially after Union reverses in Virginia during 1862. Volunteering had slackened, requiring the use of a militia draft in some states. Obviously the pool of willing soldiers was drying up. Accepting blacks into the army would ease the strain, but first they must be freed. Only a few Negro units had been organized by field commanders before the Proclamation. It was a touchy subject. The pride of many white soldiers was insulted at the idea of serving alongside blacks. But as the casualty lists lengthened, pride gave way to the instinct for self-preservation. This was particularly true after the Enrollment Act of March 1863, with its provisions for a Federal draft. The fewer men who had to be drafted, the fewer enemies the administration would make, and the less unpopular the war would become. "I thought," President Lincoln once remarked, "that whatever negroes could be got to do as soldiers, leaves just so much less for white soldiers to do in saving the Union." Many antislavery spokesmen made the same point to their audiences, sometimes in a style disparaging to blacks. The Republican governor of Iowa stated publicly that he would "prefer to sacrifice the lives of niggers rather than those of the best and bravest of our white youths." And in 1864 General John A. ("Black Jack") Logan, a Democratic convert to extreme Republicanism and the postwar commander of the Grand Army of the Republic, told an audience in Springfield, Illinois, that he would "rather six niggers be . . . killed than one of his brave boys."

Faced with a shrinking labor supply and rising wages, Northeastern businessmen and politicians lobbied for a law permitting state draft quotas to be credited with blacks recruited in occupied parts of the South. With Lincoln's help they succeeded, and about 1000 state agents set out for Dixie and eventually rounded up about 5000 recruits. Negro "volunteers" were pressed into the army at the point of a gun, shot without trial for resisting or deserting, and hunted through the swamps by bounty-hungry recruiters. A Massachusetts army officer who saw the system in operation said that "this traffic of New England towns in the bodies of wretched negroes, who are deluded, and if some of my affidavits . . . are true, tortured into military service, forms too good a justification against the Yankees." Another Massachusetts man on the South Carolina coast wrote, "I can conceive of nothing worse on the coast of Africa. These men have been hunted like wild beasts and ruthlessly dragged from their families," and then robbed of their bounties. Blacks could now be hired as substitutes, too. John G. Nicolay, Lincoln's private secretary, avoided service by doing so; his replacement eventually was killed in action.

First to last, about 180,000 blacks served in uniform, the great majority being recruited in the slave states. They were segregated, paid less than whites, and commanded almost exclusively by white officers, who were often held in contempt by their colleagues in white regiments. The predicament of the Negro soldier in combat was not an enviable one. Some Southern soldiers did not take black prisoners, and some Northern soldiers, taking advantage of the confusion of battle, killed them out of sheer race hatred. Although an increasing number of blacks saw combat from mid-1863 on, most remained on garrison duty and the like. A total of 2870 were killed in action or mortally wounded, somewhat less than the number of Union soldiers killed at Gettysburg. Deaths from disease came to more than 30,000. Considering that most served for less than two years — many much less — these were rather heavy losses. Despite discouragements and mistreatment, however, many blacks volunteered for service, and black soldiers fought bravely on numerous occasions. Their net contribution to the Union's army strength is impossible to estimate because it is not known how many Northern whites they relieved from service.

Enlisting blacks had other than a military function. The idea was, as Union armies advanced, to keep the freedmen in the South by enlisting them and assigning them to garrison duty. Those not put in the army were often used as military laborers or compelled to work on "abandoned" plantations. For these and other reasons the vast majority of freedmen did stay in the South. Northern fears of a black immigration subsided. By the time of its National Convention in 1864, the Republican party felt able to call for a constitutional amendment abolishing slavery completely. While publicly espousing this Thirteenth Amendment, Lincoln clung tenaciously to his hopes for gradual, compensated emancipation coupled with colonization. With his deep understanding of human nature and his keen insight into the temperament and prejudices of his fellow whites, Lincoln feared that emancipation was only an early chapter in a long and unhappy story.

RECONSTRUCTION DURING THE WAR

Historians' discovery in the 1950s and 1960s that Republicans did not stand as a solid phalanx on economic policies either during the war or immediately afterward has led some scholars to commit a logical fallacy. They have concluded that because Republicans disagreed on economic matters, their motives must have been largely disinterested and idealistic when they championed abolition, Negro suffrage, civil rights, and the other policies associated with congressional, or Radical, Reconstruction.

In fact, economic divisions were present at the party's birth. They fell along sectional lines mainly, Northeast versus Northwest, and naturally persisted into the war years. The party arose in spite of such divisions because of even greater antagonism to Democratic policies and a complete agreement on the overriding purpose of supplanting the Democrats as the nation's ruling party. The Republicans' line of reasoning has been suggested earlier; it was relatively simple. To make their party a permanent majority, they would impoverish the Southern Democrats by abolition, thus destroying them as an office-holding class, and then consolidate their victory by a political reconstruction that would Republicanize the South. They were merely doing what every party does: trying to stay in office indefinitely. That, indeed, was one economic goal they all agreed on, office-holding having become a distinct form of business enterprise. Republicans differed among themselves as to means, hence the use of categories such as Radical, moderate, or conservative; as to the end, they differed only with the Democrats. This is no obscure deduction based on circumstantial evidence. Republicans readily avowed what seemed to them to be a normal, laudable, and patriotic ambition.

Just how to achieve that goal gave the Republicans no little trouble. To a large degree, tension over radical versus moderate means was a function of the far more serious contest between Congress and the executive branch over which would control Reconstruction. Because Reconstruction was the fundamental issue of the war and involved immense patronage and influence, control of the process carried with it leadership of the party. Lincoln, like other presidents, was determined to be his party's leader, but congressional Republicans were unwilling to trust one man with a matter that might determine their collective political fate. Besides, Lincoln's approach made them nervous. He refused to admit that secession was possible in a constitutional sense or that the seceded states had changed in any essential way. They were out of their proper practical relations with the rest of the country; that was as far as he would go. In initiating Reconstruction he tended to rely heavily on conventional political techniques: patronage, persuasion, conciliation. Necessarily, then, he could not be doctrinaire ("my policy is to have no policy"), but adapted measures to changing circumstances. At the same time he made certain that his actions had at least the appearance of constitutionality, and so he set indefinite yet real limits on the means he could employ.

Lincoln's style did not suit the more extreme Republicans, who argued that the rebellious states had ceased to exist and should be governed as conquered provinces or undergo a territorial stage before statehood would be considered. Territories were the creatures of congressional legislation, clay in the hands of the potter. The political and entrepreneurial possibilities implicit in this subject have been described in connection with Kansas, and territorialization under another name was the formula that Congress ultimately would impose on the South. In contrast to the President's flexibility, congressional programs were prescriptive, spelled things out, left nothing to chance, and rode roughshod over constitutional barriers.

Rivalry between Lincoln and Congress over control of Reconstruction existed from the early months of hostilities. Although it fluctuated in intensity, overall it increased steadily as the occupation of more Southern territory gave the issue substance and urgency. As commander-in-chief of the forces occupying the South, Lincoln had the advantage as long as the war continued, and he set in motion several different plans, such as holding congressional elections in districts taken from Confederate forces, recognizing a Unionist governor of Virginia, promoting the formation of West Virginia, and so on, and he partially disarmed congressional opposition by his shift toward emancipation.

By late 1863 Union armies had subdued almost all of Tennessee, much of Arkansas, a significant portion of Louisiana and Mississippi, and some areas in all the other Confederate states. At that time Lincoln announced a general policy of Reconstruction to be implemented directly by the executive branch. It was described in a proclamation of December 8, which he explained and defended to Congress in his annual message of the same date. He derived his authority from the pardoning power and from the injunction that the United States shall guarantee to each state a republican form of government, and shall protect each from invasion and domestic violence. (Constitution, Article II, Section 2, Article IV, Section 4.) He offered a pardon to all those who had participated in the "rebellion" if they would take an oath of allegiance to the Federal Constitution and would promise to obey all presidential proclamations and congressional legislation dealing with slavery. Excluded from amnesty were highranking Confederate civil officials, army officers above the rank of colonel, navy officers above lieutenant, and all former members of the U.S. Congress, courts, army, or navy who had gone over to the Confederacy.

In any of the seceded states except Virginia, where a Unionist government was already functioning in the Northern counties, when voters equal in number to one-tenth of those who had voted in 1860 took the prescribed oath of loyalty they could then "reestablish" the state government. Slavery would be eliminated, but Lincoln agreed to accept temporary arrangements arising out of the freedmen's "present condition as a laboring, landless, and homeless class" that would recognize their permanent freedom and provide them with education. Such reestablished governments could send representatives and senators to Congress, which would then, as was its constitutional prerogative, decide if they should be admitted. The plan was a good example of Lincoln's pragmatic, conciliatory approach, which made use of political rewards and inducements.

The President promoted this method of Reconstruction in several states, concentrating his efforts on Louisiana. Soon that state was regarded as the test of Lincoln's policy. Early in 1864 General Banks, acting under Lincoln's orders, held elections for state offices and a constitutional convention. The Lincoln-Banks slate defeated Treasury Department candidates, who were more radical and were dedicated to replacing Lincoln with Secretary Chase. Restoration was sufficiently far advanced in the spring of 1864 in Louisiana, Arkansas, and Tennessee for those states to send delegates to the Republican National Convention, where they voted for Lincoln's renomination.

Congressional Republicans were pleased that Lincoln had made emancipation a condition of Reconstruction. However, a hostile reaction quickly developed because the President's plan did not go far enough toward guaranteeing Republican supremacy. Alternatives put forward included Negro suffrage, but as the presidential canvass drew near, most Republicans backed away from a step that was anathema to Democrats, who realized that the blacks would vote for their opponents, and to many Republican voters fearful of eventual Negro equality in the North.

The final product of congressional deliberations was the Wade-

Davis bill of July 1864. According to this program, the President was to appoint a provisional governor for each state with the Senate's concurrence. At the end of hostilities, all white male citizens would be enrolled. If a majority took the oath of allegiance, the governor would then summon a state constitutional convention. No one could vote for or serve as a delegate who had voluntarily aided the Confederacy. The new constitution was required to prohibit anyone who had held civil office under the Confederacy or any of its states, or military rank of colonel or above, from voting for legislative or gubernatorial candidates, or serving in those offices. It was further required to abolish slavery and repudiate the Confederate debt. The constitution would be voted on by the same restricted electorate that had chosen the convention. If approved, the constitution was then to be scrutinized by Congress and the President to see if it established a republican form of government. If it passed muster, the new state government could elect members of Congress. Every person who held civil or military office under the Confederacy after the Wade-Davis bill became law would be stripped of U. S. citizenship.

The contrast between this scheme and Lincoln's is an excellent illustration of the rivalry between the two branches of the Federal government and of the political objectives sought by Republicans generally. The Wade-Davis plan would postpone Reconstruction until the war was over, when the role of the executive would be greatly reduced. Lincoln would now have to seek senatorial approval for his appointments to provisional governorships, and the new state governments would need congressional as well as presidential recognition. The state-making process would exclude from participation the vast majority of white Southerners, leaving affairs in the hands of the Unionist minority and those Republicans who were expected to go South after the war to exploit the opportunities thus created. They would find their path smoothed by the political proscription of the old office-holding class, the "Slaveocracy," which was already crippled by emancipation and various forms of confiscation. Furthermore, the "ironclad oath" was still in force, dating from a law of July 1862 that barred from Federal office (except the presidency) anyone who had held office under or who had voluntarily supported the Confederacy.

Lincoln vetoed the Wade-Davis bill, explaining that he was doubtful of Congress' constitutional power to abolish slavery in a state, was unprepared to have the provisional governments in Louisiana and Arkansas "set aside and held for naught," and was himself unwilling "to be inflexibly committed to any single plan of reconstruction." However, any Southern state was free to adopt the Wade-Davis formula if it wished to do so. Wade and Davis responded in a public "manifesto" abusing Lincoln, accusing him of "dictatorial usurpation," proclaiming the authority of Congress to be paramount, and hinting at impeachment. The same issues and the same threat would face Andrew Johnson a few years later.

Lincoln's decision is understandable. Once signed into law, the Wade-Davis plan would have become the official Republican platform in the presidential election, and the party would have been irrevocably and conspicuously committed to the principle of no peace without abolition. Given the gloom and war-weariness that prevailed in the summer of 1864, this would have been political suicide. From every quarter in the party came warnings that defeat in the fall elections was inevitable should abolition be made a condition of peace. At one point in the desperate month of August, Lincoln stood on the brink of opening negotiations with the Confederacy without insisting on abolition, but he pulled back, convinced that such a course would also be fatal both politically and militarily. In a letter he wrote but did not send, he said that should the Negro be left in slavery:

> All recruiting of colored men would instantly cease, and all colored men now in our service, would instantly desert us. And rightfully too. . . . The party who could elect a President on a War & Slavery Restoration platform, would, of necessity, lose the colored force; and that force being lost, would be as powerless to save the Union as to do any other impossible thing. It is not a question of sentiment or taste, but one of physical force.

The administration's mature campaign strategy was characteristically Lincolnian: it avoided both extremes and was sufficiently ambiguous to reassure all shades of opinion. In explaining the policy, Seward dazzled the voters with a metaphysical virtuosity capable of proving a horse-chestnut to be the same thing as a chestnut horse, to adopt one of Lincoln's homely expressions. All measures taken against slavery thus far (such as the Emancipation Proclamation) had been taken to preserve the Union. They were war measures, he said. Their effect would cease with the fighting, at which time the status of slavery would be decided by legislative and judicial means. But since slavery was the root of the rebellion, when the rebellion was crushed, slavery would perish. Seward had a knack for leaving his audiences empty but satisfied.

Lincoln continued to be haunted by the problem of Reconstruction. After the election efforts were made to reach an accommodation with Congress; all were unsuccessful. In the meantime, well before the election, Lincoln had talked with men who were in touch with the Confederates, and he told them that slavery would not stand in the way of peace. At the famous Hampton Roads Peace Conference in February 1865, when Lincoln and Seward met high-ranking Confederates, the President offered the South generous terms if it would lay down its arms. He believed that gradual emancipation was still possible, he said; he was willing to compensate slaveowners, and would use his executive authority to protect Southerners from the consequences of punitive laws such as the Confiscation Acts. He believed that when resistance ceased, the Southern states should be restored to the Union immediately and admitted to representation in Congress. Seward suggested that if the Southern states wished to head off emancipation, they should rejoin the Union and vote against the pending Thirteenth Amendment. Lincoln repeated that proposal to one of Calhoun's old lieutenants early in April, while reminding him that the permanent effect of the Emancipation Proclamation would be determined by the courts. Lincoln did, in fact, return from Hampton Roads and propose to the cabinet that $400 million be appropriated, half to be paid before and half after ratification of the Thirteenth Amendment, these concessions to be accompanied by an executive pardon for all political offenses and the release of all property, except slaves, subject to confiscation or forfeiture. His recommendations were buried under the cabinet's unanimous disapproval.

Nevertheless Lincoln persistently tried to negotiate with the Southerners in such a way as to deal with the existing state governments. He feared that in the absence of a negotiated peace all civil authority might dissolve. Anarchy and guerrilla warfare would play into the hands of extremist Republicans who wished for a vengeful peace and an oppressive form of Reconstruction. Such a situation would greatly enhance the influence of congressional Republicans. Time was of the essence. Congress adjourned on March 4 and would not reconvene until the following December. If Lincoln could stop the fighting immediately and even temporarily work with the existing state governments to start the process of restoration, he would have more than six months in which to establish loyal regimes such as those he had already sponsored in Louisiana and elsewhere. He could then present Congress with an accomplished fact in December.

Beyond considerations of immediate political advantage, Lincoln seemed to have a deepseated aversion for the Radicals' approach to Reconstruction. No doubt his instincts told him that their solution could not last. He apparently wished to use conciliation and leniency to rebuild a party closely resembling the old Whig coalition of which he had once been a faithful member. He tailored his policy to appeal to the Southern Whigs with whom he had worked and campaigned in happier times. With its Southern allies and War Democrat recruits, this Whig-Republican party might well command a popular and electoral majority, one that would rest on a firmer foundation than a majority based on the disfranchisement of Southern whites and enfranchisement of the ex-slaves — the policy ultimately adopted by Congress after the war. Had the party followed Lincoln, there might well have been a Compromise of 1865 instead of a Compromise of 1877, and the course of Reconstruction might well have been very different.

Chapter VIII

The Confederacy: Government, Diplomacy, and War

PRESIDENT AND CONGRESS

The Confederacy was a government of men, not of parties. The tendency to abandon party for section gained strength in the 1850s, when Southerners closed ranks to meet the Republican attack, and it became a conscious policy when the Confederacy was born. There were lingering echoes of the old Whig-Democrat divisions, a distinction that coincided fairly closely with the secessionist-conservative groupings of 1860; and later, when the war began to go badly, there would be divisions based on opposition to or support for the administration of Jefferson Davis. Political factors were present and influenced events, but without a party system they were not as obtrusive or as dangerous to effective prosecution of the war as in the North. Their most conspicuous manifestation took the form of championing states' rights, which was a product of the Southerner's devotion to local independence and correlative constitutional principles, as well as a reaction to military invasion and the growing burdens of war. The state government and the state's delegation in Congress were the only political means of addressing these local problems, and they sometimes collided with the central government, which had to keep in view the needs of the whole Confederacy. The same situation existed in the North and would have been greatly magnified if war had scourged that section as it did the South. Much more striking than the states' rights phenomenon was the Richmond government's exercise of unprecedented powers, which it combined, rather paradoxically, with a remarkable respect for civil and political liberties.

On February 9, 1861, the Montgomery Convention elected Jefferson Davis provisional president of the Confederate States. Some accounts assert that most of the state delegations favored someone else, Robert Toombs of Georgia being frequently mentioned, and make much of the alleged bitterness of Toombs or Robert B. Rhett or William L. Yancey at being passed over. Davis's election has been attributed to a misunderstanding as to the identity of Georgia's favorite son, who was rumored to be Howell Cobb, causing the other delegations to unite behind Davis in order to block Cobb. The net effect has been to picture Davis as an accidental and not very popular choice, an impression that distorts the real events.

All things considered, Davis was probably the most distinguished Southern statesman alive and was from the first an obvious contender. Mary Boykin Chestnut, the astute diarist whose husband was a member of the convention, reported that "everybody wanted Mr. Davis to be either General-in-Chief or President." The mystery surrounding his selection stemmed from the convention's "mania for unanimity," its anxiety to avoid a division in the midst of crisis. Howell Cobb, president of the convention, wrote his wife shortly before Davis was picked: "The truth is — and it is creditable to our public men here — there is no effort made to put forward any man, but all seem to desire in everything to do what is best to be done to advance and prosper the cause of our independence." He predicted that Davis would be chosen. Whatever individual heartburnings there may have been, Davis's election was well received by the people and the politicians. Thereafter his public reputation followed closely the fortunes of the Confederacy, and much of the blame for Southern defeat rested on his shoulders. Precisely the opposite process occurred, incidentally, in the case of Lincoln's reputation.

Davis has not fared well at the hands of the historians. They have depicted him as uncompromising, opinionated, and prejudiced. He has been accused of immersing himself in countless trivial details, of not seeing the woods for the trees, of making mere clerks of his cabinet officers, of clinging to incompetent favorites while discarding able men he happened to dislike, and so forth. This portrait of Davis does him less than justice. Certainly he had the defects of his virtues. He was a man of great courage, rigid morals, and complete integrity; his cast of mind was logical and legalistic. These qualities meant that he was sometimes blunt when he should have been conciliatory, argumentative when he should have been tactful. He also had the habit of being right and winning arguments, which those who were wrong or out-argued found highly irritating. But Davis could also be surprisingly flexible and tolerant. Furthermore, he realized the need for bridging the gap between government and the people. Three times he toured the Confederacy, twice as far as Mississippi, once as far as Alabama, visiting the armies, addressing civilian gatherings, and trying to invigorate Southern morale.

The best way to arrive at a true estimate of Davis's historical stature is to compare him with his contemporaries, North as well as South. The Montgomery Convention undoubtedly picked the best available man. The same cannot be said of its choice for vice-president, Alexander H. Stephens. He came from Georgia, the most populous Deep South state and one that many thought should be conspicuously represented in the new government. Stephens had been one of the best-known Southern members of the Federal Congress and an archdefender of states' rights. He was also an archenemy of secession who only bowed to the inevitable. Stranger than any prominent statesman since John Randolph, this wizened, sickly, frail, despondent, unhappy little man used the South's struggle for national existence as the occasion for undermining the Davis administration on the pretext of defending states' rights. Many of Davis's more rational opponents were reconciled to his incumbency when they considered that should Davis go, Stephens would be president.

Davis and Stephens were both regularly elected under the permanent Confederate constitution in November 1861. Because of the continued desire to avoid internal divisions, no other candidates were put forward, and indeed, at the time, there was no desire to do so.

The President's cabinet contained men of experience and talent, and it enjoyed considerable continuity in membership. Secretary of the Navy Stephen Mallory and Postmaster General John H. Reagan served throughout the war. After short terms as attorney general and secretary of war, Judah P. Benjamin became secretary of state in March 1862, a position he held until the end. Christopher Memminger was secretary of the treasury for more than three years. Even in the war department, which had a total of five secretaries, James Seddon held office from November 1862 until January 1865. The quality of Davis's official family was in the main quite high. Of all the executive departments, only the Treasury Department failed badly, probably for reasons beyond the secretary's power to remedy. The President refused to allow partisan political claims to control his appointments at any level, although he seemed to have given some weight to state pride in the distribution of cabinet offices.

The Montgomery Convention became the provisional congress and moved to Richmond in July 1861 after that city became the seat of government. It was replaced by the first regularly elected Congress, which convened in February 1862. The Second (and last) Congress served from May 1864 until March 1865. All three had a large leaven of experienced legislators. Of the total of 267 men in all the congresses, nearly one-third had been members of the U. S. Congress and still others were former state legislators. Among them were men of parts. The flood of criticism that overflowed Congress when things began to go wrong cannot conceal the accomplishments of men such as Benjamin Hill, James L. Orr, James Chestnut, Robert M. T. Hunter, and James M. Mason. Yet the level of Southern statesmanship had obviously declined when compared with the first half of the century, as it had in the country at large. No giants such as Madison or Clay or Calhoun graced the halls of the Confederate Congress, and some men thought to have been of the first rank, such as Toombs and Stephens, revealed an appalling meanness of spirit during the war. There were times when the behavior of Congress was embarrassing. It could be unruly or even violent, although one historian's description of it as "little better than a bear garden" goes too far. A good part of its proceedings will never be fully discovered, because it often met in secrecy. Even though there were good reasons for the practice, some Southerners, especially newspaper editors, regarded closed sessions with suspicion.

The weaknesses of Congress did not prevent it from passing a corpus of legislation unprecedented in scope and boldness, demonstrating a willingness to confront painful choices whether the subject was conscription, taxation, impressment, control of commerce, or some other policy that was bound to be unpopular with many citizens. The President exercised important leadership in proposing legislation and in correcting, by veto, defective bills. The number of Davis's congressional critics grew as time passed, particularly after the Second Congress, elected in the fall of 1863, convened. Many of his staunchest allies during the last half of the war were men from Union-occupied areas who had often been elected by soldiers and refugees or appointed by a governor in exile. For obvious reasons, they usually voted for vigorous measures. Fairly consistent opponents of the administration made up about 40 percent of the Second Congress. They were mainly responsible for refusing Davis's request for greater executive control over military exemptions and the suspension of habeas corpus, and for thwarting the administration's fiscal policies. Generally, however, Congress cooperated far more than it resisted, and it was less prone to interfere with the President's running of the war than the Federal Congress was. One scholar who has studied the workings of the Confederate legislators in detail concludes that the Southern government "ran more smoothly than did that of the United States and Lincoln was far more bothered with politics than was Davis."

THE SOUTH AMONG THE NATIONS

Foreign intervention tipped the scales in the first war of secession — the American Revolution — and like Patriot leaders the Confederates entertained high hopes of receiving aid from abroad. If they had, the scales would again have been weighted on the side of independence; they did not, of course, and went down to defeat.

The phrase "King Cotton Diplomacy" is used to describe the South's quest for European assistance. It refers to the hope or expectation that the British and perhaps the French economy would suffer so much from the loss of Southern cotton as to require decisive intervention on behalf of the Confederacy. Another inducement was the prospect of a virtually tariff-free Southern market that would absorb larger quantities of European products. Some Southerners also believed that the English aristocracy, whose social system they had long admired and emulated, would feel a reciprocal sympathy for their embattled counterparts across the sea. Napoleon III's Mexican venture, leading to the establishment of a puppet state under Maximilian, supposedly made the French emperor vulnerable to the argument that this piece of flamboyant imperialism could not survive either a triumphant North wielding the Monroe Doctrine or a successful Confederacy embittered by French indifference. The best safeguard for Maximilian's regime, this argument ran, would be an independent South under obligations to France for timely assistance.

France would not act except in concert with Britain, and so British nonintervention meant the failure of King Cotton Diplomacy. The factors militating against intervention were numerous and complex. It was true that literally hundreds of thousands of workers depended on the British textile industry, which bought the lion's share of its raw cotton from the South. It was also true, unluckily for the Confederates, that during the two decades preceding the war the relative importance of textiles to the economy as a whole had diminished. Furthermore, in 1861 there was an enormous glut of both raw and manufactured cotton lying in British warehouses. The cotton famine that Confederates believed would occur early in 1862 did not appear until the fall; even then it was not as acute as expected. There was severe unemployment in the Lancashire mill districts, although it is possible that these layoffs were caused partly by factors other than a real cotton shortage. From the end of 1862 onward the supply of cotton increased, and by the end of the war Britain was receiving three-fourths of its normal imports. And despite suffering in Lancashire, total unemployment in England and Wales apparently did not exceed the levels that prevailed during the years immediately before the war.

The cutback in cottons stimulated other textiles and thus lessened the impact of the famine. Gigantic orders of war matériel added to the prosperity of manufacturing as a whole. Britain's volume of foreign trade was 34 percent higher in 1864 than in 1860. The war, then, was most profitable. Intervention would mean a shorter war and an independent Confederacy. There were, as one authority observes, "large interests" in Britain that stood to profit from prolonged hostilities, and still others that would suffer by a Union defeat. British investors had sunk hundreds of millions of dollars in public securities and private businesses in the United States. A permanent division of the country would bring a collapse of government credit, a financial panic, and a round of bankruptcies that might wipe out those investments.

These economic arguments were persuasive; even more convincing were the realities of European international politics. Revolutions, wars, and national consolidation marked the years since 1848. The Crimean War had embroiled most of the great powers. In 1859 the process of Italian reunification began, touching off a war between France and Austria-Hungary. Bismarck became minister president of Prussia in 1862 and thereupon embarked on a program of German unification that would involve wars with Austria and France before its completion in 1871. The Poles revolted against Russian rule in 1863, and in 1864 there was a little war over the provinces of Schleswig and Holstein. Continental Europe, in other words, was in a state of flux; the balance of power was undergoing major changes. Should Britain become too deeply entangled in American affairs, its capacity to influence events on the Continent would suffer. For France the risk would be even greater, with a powerful Germany rising on its eastern frontier. Even the Emperor's Mexican project was too much of a diversion, and it was in the course of liquidation before the Civil War ended.

The limited role of the United States in the balance of power also came into play. In the view of the prominent British statesman, William Gladstone, then chancellor of the exchequer, Confederate independence might well provoke a vengeful North to recoup its losses by taking Canada; and an imperialist South, free from Northern restraint, might annex parts of Latin America. Russia took a decidedly pro-Northern stand, mainly because a strong Union would provide a partial counterbalance to the Royal Navy, on which British foreign policy relied to keep Russia out of the Mediterranean.

These were, then, the major reasons against interference in the Civil War. As far as the British were concerned, they were reinforced by the fact that any formal step on behalf of the South carried with it risk of war with the United States. Seward from the first announced that diplomatic recognition of the Confederacy would be considered a hostile act, with the clear implication that war would probably follow. Even if victory were certain, war was expensive, whereas neutrality was profitable and carried no risks. Therefore the British would do nothing to help the South until they were somehow compelled to accept the risks of war and sacrifice the advantages of neutrality. Even then, barring some extraordinary provocation, they would act only in association with France and Russia.

Into these dark and troubled waters sailed the Confederacy's emissaries, filled with faith in King Cotton and the righteousness of their cause. Some were men of respectable accomplishments, notably James M. Mason and John Slidell, accredited respectively to London and Paris; but on the whole they were an unimpressive lot. It probably mattered little. An embassy of Talleyrands could scarcely have untwisted the perplexities afflicting the Confederacy's foreign affairs. The powers, led by Britain, did recognize the South as a belligerent, entitling it to be treated according to the law of nations, not merely as a pack of rebels, but even this was the result of Lincoln's proclamation of a blockade and not of Southern diplomatic skill. Otherwise little was gained. Foreign governments officially refused to receive Mason, Slidell, and the rest; an occasional unofficial conversation was all the attention they got. Their protests against the Federal blockade as ineffective and hence illegal under international law were brushed aside by Britain, especially since the United States had reversed its traditional policy and expediently adopted the British outlook on the rights of a blockading belligerent. Although some cruisers, such as the *Alabama,* did escape from British ports, promising Confederate shipbuilding programs in France and Britain were cut short by Northern hints of war. The free use of European shipyards would have proved fatal to the Union blockade.

Britain appeared to be contemplating the possibility of recognition in the fall of 1862, when the cotton famine was at its worst and

Southern armies were on the offensive. Then McClellan turned back Lee's invasion of Maryland, and the cabinet postponed the subject. As Lord Palmerston, prime minister, informed Lord John Russell, foreign secretary, "I am very much come back to our original view of the matter, that we must continue merely to be lookers-on till the war shall have taken a more decided turn." A few months later, early in 1863, France made a halfhearted offer of mediation that the North promptly repelled. Further than that the nephew of Bonaparte was unwilling to go.

There was one time when a miscalculation would probably have produced war between Britain and the North. On November 8, 1861, the British mail steamer *Trent,* bound from Havana to St. Thomas in the Danish West Indies, was intercepted by the *U.S.S. San Jacinto.* Charles Wilkes, captain of the *San Jacinto,* sent over a boarding party and seized Mason, Slidell, and their secretaries, who were passengers en route to Europe. They were taken to Boston and imprisoned. The North was exultant at this defiance of the ancient enemy. Its newspapers praised Wilkes to the skies. The House of Representatives passed a complimentary resolution. For their part, the British were hotly indignant and demanded an explanation and restoration of the diplomats. Troops were sent to Canada and plans laid for a crushing naval war should the United States refuse to comply. Although Seward was willing to threaten hostilities to forestall actions that would significantly increase the prospects of Confederate independence, he was not so mad as to risk ruin over Mason and Slidell. The inflamed temper of public opinion on both sides of the Atlantic made the situation awkward to manage, but an accommodation was reached because neither government wanted war. Seward released the Confederates and denied that Wilkes had acted by authority. However, with his ear attuned to public reaction, he did not apologize; instead he adroitly turned his compliance into a ringing vindication of America's time-honored stand against the right of impressment.

The *Trent* affair was as close as foreign intervention ever came, and the only role played by Mason and Slidell was to be captured by the enemy. The episode symbolizes the impotence of Southern foreign policy. Indeed, by mid-1863 all lingering hope of outside help had been abandoned. One wit proposed that the Great Seal of the Confederacy represent a man all alone paddling his own canoe. The grim fact was that the new nation would have to win its independence before anyone would recognize it. The motto carried on the wheel of the *C.S.S. Alabama* was the perfect motto for Confederate diplomacy: *Aide toi et Dieu t'aidera.* God helps him who helps himself.

CALL TO THE COLORS: THE CONFEDERACY

The Confederacy, like the Union, at first relied on volunteers to fill up the ranks, and in the beginning there was no lack of men willing to fight. Congress passed a series of laws in the spring of 1861 authorizing the President to accept a maximum of 400,000 men for terms varying from six months to the duration of the war. The Secretary of War stated that during the summer of 1861 he turned away 200,000 volunteers because he had no weapons for them, indicating that approximately 500,000 enlisted or tried to do so — an outpouring unique in American history. By January 1, 1862, the Confederate army carried 318,000 men on its muster rolls.

Many Southerners expected the fight to be short and were in a fever to "get their Yankee" before it was all over. The stunning victory at Manassas created a fairly widespread impression that the war was won. Yet somehow it dragged on. The fiercely individualistic Southerner often did not take kindly to disciplined camp life; he was used to coming and going as he pleased, taking orders from no one. With the big battle over, what was the point of staying in the army? Volunteering dropped off, and many of those who had enlisted for 12 months — a majority of the army — looked forward to the expiration of their terms.

Congress endeavored to encourage reenlistments by the Furlough and Bounty Act of December 11, 1861. This piece of legislative imbecility offered a $50 bounty to new recruits who would enlist for three years or the duration, and to the 12-month men a 60-day furlough besides. Upon reenlisting they could elect their regimental officers from colonel down, although subsequently vacancies were to be filled by promotion, except for second lieutenants. These elections had the support of Jefferson Davis, who should have known better. A hugely outnumbered army was invited to go home for two months and then to demoralize itself by the popular election of officers!

The next month Congress passed a law that could have turned out to be the most effective and least divisive method of recruiting. It empowered Davis to call on the governors for troops. Some states already had passed conscription acts, and this system would have appealed to state pride while it deferred to states' rights. However, the military emergency rapidly became too acute for reliance on state mediation. Generals in the field faced the possible decimation of their armies when the 12-month enlistments expired in April and May. Quick action was necessary. On April 16, 1862, Congress passed the first conscription act in American history, making liable for military service for three years or the duration all men between the ages of 18 and 35. In September the upper age limit was set at 45, and in February 1864 the limits were expanded to 17 and 50, with the newly eligible men to serve in the state reserves. One important feature of conscription was that it filled up veteran regiments, in contrast to the Northern practice of sending in green regiments. Substitution was allowed, but it was criticized severely and abolished early in 1864; all those who had hired substitutes were made liable for service. Commutation was not permitted except for conscientious objectors, such as Quakers.

The system created was a selective service. Later laws allowed exemptions for occupational as well as medical reasons. The list of the former was very extensive and included Confederate and state officials, mail carriers, telegraph operators, textile mill workers, teachers, ministers of the gospel, druggists, editors, and so forth. The most controversial decision was to exempt one overseer or other white male for each 20 (later 15) slaves. This stirred complaints about a "rich man's war and a poor man's fight," although probably no more than 2000 men were excused in this way. During the last year of the war, Congress made occupational exemptions more difficult to obtain. Medical exemptions were always hard to come by. "Blindness, excessive deafness, and permanent lameness, or great deformity" were "obvious reasons for exemption," as were tuberculosis and "large incurable ulcers." Moderate deafness, the loss of one eye or of several fingers were no bar to service. The rule was that if a man was leading a normal civilian life, he was fit for the army.

If truth be told, a decided fraction of Southern manhood had no stomach for war. There was a sudden influx into exempted occupations. Apothecary shops and schools popped up like mushrooms. Government jobs were popular. The well-to-do slacker could buy a newspaper and become an editor, or buy counterfeit discharge papers, or slip through the blockade to Europe. Some men of military age experienced a sudden deterioration in health. A Richmond newspaper observed that "rheumatism, which was once dreaded as a torturing fiend, has become as popular as a beautiful coquet [sic], tormenting and yet enchanting her spellbound victims. . . . Gout it also much sought after; but in these hard times few can get above rheumatism." In February 1865 in all the Confederate states east of the Mississippi except Tennessee, the number of men exempted for all reasons came to 13 percent of those carried on the army muster rolls. The small number of substitute brokers vanished when substitution was eliminated, and except for token sums paid by the Confederate government, there was no bounty system and hence no duplication of the frantic scramble to buy and sell recruits that prevailed in the North.

Conscription was resisted by states' rights extremists, Unionists, and by those who believed that it chilled the patriotic spirit, or those who merely wished to stay out of the army. Opposition was most pronounced in the Appalachian plateau — western Virginia, western North Carolina, the northern counties of Georgia and Alabama, and East Tennessee — where Unionist sentiment had always been strong. Armed defiance of conscription officers was not uncommon in these areas, which nevertheless provided many volunteers for the Confederacy.

Conscription is usually described as a failure whose main effect was to stimulate volunteering. Even that claim is doubtful, because the inducement of large bounties was absent. Although conscription may not have been the best way to raise troops, especially because of the political dissension it caused, it certainly did not keep men out of the army. After all, the Confederacy put into the field three-fourths of its white men of military age. Even with no exemptions or desertions, Southern armies would have faced nearly two to one odds.

A large proportion, perhaps a majority, of army deserters apparently came from Unionist areas; they were men who had never sympathized with the Confederate cause and who remained loyal to the Union from the start. The patriotism of others was very parochial; when their home neighborhoods were conquered, they often lost interest in fighting. Otherwise the two most important causes of desertion seem to have been a belief that the South had lost the war and the suffering of destitute families at home. The fall of Atlanta and subsequent disasters convinced large numbers that independence could never be won. During the fall and winter of 1864-1865, civilian sufferings reached new levels, and the flood tide of desertions began in October 1864. By March 1865 the Bureau of Conscription had reported 100,000 deserters to be at large. One soldier court-martialed for desertion presented in evidence a letter from his wife.

> My dear Edward: — I have always been proud of you, and since your connection with the Confederate army, I have been prouder of you than ever before. I would not have you do anything wrong for the world, but before God, Edward, unless you come home we must die. Last night, I was aroused by little Eddie's crying. I called and said "What is the matter, Eddie?" and he said, "O mamma! I am so hungry." And Lucy, Edward, your darling Lucy; she never complains, but she is growing thinner and thinner every day. And before God, Edward, unless you come home, we must die. (From Ella Lonn, *Desertion during the Civil War.*)

Many men could not make such a sacrifice for a lost cause.

THE CONFEDERATE HIGH COMMAND

The disparity of resources and the facts of geography compelled the Confederacy to fight a defensive war. The Union's control of navigable rivers meant that the only possible avenue for invading the North lay between Washington and the Ohio River, a corridor largely mountainous and devoid of north-south railroads. Logistically, the only practicable route lay athwart the upper Potomac, where Lee crossed in 1862 and 1863. His invasions were no more than large-scale raids; with no means of supply, they could not have been otherwise. The best the Confederates could do was to mount

local offensives in hopes of disrupting Federal campaigns and ultimately to exhaust the enemy's will to fight, a policy known to
military historians as the offensive-defensive. Thus the Confederates could not develop an overall strategic plan. The offensive-
defensive is by nature opportunistic; it can do no more than devise
temporary expedients. It necessarily surrenders to the enemy the
priceless advantage of the strategic initiative.

Southern geography greatly facilitated Union offensives. The
decisive strategic fact of the war was the extent to which the South
was surrounded and penetrated by navigable waters. Had the
Confederates been able to build a navy capable of meeting the
Federals on equal terms, a Northern victory would have been
impossible. In the Virginia theater the Union's naval supremacy
gave its armies much additional mobility and supply lines usually
invulnerable to attack. In the West geography was fatal to the
Southern cause. A classic example is the sequel to Grant's capture
(February 1862) of Fort Henry and Fort Donelson on the Tennes-
see and Cumberland rivers, respectively. Up to that moment the
Confederate line of defense ran from Columbus, Kentucky, on the
Mississippi, to Henry and Donelson just below the Tennessee line,
then up to Bowling Green in central Kentucky, and from there to
Cumberland Gap in the mountains. Much of Kentucky and all of
Tennessee were in Confederate hands. Grant's victory at one stroke
opened the Cumberland River to beyond Nashville and the
Tennessee to Muscle Shoals in northern Alabama. These rivers,
now available to Union gunboats and armies, cut across the Confederates' lines of communication. There was nothing to do but abandon Kentucky and most of Tennessee and fall back to Alabama and
Mississippi. The Federals occupied Nashville, which became their
base of operations against Chattanooga. Chattanooga in turn
became Sherman's base for the Atlanta campaign. Had the Confederates been able to hold Henry and Donelson, the Atlanta campaign would not have been possible. The loss of Kentucky and
Tennessee meant the loss of military stores, manufactories, raw
materials, and indispensable food supplies.

Another obvious consequence of Union naval power was the
capture of New Orleans, the South's largest city and most active
port. Its occupation severely curtailed the movement of men and

supplies from the trans-Mississippi states and diverted troops that could have defended Vicksburg against Grant.

These geographical and technological factors, when added to the other advantages the North possessed, confronted the Confederate high command with a task that was formidable indeed. Jefferson Davis was keenly aware of his country's peril. A West Point graduate, he had commanded a regiment in the Mexican War, presided over the War Department under Pierce, and served as chairman of the Senate's Military Committee. He had great confidence in his ability to be commander-in-chief in fact as well as title. His intimate knowledge of the officer corps, based on his antebellum career, made him a supremely confident judge of men and sometimes led him to tolerate inept commanders long after their failings had become painfully apparent to others. Yet on important occasions he sank his own opinions, took the advice of others, and appointed men in whom he had little faith. He quickly identified the genius of Lee at a time when others little appreciated him. The overall quality of Confederate generalship suggests that Davis was more often right than wrong. One reason for his success was his policy of appointing and promoting on the basis of military instead of political considerations. The purely political general was a rare bird in the Southern service and never enjoyed departmental or army command. Men without military background who attained and kept high command — Nathan Bedford Forrest is the premier example — came up through the ranks. The one exception was John C. Breckinridge, vice-president under Buchanan and a presidential candidate in 1860, who received a brigadier general's commission in 1861, later rose to divisional command, and early in 1865 became secretary of war. Banks, Butler, and the rest had no Southern counterparts. Although Davis did not believe that parceling out generalcies to ambitious politicians was necessary to the prosecution of the war, he found, like Lincoln, that political realities could put distinct and sometimes damaging limits on military policy. Lee pleaded for reinforcements from the Georgia-Carolina front, where Confederate troops equaled or even outnumbered Federal forces, but Davis refused, evidently fearing the political repercussions of depleting the coastal defenses. Not until Richmond itself was in great danger did Beauregard come to Virginia.

And in the fall of 1862, as the Federal campaign against Vicksburg was taking shape, Davis reportedly would not order reinforcements from Arkansas lest the people of that hard-pressed state go over to the Union.

Davis's management of the War Department has not been the object of great admiration. His first secretary was unqualified and soon disappeared. It is often charged that the other four, although capable, were "mere clerks" in the President's estimation. Most such criticisms came from subordinates in the department whose diaries have been taken at face value by some historians. Critics who have accused Davis of being obsessed with administrative details usually have reference to the War Department. This trait was not peculiar to Davis, as any reading of Lincoln's correspondence will show.

The fruits of Davis's judgment of military talent and his refusal to make political appointments can best be seen on the Virginia front. For practical purposes, the army there had only two commanders throughout the war, while the Army of the Potomac had seven, of whom three were appointed and one removed for substantially political reasons. Superior leadership allowed the Confederates to fight the Federals to a standstill in Virginia for nearly four years despite heavy odds.

The Western Theater, from the mountains to the Mississippi, was a different story. The commander Davis selected for that vital responsibility was Albert Sidney Johnston. With a lofty character reminiscent of Lee and with a reputation as perhaps the South's best soldier, he was killed early in the war at Shiloh, after driving Grant's army to the brink of destruction. In Davis's view there was no one who could fill his place. " . . . The fortunes of a country," he wrote after the war, "hung by a single thread of the life that was yielded on the field of Shiloh." Thereafter the President intervened in Western military affairs far more than he would have done had Johnston lived, and far more than he did in Virginia.

Pierre Gustave Toutant Beauregard, hero of First Manassas and second in command to Johnston at Shiloh, took charge of what was to be the Army of Tennessee, next to the Army of Northern Virginia in size and chief defender of the Confederate heartland. Davis blamed Beauregard for losing Johnston's "victory" at Shiloh and took the earliest opportunity to replace him with Braxton Bragg, who commanded the army for half of its effective fighting career. Bragg had won a well-deserved reputation as an artillerist in Mexico and had performed creditably at Pensacola and Shiloh. He was a soldier of considerable imagination, a stern disciplinarian, courageous, and wholly dedicated to the cause. Unfortunately, his personality made him his own worst enemy. Like so many of that generation he suffered from "dyspepsia" — probably ulcers — although it is not clear whether the ulcers gave him his personality or vice versa. He was bitingly critical, contentious, ill-humored, and managed to win the hatred of one high-ranking subordinate after another. Neither was he loved by the common soldiers or the civilian population. Worse yet, he had a penchant for losing won battles. A brilliant invasion of Kentucky in the fall of 1862 came to nothing when Bragg declined battle at the crucial moment. After a successful attack on the army of William F. Rosecrans at Murfreesboro, Tennessee (December 31 to January 3, 1862-1863), he retreated. He broke the Union line at Chickamauga Creek (September 19-20, 1863) and drove the Federals back to Chattanooga in headlong retreat, yet failed to exploit his costly triumph. Finally, he allowed himself to be defeated in humiliating fashion at Chattanooga in November 1863. Thereupon Davis accepted his resignation and made him military adviser to the President!

Davis's tolerance of Bragg was not quite as egregious as this bald recital might suggest. After the Kentucky campaign, Davis had placed Joseph E. Johnston in overall command of the Western Theater, and after Murfreesboro asked him to decide if Bragg should be replaced. Johnston said Bragg should remain in command. Then Johnston was ordered to take charge of the Army of Tennessee himself. Finding Bragg distracted by the illness of his wife, Johnston procrastinated and then fell ill, so Bragg stayed on. Davis had an excellent chance to remove Bragg when he visited the army after its wasted victory at Chickamauga and listened to the angry complaints of Bragg's officers. But he did nothing. This was a costly mistake for which there is no satisfactory explanation. The President made an equally bad error the following year by relieving Johnston when the Army of Tennessee faced Sherman before Atlanta. He made matters worse by giving the army to John B. Hood, who lost Atlanta, recklessly invaded Tennessee, and allowed his tattered army to be destroyed before Nashville. A similar failure of judgment was Davis's persistent support of John C. Pemberton, even after the latter had lost his army at Vicksburg.

Such mistakes must be balanced against the many excellent brigade, division, and corps commanders in the West, and competent departmental commanders such as Richard Taylor and E. Kirby Smith. After A. S. Johnston's death, the great problem was to find an army commander. It may well be that Bragg and J. E. Johnston were the best available, and between them they led the Army of Tennessee for about 80 percent of its career after Shiloh.

On several occasions President Davis took an active part in directing military operations in the West, although he usually did so only after a serious defeat or when a crisis impended. Here, also, his record was mixed. One of his most daring moves was to strip the seaboard from Charleston to Texas of almost all troops to reinforce A. S. Johnston after the fall of Fort Henry and Fort Donelson, thus taking a calculated risk of having the Federals descend on a defenseless coast. Johnston was thereby enabled to counterattack at Shiloh. Davis's decision late in 1862 to detach troops from the Army of Tennessee to reinforce Pemberton in Mississippi over the protests of both Bragg and Johnston was a costly mistake. Nine months later, however, the detachment of James Longstreet's corps from Lee's army to reinforce Bragg in northern Georgia made possible the victory at Chickamauga.

Davis's greatest mistake, perhaps the greatest strategic error of the war, was his refusal during the Atlanta campaign to allow Forrest to leave Mississippi and attack Sherman's rail communications, which stretched for hundreds of miles from northern Georgia to Louisville on the Ohio River. Lee, Johnston, and Governor Joseph Brown of Georgia all recommended that a major effort be made to break Sherman's railroads. Confederate cavalry in the West were still superior to Union horsemen, and there was no Federal general who could handle Forrest. Sherman was in mortal fear lest "that devil Forrest" get loose in Tennessee, and he sent one diversionary expedition after another into northern Mississippi to keep the devil occupied. Had all available cavalry been put under Forrest and sent into Tennessee and Kentucky, Atlanta would probably have been saved and the presidential election lost for Lincoln. But Davis stubbornly refused; Forrest, he said, was needed in Mississippi. Then Atlanta fell, and the Confederacy's last chance was gone.

When all things are taken into account — the successes and the failures, the victories in the East along with the defeats in the West, the oppressive disparity in resources — the Confederate high command performed well. Sometimes coordination was poor, but it was freer of politics and functioned more efficiently than its Union counterpart. Above all, it secured a better quality of leadership. This conclusion should come as no surprise. Had it been otherwise, could the Confederacy have resisted for so long against such odds?

Chapter IX

The Confederacy: Economic and Social Problems

FINANCES: THE STRUGGLE AGAINST BANKRUPTCY

The Confederacy battled throughout the war with varying degrees of success to overcome fundamental economic weaknesses. Its most dismal failure was financial. It was able neither to maintain a reliable currency nor to provide the government with an adequate income; the results of this were far-reaching and very harmful.

In 1861 the Confederacy's banks held only $26 million in specie, with perhaps another $20 million in the hands of private citizens. Even if all of this had been available to the government, it still would have supplied only a fraction of the need. The pressing requirements of the treasury led to the issuance of $135 million in bonds and $311 million in Treasury notes by the end of August 1861. Since a mere $46 million in specie could not have funded such a large obligation, it was essential to convert the South's great staple commodities, mainly cotton, into money. Here the problem was threefold. When the Confederacy was organized, by far the greater part of the 1860 crop had gone abroad or to Northern textile mills; another crop would not be ready until late in 1861. Second, even when cotton was available again, Congress hesitated to impose massive taxation on a people the vast majority of whom had never paid a penny directly to the central government. Third, Secretary Memminger, like so many Confederates, believed that if cotton was held off the world market, England and France would probably intervene; the Treasury was not interested in buying and shipping cotton until the war was almost a year old. Finally, although this by no means exhausts the complexities of the situation, there was the Union blockade, which, although leaky, kept many foreign vessels from trying to enter Southern ports. As it became somewhat more efficient, and especially after many ports had fallen to Union troops, exportation became more difficult. In normal times cotton would have bought the specie with which to back the currency, but as Memminger said in September 1863, "The blockade prevents the shipment of more cotton than such is absolutely necessary to pay for munitions of war and supplies. . . . " By the end of 1863 his department had shipped abroad on its own account a paltry 574 bales. The Treasury had only very limited success in trying to sell to foreign investors bonds and certificates secured by government-owned cotton located in the Confederacy.

Three obvious expedients were left: printing money with nothing to back it, taxing the actual products of the land (a sort of fiscal barter system), and impressment (forced sale) of those products. The latter two caused much resentment and many administrative problems, and were hampered in their execution by the deteriorating transportation system. Yet these practices, although deficient, were the quintessence of success when compared to the production of income by printing paper money. The stock of money in the Confederacy — bank notes, deposits, Treasury notes, and private currency — had increased more than nine times over by early 1864. As Union armies advanced, this bloated supply of money circulated in a smaller and smaller area that contained a constantly shrinking supply of goods. Inevitably there was a drastic depreciation of Confederate currency in terms of gold (20 to 1 by the end of 1863, 40 to 1 a year later) and prodigious price inflation (an increase of 28 times by the beginning of 1864), a repetition of the experience of Continental money during the dark days of the Revolution. From October 1861 until March 1864 prices rose on an average of 10 percent a month. The natural impulse was to spend money before it lost any more value, thus reinforcing the inflationary pressure. Wages lagged behind prices, as they always do in an inflationary crisis, and real income probably fell by one-half. However, wage earners had the great majority of Southerners as companions in hardship, from once-wealthy planters with their rotting cotton to the haggard soldiers in the trenches. The Confederacy's productivity decreased along with its wealth; by the end of the war poverty was the common lot.

Until the last months of the conflict, military reverses had much less to do with inflation than shortages of goods and the velocity and stock of money. Congress, at Davis's urging, curtailed the currency early in 1864 with some success. Prices were actually lower in November than they had been in March. Then the inflationary avalanche resumed, never again to be stopped. When all was over, the Confederate government had raised 5 percent of its income by taxation, 30 percent by borrowing, 60 percent by printing money, and 5 percent from miscellaneous sources. (Comparable figures for the North are: 21, 62, 13, and 4 percent.) Its total obligation in Confederate currency came to $712 million in funded debt and $1,554 billion in Treasury notes.

The historian, made eagle-eyed by hindsight, can easily perceive the formula for Confederate solvency. The government should have acquired by taxation or borrowing as much as possible of the 1861 cotton crop, which amounted to about 4 million bales, and begun exporting early in 1862 when the blockade was still very porous and no major ports had fallen to the enemy. Just 10 percent of the crop would have grossed $150 million in specie at Liverpool in the fall of 1862, a sum that could have bought up the entire amount of Treasury notes then in circulation, with $35 million in specie to spare. Even this measure of success would have significantly reduced the rate of inflation. Obviously such a policy would have represented a high level of statesmanship, considering the financial and political conventions of the day, the hope of foreign intervention, and the expectation of Northern financial collapse. Yet, as Clement Eaton points out, more remarkable than financial failure was

> the amazing phenomenon of a nation waging a long war chiefly with fiat money, paying possibly eight hundred thousand soldiers, buying supplies of war and naval vessels in Europe, and carrying on a civil government for nine million white and Negro people.

TRADE

Much of the South's commercial life was bound up in the exportation of cotton, causing a longstanding bias toward free trade. The coming of war reversed that tendency and drastically restricted the cotton trade. The impact of the King Cotton theory on overseas trade has been discussed. Jefferson Davis also hoped that the want of cotton would be fatal to Northern finances. Before the war cotton had accounted for more than half of all American exports, and Davis hoped that the loss of cotton as a medium of exchange would mean a corresponding drop in imports and hence a decrease in the tariff revenues on which the Union's public credit rested.

In May 1861 Congress indirectly prohibited the export of cotton to the United States by confining shipments to Southern seaports. As for Europe, Southern agriculturalists and the people generally united on a voluntary cotton embargo, revealing a notable spirit of self-sacrifice on the part of merchants and planters. Congress discussed but never passed a legal ban on exports to Europe, an act that Davis feared would needlessly antagonize France and Britain. The embargo lasted about a year and then began to weaken as both supplies and the likelihood of foreign assistance dwindled. By the spring of 1862 Memminger was urging the exportation of cotton. He did not believe that enough cotton would go abroad to influence the attitude of neutrals or to help the North, if it shall go there through neutral ports. But the cotton that did get through the blockade would reduce the price of foreign exchange in the Confederacy and would thereby enable Memminger to acquire cheaper credit in Europe. By 1863 all vestiges of the embargo had disappeared.

The high price of cotton on the world market and of everything but cotton in the Confederacy meant that enormous profits could be made by running the blockade. Speculators could lose a ship and cargo after two successful round trips and still make money. This was especially true of luxuries, called "blockade goods," because they were lighter and less bulky than the munitions and provisions needed by the Confederate army. Private trade injured the cause by draining cotton and scarce specie from the South, taking up valuable cargo space, and bringing in French wines, hoop skirts, and assorted gewgaws. Even the profits did not stay in the Confederacy. Most of the blockade business was in the hands of foreigners, especially British firms; the latter were loud among the voices raised against any intervention by their government that might bring the war to an untimely end.

The Confederate government bought a few blockade running vessels and operated them with great success, but they were sufficient to satisfy the needs of only the ordnance and medical bureaus. Consequently in the summer of 1863 the government ordered private ships to reserve one-third to one-half of their cargo space for its use; by early 1864 this had evolved into an ambitious and well-conceived plan for exporting and purchasing abroad. In February, Congress prohibited the importation of luxuries and gave the President complete control of the country's overseas trade. Davis in turn required all ships to reserve for the government one-half of their cargo space on both the outward and return voyage at fixed freight rates. Private shippers using the other half of the cargo space had to give bonds to import articles useful to the Confederacy. The executive established a centralized system of collecting, shipping, and selling cotton. The new program was in full operation by the summer of 1864.

Private speculators and states such as Georgia and North Carolina, which had been running the blockade on their own account, immediately raised a great clamor against the regulations. The new Second Congress attempted to weaken the work of its predecessor by exempting state-owned or state-chartered vessels, a bill that Davis killed by veto. The President steadfastly defended the system as beneficial to both finances and the war effort generally. Shipping cotton abroad for sale instead of exchanging it for supplies run through the blockade brought a far higher price — 24 pence per pound versus 6 pence. In December he reported that total exports under the regulations during July to November came to 11,796 bales, of which 1272 bales, about 11 percent, were lost. This cotton brought £320,000 sterling, equal to $1,500,000 in gold or $45 million in Confederate currency. Exports under other arrangements during the same period amounted to perhaps 3500 bales. That the President seemed so proud of this accomplishment gives some idea of the utter inadequacy of earlier policies. For example, in a single month, July 1863, 5300 bales had been exported from Wilmington alone, the great preponderance on private account — over one-third as much as the Confederate government was able to ship in the five months to which Davis referred. One reason more was not accomplished by the new policy was the location of the government's cotton; by mid-1864 most of it lay on plantations in the Mississippi Valley and was not available for export abroad. Furthermore, for various reasons, the new system did not help the subsistence bureau, and by the time Davis reported to Congress, Lee's army was literally starving on its feet. Another wise but belated action was the government's purchase of additional blockade runners. Some of them came into use during the waning months of the war and did excellent service during their brief careers.

The new policy's limited success was sufficient to show what might have been done through foreign trade had it not been crippled by the King Cotton delusion during the first year of the war and by excessive reliance on private enterprise for more than a year thereafter. The course of events might have been quite different if the system of 1864 had been adopted early in the war in combination with extensive purchases of blockade runners. As in so many things, the Confederacy moved in the right direction, but not fast enough.

Statistics of the South's foreign trade are very incomplete. Estimates of the total amount of cotton exported range from 500,000 to 1,250,000 bales, amounts that can be compared to 1860 exports of 3,774,000 bales. The larger estimate would give a monthly average of 26,000 bales throughout the war, or 35,000 bales after the embargo began to weaken, and is almost certainly too high. My guess, based on a variety of fragmentary evidence, falls between the extremes: 800,000 bales, including exports through Mexico and cotton that went to the North by way of neutral countries, but excluding direct trade with the North.

The imports produced by this trade fell far short of meeting the needs of either government or people. From March to December 1864, for instance, total government exports came to 3000 bales per month, whereas the War Department alone required supplies that would cost 6000 bales; the same gap existed in imports. Still, the Confederacy could not have lasted long without its foreign trade, inadequate as it was. Incomplete figures show government imports of about 300,000 small arms; in the year beginning September 1863, three times as many were imported as were manufactured at home. Probably 200 cannon came through the blockade, plus millions of rounds of ammunition, millions of pounds of nitre for making powder, and over 2 million pounds of desperately needed lead. After the autumn of 1863 virtually all copper, which was indispensable in making percussion caps, came from outside. About 750,000 pairs of boots and shoes and 400,000 blankets were run in. There was less success in procuring food; perhaps 11 million pounds of meat were obtained, most of it in 1864 and 1865. This was not enough to feed Lee's army adequately, and yet without it the end would have come sooner.

In brief, trade through the blockade and with Mexico provided the margin of survival for four years. The main effect of the Union blockade, as mentioned, was more to keep ships away than to capture them. Far more damaging to commerce was the capture of Southern ports. New Orleans, through which more than one-fourth of the country's exports passed in 1860, fell in April 1862. By that time the North Carolina Sounds and Chesapeake Bay were sealed off by Union garrisons and forts. The capture of Fort Pulaski in April 1862 severely limited access to Savannah. Pensacola, blocked by Fort Pickens from the onset of hostilities, fell in May 1862. Parts of the Texas coast were taken in 1863; Mobile, next to New Orleans, the largest Gulf port, was substantially closed in the summer of 1864; and the greatest blockade port of all, Wilmington, was captured in January 1865. Only Charleston remained, and the Confederates were forced to abandon it in March. The efficiency of Union blockaders increased in inverse proportion to the number of ports they had to watch.

The loss of ports generated growing pressure to trade with the enemy. States bordering the Mississippi grew half of the South's cotton. The Atlantic states produced only 27 percent, and that was the first to go through the blockade. As the railroads wore out, the transfer of Mississippi Delta cotton to available ports became so difficult that the only alternative to its eventual destruction or theft was sale to the North. Jefferson Davis faced that prospect with the utmost distaste, particularly during the first two years. He and other officials feared that cotton would relieve the Union financially as well as diplomatically. They also suspected that the people's allegiance might be weaned away by such unnatural traffic. The most anxious proponents of the trade were to be found in the War Department, where the suffering of the armies was most sharply felt. The subject became more urgent as large sections of the cotton-rich Mississippi Valley fell to the Federals in 1862 and 1863, along with commercial centers such as New Orleans, Memphis, and Vicksburg. Indeed, for civilians along the military frontier, trading through the lines was often a matter of sheer necessity. The trade increased as scarcities grew worse from 1863 onward. Commanding officers, Lee among them, urged that it be sponsored and regulated by the government so as to realize maximum benefit for the army.

Davis never gave his approval to interbelligerent commerce, but he finally allowed the War Department to go its own way. Agents went North to contract for the delivery of goods for the Confederate army. Supplies came in by steamboats plying rivers and coastal waters, overland through Memphis and other cities, and by ship, sometimes running the blockade directly from New York, other times by breaking bulk and shipping through neutral ports. Of the 1 million bales imported by the North, roughly 700,000 must have come directly from the Confederacy. It was paid for with guns, including cannon, ammunition, uniforms, boots, salt meat, medicines, and so forth. The exact volume of the trade cannot be ascertained because of its largely clandestine nature, but comments from Southern officials leave no doubt that it was of substantial assistance. If the Confederates had put it on a systematic basis early in the war, they could have translated their enemies' entrepreneurial appetites into an important source of strength.

INDUSTRY AND AGRICULTURE

The South tried to compensate for the derangement of its normal commercial relations by making a strenuous effort to become self-sufficient. It was not able to transform an agricultural economy into a manufacturing economy; it did not bring about an industrial revolution in the normal sense of the term. Yet Professor Luraghi believes that "what the South accomplished is astounding." He is especially struck by what happened "when private interests collided with public ones; possibly, never before had America seen so ruthless a violation of the sacred rights of private property. No country, from the Inca Empire to Soviet Russia has ever possessed a similar government-owned (or controlled) kind of economy."

The Richmond government consciously manipulated private business by its control of manpower and its extensive purchases of cotton, by its requirement that factories reserve at least two-thirds of their output for military use, and so forth. With the exception of the Tredegar Iron Works in Richmond, which turned out over 1000 cannon, large quantities of ammunition, warship armor, and so on, the most important manufactories were those built and owned by the government. With pardonable pride Josiah Gorgas, Pennsylvania-born chief of ordnance, reported in November 1863 that among the items fabricated in government workshops during the year were 113 pieces of artillery, 300,000 rounds of artillery ammunition, 27,000 small arms, plus another 127,000 repaired, and over 36 million rounds of small arms ammunition, 1,417,000 pounds of powder, 6800 saddles, and many other essential articles. Virtually none of these, including gunpowder, had been made in the South before the war. As Gorgas recorded in his diary in the spring of 1864, "Where three years ago we were not making a gun, a pistol nor a sabre, no shot nor shell (except at the Tredegar Works) — a pound of powder — we now make all these in quantities to meet the needs of our large armies."

The most striking example of government enterprise was Augusta, Georgia. There were constructed the world's second largest powder mill, a factory with 1500 women employees making army uniforms, shops that made uniforms and shoes for the navy, an arsenal, a cannon foundry, and a giant military bakery. Richmond, Selma, Macon, and Atlanta were other such centers. A military-industrial system had been built from scratch.

The South's worst failure in industrial management was its handling of the railroads. Fighting the first major war in history in which railroads were a strategic factor, the South found its rail lines to be deficient in the quality of construction, in miles of track, in uniformity of gauge, in repair shops, in skilled workers, and in everything else. Such a precious and limited resource demanded careful direction and conservation. The railroads got neither. As track and rolling stock wore out or fell into enemy hands, they were replaced neither by domestic manufacture nor by importation. The former could have been done at the Tredegar Works and elsewhere; the latter certainly should have been feasible. In contrast to its assumption of economic control in other sectors, the government was strangely reluctant to take responsibility for the railroads. It moved in that direction only when pressed by dire emergency. Congress, President Davis, the states, and the companies were all to blame for this condition of affairs. The breakdown of the rail system caused virtual starvation in Lee's army, crippled its strategic mobility, reduced the amount of cotton available for shipment through the blockade, gave rise to wide price variations from place to place, and made all forms of economic endeavor expensive and uncertain. Congress at long last gave the executive the power it required — two months before Lee surrendered.

Few people thought that an agricultural nation like the Confederacy would go hungry. But Southern agriculture was very vulnerable to disruption. Because of its specialization, it depended on unfettered intraregional and interregional trade in foodstuffs and on access to manufactured articles from outside the South. Lower Mississippi planters, for example, normally imported huge quantities of food from states further upstream.

The case of pork offers the best illustration of why starvation became a reality. This meat, along with corn meal, was the backbone of the average Southerner's diet and of the Confederate soldier's ration. However, swine production was geographically uneven. Virginia, the Carolinas, Florida, Georgia, Alabama, Mississippi, and Louisiana all imported pork, even in peacetime. Fifteen percent of the hogs raised in the 11 Confederate states came from Tennessee, mainly the central and western parts of the state, sections wholly or partially occupied by Union troops as early as the spring of 1862. Another 9 percent came from Texas, completely cut off from the eastern Confederacy by the summer of 1863, and

7½ percent came from Arkansas, which was overrun even earlier. Additional losses occurred when the Federals took the pork-producing counties in eastern North Carolina and southeastern Virginia in 1862, and the Mississippi Delta counties in 1863. By mid-1863 the Confederacy had lost possession or access to almost one-half of its hog-producing areas. The normal pork supply was further reduced by a savage epidemic of cholera that began before and continued into the war. As early as August 1861, Commissary General Lucius Northrop warned that there were not enough hogs in the Confederacy to feed both the army and the slave population.

A similar problem of inaccessibility applied to cattle. No less than one-third of all the beef in the Confederate states was grown in Texas. Thirty percent of the corn production was lost with Texas, Arkansas, and Tennessee. Virginia, which raised over 40 percent of the wheat, was the first state to suffer invasion, and large stretches of it soon were devastated or in Union hands.

The loss of these food-producing areas was aggravated by a variety of other problems. Manpower was scarce because of the needs of the army and the impressment of slaves to perform military labor. Unlike his Northern counterpart, the Southern farmer could not substitute machines for people. The lack of qualified overseers impaired efficiency, as did the inability to replace wornout tools, the depletion of draft animals, taken in large numbers by the military, and the lack of salt, which was needed to preserve meat as well as to prevent hoof and mouth disease. Bad weather damaged crops extensively in 1862 and 1863, especially hurting corn and wheat production. Vast sections of the Confederacy were ravaged by Union armies, which served as magnets for large numbers of runaway slaves. Fences were used for firewood by friend and foe alike and were replaced with great difficulty, if at all. Farming was, of course, impossible without fences to keep stock out of the crop fields.

Southerners took various measures to meet these new and discouraging conditions. Many states passed laws encouraging planters to shift from cotton to food crops; corn was the favorite substitute. Cotton production did drop sharply after 1861, although this was due partly to invasion and other factors. The 1862 corn crop may have been larger than in antebellum years; if so, that experience was not duplicated during the rest of the war. The states also tried to conserve grain by severely limiting whiskey production. There were not a few who resisted this supreme sacrifice, and the law was difficult to enforce. Expanded trade with the Federals was another result of the food shortage.

In the spring of 1863 the combination of shortages and financial embarrassments led Congress to pass the impressment and tax-in-kind acts. The latter was a tax paid in agricultural products instead of in money; impressment, forced sales at a set price, was used only as a last resort. Both laws met with strenuous opposition, were troublesome to execute efficiently or fairly, and certainly contributed to disaffection among a people who were fighting a losing battle to make ends meet. More to the point would have been a law early in the war to require a shift to food crops. Congress debated the subject, but because of constitutional objections and apprehensions that other parts of the world would supplant the South as the great supplier of cotton, it did no more than issue exhortations. Cotton could be a tyrant as well as a king.

At war's end agriculture in the Confederate South lay in ruins. Stocks of cotton had been largely burnt, stolen, or exported, and productive capacity generally had been crippled and remained so for many years. Next to the loss of life, this was the most grievous wound the South suffered in its bid for independence.

DISLOYALTY, DISAFFECTION, AND STATES' RIGHTS

Some Southern Unionists who opposed secession rallied to the Confederacy once the decision had been made, especially after Lincoln's call for troops. Others continued to oppose the movement for independence and formed the nucleus of a growing opposition to the war. Unionist dissent was mainly passive or rhetorical as long as active support for the Confederacy was not required. But with military conscription, the periodic suspension of habeas corpus, impressment, and the tax in kind, Unionists gathered new recruits and began to resist openly. Still more joined the peace movement as the hardships of war multiplied. They organized secret societies, sheltered deserters, and collaborated with the Northern armies. As with desertion, disloyalty was most common in the mountains and in other areas settled mainly by poorer whites, who had a long history of opposition to anything favored by low country slaveowners.

Those who remained fundamentally loyal to the Confederacy could express dissatisfaction forcefully — even violently. They too suffered from the hardships and complained about the inequities of the times. They accused the government of fostering or at least tolerating profiteers and speculators who fattened off the misery of the common people. Workers who saw their wages buy less and less struck for more money. Hungry women and children participated in "bread riots," breaking open stores and seizing the food that they were unable to buy. As the fortunes of war turned even more decidedly against the Confederacy, civilians as well as soldiers became less willing to give of their own to bolster a lost cause.

The most obvious form of opposition to the government's policies was the invocation of states' rights, which one scholar has seen as fatal to Confederate independence. According to this view, states crippled the war effort by putting their respective needs before that of the nation as a whole. They were accused of restricting the size of the Confederate army early in the war by withholding arms, and later of diverting 100,000 men into state defense units when they were urgently needed at the front. They monopolized half of the country's cotton mills, competed with the government in blockade-running, and hoarded clothing and other supplies. State governments solidly opposed the suspension of habeas corpus and sometimes obstructed the work of conscription officers. States' rights were used as a political platform by Vice-President Stephens and his irresponsible claque, whose first purpose and greatest joy was to thwart and vilify Jefferson Davis.

There is much truth in this estimate of the baneful effects of states' rights, but preoccupation with the dark side of the question has diverted attention from the states' important contributions to the common cause. For example, some of the weapons in state arsenals had been purchased in the reaction to John Brown's raid, before there was any Confederate government, and although the states withheld some weapons, they put a far larger number into the hands of regiments that they raised at their own expense and sent into the Confederate service. Facing as they did an aggressive enemy in command of the sea and having to rely on a central government as yet untested, the states naturally wanted to keep some arms and men at home to repel possible invasions.

Meat bought by the states early in 1861 significantly eased the task of the Bureau of Subsistence. They sent clothing and other necessaries to their troops, thus assuming an obligation properly belonging to the Richmond government. They lent money with a generous liberality to the national treasury, and most of them pledged their credit to guarantee the Confederate debt. Their complaints about conscription and impressment usually addressed abuses, not the laws themselves. The states took steps to provide for soldiers' dependents by passing stay laws and appropriating money for the needy. They started factories, tried to control prices, bought and operated blockade-runners, and traded through the lines for necessary supplies. In these and other ways the states sought to sustain the war. In the end, of course, they failed. Like the Confederacy, they could not make bricks without straw.

The Confederate government and people manifested a remarkable solicitude for the preservation of civil liberties and states' rights even in the midst of a struggle for national survival. So dedicated to constitutional rights were leaders such as Jefferson Davis that the government did not suppress a single newspaper. Nor did the President presume to suspend the writ of habeas corpus by executive decree whatever the crisis, regarding that power as belonging exclusively to Congress. Congress suspended the writ grudgingly and only for limited periods, and the President acted under the suspension with great restraint. In contrast to the North, there was no imprisonment of thousands of civilians by executive warrant. Professor David Donald has argued that such extreme libertarianism killed the Confederacy by preventing the government from enforcing conscription and stamping out sedition. "The real weakness of the Confederacy was that the Southern people insisted upon retaining their democratic liberties in wartime." The Confederacy, he writes, "died of democracy." However, given the odds, it is doubtful if an authoritarian policy, even if politically possible, could have squeezed from the Southern people enough additional resources to turn the tide of battle.

THE NEGRO IN THE CONFEDERACY

One of the main purposes of the Deep South states in seceding was to settle the status of slavery once and for all. The outbreak of war, however, quickly unsettled the institution to such an extent that even if the Confederacy had been able to maintain its independence, it seems possible that slavery would have emerged from the war in a distinctly shaky condition.

The war made Southerners look at slaves in a new light: they seemed both more useful and more dangerous. The possibility of an uprising could not be overlooked; Lincoln's Emancipation Proclamation was regarded as an incitement to rebellion. State legislatures made the criminal code more severe in some respects and tried to tighten the patrol system. Lack of manpower largely nullified these precautions; consequently there was less supervision of blacks than in normal times. Some plantations had no adult white males in residence, leaving the management of slaves to women and Negro drivers. Such conditions created some uneasiness among whites, and from time to time there were rumors of plots and uprisings. Yet the fact remains that Southern whites had sufficient confidence in their slaves to leave large areas virtually in the hands of blacks, suggesting that historians have perhaps overestimated the whites' fear of slave insurrections.

The impressment laws applied to slaves as well as other forms of property, and military authorities took many thousands from their owners to labor on defensive works and for other noncombatant purposes. In Virginia alone 35,000 slaves were used. The practice was not popular with the owners. It was observed that some planters who willingly sent their sons into battle objected bitterly to having their slaves dig trenches. Slaves — and free blacks — worked for the Confederacy voluntarily and otherwise on railroads, in factories, as artisans, cooks, teamsters, and in many other capacities. Their contribution to the South's military capability was significant. As white manpower dwindled, there were those who advocated imitating the North and filling up depleted ranks with black soldiers. The subject was openly discussed following the defeats at Vicksburg and Gettysburg. After alluding to Northern enrollment of slaves, the Alabama legislature recommended that

Congress consider using male slaves "in some effective way . . . to perform such services as Congress may direct." Proponents of arming blacks sometimes conceded candidly that this amounted to a tacit admission of equality with whites. In a private circular to his colleagues in the Army of Tennessee, General Patrick Cleburne called for the emancipation and enlistment of blacks. In February 1864 Congress in effect made free blacks subject to conscription for noncombatant service. They were to be given the same pay as white soldiers.

Moved by the continuing loss of white manpower, President Davis proposed in November 1864 that Congress approve the purchase of 40,000 slaves for use as noncombatants, with emancipation as the reward for faithful conduct. For Davis this was not quite as radical a break with the past as it may seem. He had believed ever since the formation of the Confederacy that even if independence were won, "slave property will be lost eventually." His request, however, was received with hostility by most of the editors and politicians who expressed themselves on the subject; an exception was the governor of Virginia, who advocated arming the slaves even if it meant emancipation. Early in 1865 General Lee advised the use of black soldiers, giving them freedom upon enlistment and freedom for their families upon completion of service. Lee's immense prestige finally levered Congress into action. In March 1865 the legislators authorized the enlistment of up to one-fourth of the male slaves 18 to 45 years of age in any state. The Constitution forbade congressional interference with the rights of slaveowners, and so the law stipulated that "nothing in this act shall be construed to authorize a change in the relation which the said slaves shall bear toward their owners and of the states in which they reside." However, the War Department refused to accept any slave as a recruit "unless with his master conferring, as far as he may, the rights of a freedman," and it enjoined on officers in charge of Negro soldiers to exercise "kindness, forbearance, and indulgence" and to "protect them from injustice and oppression." Once the decision to enlist Negroes was made, political opinion endorsed it. The army managed to put a few companies into uniform before the final collapse, but there was no time to give the experiment a fair trial.

Simultaneously with the debate over arming the slaves, President

Davis and Secretary of State Benjamin sent Duncan F. Kenner, a large slaveholder from Louisiana, on a secret mission. He was to make unofficial inquiries to discover if a promise of emancipation could buy British or French recognition of the Confederacy. Kenner sailed from New York in disguise and consulted with Mason and Slidell upon his arrival in Europe. Subsequent conversations with Lord Palmerston and Napoleon III proved, if further proof was needed, that only the establishment of independence by victory on the battlefield would bring recognition. *"Sic transit gloria mundi,"* said Mason.

Jefferson Davis was probably correct in believing that slavery was doomed even if the Confederacy survived. The wartime damage sustained by the institution doubtless reinforced his opinion. There were also signs raising at least the possibility that in an independent South slavery might eventually be reformed out of existence. Before the war some moderate Northerners, such as Daniel Webster, argued that had it not been for the Northern assault on slavery, a Southern abolitionist movement would have arisen. Antislavery sentiment was by no means unknown in the antebellum years, particularly in the upper South, and there were those who would have welcomed gradual emancipation under Southern control. As Lee wrote to his wife late in 1856, "In this enlightened age, there are few, I believe, but what will acknowledge, that slavery as an institution, is a moral and political evil in any country." As did many of his class in the border and upper South, he believed that emancipation would "sooner result from the mild and melting influence of Christianity, than the storms and tempests of fiery controversy."

Southern independence, brief though it was, gave rise to a movement for the reform of slavery, although not for its abolition. The impulse came mainly from religious leaders and gathered strength during the last two years of the war. Their program called for forbidding the separation of mothers and children by sale; eliminating laws that forbade teaching slaves to read and hence deprived them of the grace and comfort of the Holy Scriptures; legalizing slave marriages; and admitting slave testimony in court so as to protect slaves against cruel masters. Although there were a few state laws passed to promote more humane treatment, the general response was that no matter how meritorious the reform might be, action on so sensitive a matter should be postponed until peace came.

The reaction of Negroes to the Civil War was as varied as human nature and the circumstances in which they found themselves. When the fighting was at a distance, plantation life went on much as usual. If Union forces established themselves nearby, runaways and insubordinate behavior increased markedly. Occupation by the Federals sometimes elicited wholesale desertion. Historians have both challenged and confirmed the tradition that field hands on large plantations were usually the first to go, while house servants, living in close contact with their white owners, were more loyal. As might be expected, harsh masters were more likely to lose their slaves, but even the most benevolent found that kindness did not guarantee loyalty. Often Union officers took unwilling slaves from their masters by force, selecting, as one of the Federals said, "the ablebodied men" and "the youngest and best looking women." Far more came of their own accord, and after every invading army trailed a long caravan of blacks. The plight of the fugitives was never enviable; often they were left behind and had to fend for themselves. The death rate among these unfortunates was sometimes fearful. At one contraband camp near Helena, Arkansas, more than one-half of the inmates died in a month, while more poured in to take their places. The freedmen whom Union authorities kept on the plantation suffered least; they lived and worked much as before, although now under wage contracts. Others less fortunate were summarily impressed into the army or, especially in the cities, indiscriminately jailed. Some who had run away from their masters later ran away from the Federals. Two desires seemed to be uppermost in the hearts of most freedmen: to be able to move about from one place to another — the acid test of liberty — and to be free of white masters, whether a Southern planter or a Northern provost marshal.

A surprising number of Southern blacks apparently sympathized with the Confederate cause. Early in the war free blacks, of whom there were about 180,000, sometimes volunteered for military service. There was some disposition in several states to accept them, and a few units were mustered in, but the War Department's policy was to decline such offers politely. Donations of labor were quickly accepted. Some slaves made charitable donations for the relief of soldiers' families and purchased Confederate bonds. Some expressed a willingness to fight for the South. According to a surgeon in charge of a military hospital, 60 out of 72 hired male slaves said that they would "take up arms to protect their masters' families, homes, and their own from an attacking foe, would volunteer to go to the trenches and fight to the bitter end."

Some slaves did go to war with their masters as personal servants, and they proved to be enthusiastic Confederates. They naturally had many opportunities to desert, yet the evidence for the loyalty of these men is overwhelming. They sometimes took such an active part in the fighting that there was a fairly general impression among the Federals that blacks were enlisted in the Southern armies. There were numerous instances of their killing and capturing Union soldiers. Colonel Arthur Fremantle of the Coldstream Guards recorded the following incident on Lee's retreat from Gettysburg:

> I saw a most laughable spectacle this afternoon — a Negro dressed in full Yankee uniform, with a rifle at full cock, leading along a barefooted white man with whom he had evidently changed clothes. General Longstreet stopped the pair, and asked the black man what it meant. He replied, "The two soldiers in charge of this here Yank have got drunk, so for fear he should escape I have took care of him. . . . " This little episode of a Southern slave leading a white Yankee soldier through a Northern village, *alone and of his own accord,* would not have been gratifying to an abolitionist.

The reactions of Confederate blacks to the war were so varied as to make generalizations risky. The small free black elite of successful business people and slaveowners had little to gain and possibly much to lose should the North triumph. To other free blacks, who knew the limitations as well as the advantages of liberty in a white society, emancipation meant an enormous enlargement of the free labor force that might well drive down wages for all. As for the slaves, the great weight of evidence shows that the vast majority wanted to be free, and very few regretted the passing of the peculiar institution, however disappointing the reality of freedom when compared with vague and roseate expectations. There is also much evidence to show that slavery had not made blacks hate whites, although they might hate slavery itself. The physical separation of blacks and whites that freedom brought and the use of the wage system, sharecropping, and tenancy rapidly destroyed personal relationships that had existed between masters and slaves. Then the gulf between the races widened rapidly. Paradoxical though it may sound, race hatred was much more a phenomenon of freedom than of slavery. In this as in so many things the South was to recapitulate the experience of the North. Toqueville had observed a generation before, "The prejudice of the race appears to be stronger in the States which have abolished Slavery, than in those where it still exists."

Chapter X

The End of the War and the First Peace Settlement

COLLAPSE OF THE CONFEDERACY

By the time Lincoln delivered his second inaugural address, Confederate resistance was rapidly crumbling. Sherman had swept through Georgia and South Carolina and was advancing through North Carolina. A scratch force of miscellaneous garrisons and the skeleton of the Army of Tennessee could present only a feeble front to the Federal legions. Tennessee and much of Mississippi and Alabama were overrun or devastated. In the East only Lee's attenuated regiments on the Richmond-Petersburg front provided a semblance of serious resistance.

Late in March, Grant moved against the railroads that connected the Confederate capital with North Carolina. Lee countered, but his line was stretched so thin that Grant broke it, forcing Lee to evacuate Richmond and Petersburg on April 2. A week later, overtaken and surrounded by overwhelming numbers, Lee surrendered the Army of Northern Virginia at Appomattox Court House. Bowing to the inevitable, Joseph E. Johnston surrendered the Army of Tennessee to Sherman on April 26 at Greensboro, North Carolina. Confederate forces in Alabama, Mississippi, and East Louisiana followed suit on May 4, the Trans-Mississippi Department on May 26. The *C.S.S. Shenandoah,* terrorizing New England whalers in the

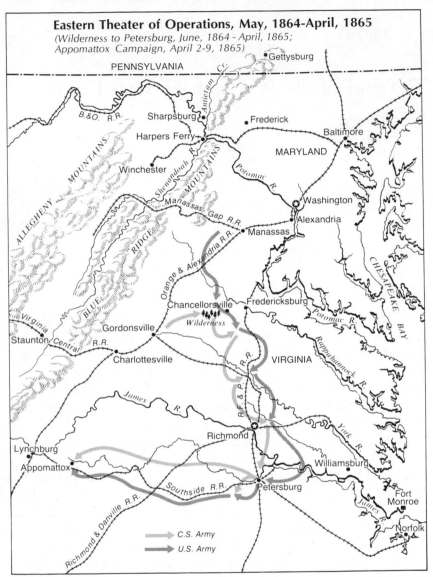

Eastern Theater of Operations, May, 1864-April, 1865
*(Wilderness to Petersburg, June, 1864 - April, 1865;
Appomattox Campaign, April 2-9, 1865)*

North Pacific, fired the last shot on behalf of the Confederacy on June 28, then learned from captured newspapers that its flag no longer had a country.

President Lincoln had come down to Grant's headquarters late in March as the final operations began. After Richmond fell he conferred with Confederate Assistant Secretary of War John A. Campbell, who had been the intermediary in the Fort Sumter negotiations, and suggested that the members of the Virginia legislature meet informally to withdraw the state's troops from the Confederate army. In exchange, Lincoln promised to return confiscated property, except for slaves, and to pardon "repentant sinners." The President accordingly ordered General Godfrey Weitzel, commanding in Richmond, to allow the legislators to assemble. As Gideon Welles recalled, Lincoln believed "the prominent and influential men . . . had better come together and do their own work. . . . Civil government must be reestablished, he said, as soon as possible. . . . " Otherwise the President feared the armies would dissolve into guerrilla bands. "These were the reasons why he wished prominent Virginians who had the confidence of the people to come together and turn themselves and their neighbors into good Union men." Secretary of War Stanton vehemently and repeatedly urged Lincoln not to proceed in this fashion. Members of the Joint Committee on the Conduct of the War were said to be "thunderstruck" by Lincoln's generosity. Lacking support from party leaders, on April 12 Lincoln rescinded his permission for the members of the legislature to meet. He gave as his reason Grant's capture of Lee's army, but inasmuch as he had known of that for the past two days, political and not military factors were probably mainly responsible for his reversal.

Lincoln still clung to his preference for a flexible Reconstruction policy, one that would treat each state according to its own special circumstances. He was relieved that Congress was not in session when the war ended and would not convene for more than seven months, because he intended to act on Reconstruction soon. The absence of party doctrinaires at the other end of Pennsylvania Avenue would speed the process. These were doubtless among the thoughts he took from his last cabinet meeting on April 14, thoughts that were obliterated by John Wilkes Booth that night.

Lincoln's attitude strongly influenced General Sherman, who had met with the President at Grant's headquarters shortly before the fall of Richmond and had concluded that Lincoln intended to work with the South's existing political leadership to bring about reunion. Therefore in negotiating with Johnston for the surrender of the

Army of Tennessee, Sherman agreed to a settlement that included universal amnesty and recognition of existing state governments. Political repercussions followed instantly. Republicans feared Northern Democrats would rally around Sherman's proposals, since they were already interested in the general's presidential possibilities. Sherman therefore had no discernible support among leading Republicans. President Johnson and the cabinet agreed that the settlement must be disapproved and Sherman instructed to offer the same terms to Johnston as Grant had offered to Lee: surrender and parole, a purely military transaction. Stanton executed this decision in a manner intended to discredit and humiliate Sherman before the Northern people, publishing slanted statements and doctored dispatches so as to suggest that Sherman's loyalty was under suspicion. Senator Zachariah Chandler, a radical among Radicals, expressed satisfaction at this opportunity to destroy the political availability of the man he believed the Democrats were preparing to seize on as their champion. The prostrate South now perforce accepted the terms that Lincoln had striven to avoid: unconditional surrender.

THE SOUTH AT THE END OF THE WAR

Some account of conditions in the South at the war's conclusion is necessary in order to appraise Federal policies and properly understand Southern reactions to those policies. A recurring complaint by Republicans during Reconstruction was the South's refusal to repent of its sins, thank the victors for showing it the error of its ways, and embrace the Union with patriotic fervor. A brief sketch of what had happened to the South may suggest that this was too much to expect of human nature.

The lives and property of noncombatants have always suffered in the theater of operations, no matter how scrupulously commanders might try to protect them. Under the best of circumstances, the South would have experienced serious losses. All the Confederate states except Texas were deeply invaded, and destruction was necessarily coextensive with the operations of the armies. To this damage must be added the deliberate devastation that was not incidental to military operations. As far as such devastation was intended to reduce the Confederacy's capacity to make war, it represented an intermediate stage between the limited, formalized warfare of the eighteenth century, when the prevailing policy was to respect the property rights of civilians, and the twentieth-century concept of total war, involving the massive destruction of both noncombatants and their property.

But most of the destruction was born of a quite different philosophy, one that sprang from a generation of anti-Southern polemics with a strong religious tincture. There was a widespread although by no means universal conviction among Union troops that Southerners were a wicked people who had deliberately started the war and therefore had no rights that the righteous were bound to respect. It was surely not coincidental that Julia Ward Howe married the crusading lyrics of "The Battle Hymn of the Republic" to the tune of "John Brown's Body," or that so many took to heart her exhortation to "trample out the vintage where the grapes of wrath are stored."

Perhaps no one represented this attitude better than General Sherman. He took as his mission the infliction on the wicked of whatever punishment was required to bring them to repentance. If necessary, he was willing "to take every life, every acre of land. . . . I would not coax them or even meet them half way but make them so sick of war that generations would pass away before they would again appeal to it."

> Satan and the rebellious saints of Heaven were allowed a continuous existence in hell merely to swell their just punishment. To such as would rebel against a Government so mild and just as ours was in peace, a punishment equal would not be unjust.

Early in 1864, in the Meridian expedition, he made, as he said, "a swath of desolation fifty miles broad across the state of Mississippi which the present generation will not forget." When he set out from Atlanta to the sea he proclaimed his intention "to make Georgia howl," and when he reached Savannah he estimated that only 20 percent of the destruction "has inured to our advantage, and the remainder is simple waste and destruction." As he was preparing to turn north from Savannah, he wrote Halleck, "The whole army is burning with an insatiable desire to wreak vengeance upon South Carolina. I almost tremble for her fate, but feel that she deserves all that is in store for her." And after the war the general observed with satisfaction, "Now the truth is we fought the holiest fight ever fought on God's earth." Sherman and the kind of warfare that he exemplified were not so much harbingers of modern total war as they were a throwback to the religious wars of the seventeenth century, or perhaps even to the wars of the Old Testament.

There has never been a full-scale study of the conduct of Union troops in the South. Such an investigation might place in perspective the American attitude toward enemy civilians in later wars, especially those in which ideology (close kin to religion) was a major component. In any case, it would be a tale replete with wanton destruction, robbery, arson, rape, torture, and murder, with both blacks and whites as victims. Such atrocities, which Northern soldiers and newspaper reporters witnessed and described in detail, often took place with the tacit or, in some instances, explicit approval of Union officers. Naturally there were many soldiers of all ranks who sincerely deplored such behavior.

When the armies had passed, some Treasury agents and occupying troops continued to plunder. The former sometimes pretended they were executing various Federal laws. Others even stole cotton by collecting the tax-in-kind once levied by the Confederacy. Secretary of the Treasury Hugh McCulloch said ruefully, "I am sure I sent some honest cotton agents South; but it seems very doubtful whether any of them remained honest very long." Besides being swindled, Southerners had to pay a tax of 25 percent on cotton that had been produced by slave labor, plus a tax ranging up to three cents per pound on all cotton. The latter drained $68 million from the impoverished South before it was repealed in 1868. Together with other levies, the cotton tax took more money from the South during the years 1865-1868 than the section received from all Federal money spent on Reconstruction and from public and private relief. Nor did the war put an end to thievery of the ordinary sort. Whitelaw Reid, militant Ohio Republican, later to be editor of the New York *Tribune,* observed in a tour of North Carolina that "the practice of regarding everything left in the country as the legitimate prize to the first officer who discovers it, has led, in some instances, to performances little creditable to the national uniform."

Statistics reflect the desperate conditions that prevailed in the postwar South. They are, however, at best abstractions. If each of two farmers has a horse to plow with, and one loses his, to say that the supply of horses is reduced by 50 percent scarcely conveys the plight of the farmer who cannot work the land.

The loss of Southern wealth was enormous. Exclusive of property in slaves, assessed property valuation in the South at the end of the war was 59 percent of the figure for 1860; if investments in slaves are included, the percentage drops to 37. By 1870 it had risen to only 63 percent of 1860 (exclusive of slaves); during the same period Northern wealth rose by 150 percent. Between 1860 and 1870 land under cultivation sank by 18 percent; South Carolina, little touched by war until Sherman marched through, lost one-third, Louisiana and Virginia almost as much. In 1880 the value of farms in the 11 states of the old Confederacy was still less than 67 percent of the value in 1860. The value of farm implements dropped 45 percent (67 percent in South Carolina) between 1860 and 1870.

Agricultural production, in this most agricultural of sections, naturally suffered. Cotton production in the eleven ex-Confederate states during the first five postwar years averaged barely half that of 1859; not until 1879 was there a crop larger than that of 1860. Corn dropped to two-thirds during the same five year period, wheat to 50 percent, rice and sugar to 34 percent and 37 percent, respectively, and so forth. Gross farm income remained below the 1859 level for all but 3 of the 15 years, 1866 to 1880, despite a population increase of 47 percent between 1860 and 1880.

Recovery was made insurmountably difficult by the lack of money. When the war ended, Confederate currency and securities were completely worthless. Many banks, corporations, churches, and colleges saw their assets reduced to zero value, while most of the people were literally left without a penny in lawful money. By 1870 bank capital amounted to only $17 million as compared with $61 million in 1860, and currency in circulation dropped from $51 million to $15 million. The South as never before became tributary to Northeastern capitalists, to whom it paid an enormous toll in usurious interest rates.

So great was the devastation and so inadequate the means of recovery that by 1900 the section had barely reached the 1860 level of economic development. Northern investors began to buy much of the South's land and resources through tax sales, foreclosures, and normal purchases. For example, John Hay, formerly Lincoln's private secretary and the future secretary of state, bought a Florida orange grove for back taxes, the owner having fallen in arrears while serving in the Confederate army. As a Northern visitor wrote soon after the war " . . . The whites [are] talking of selling their houses or lands to get bread. The fresh tide of Northern enterprise will soon sweep rudely enough against these broken remnants of the *ancien regime,* and wash them under." Old estates passed into new hands, and the "Slave Power" faded away.

Gigantic though property losses were, they could not compare to the human losses incurred during and immediately after the war. To the 300,000 dead Confederate soldiers must be added perhaps another 200,000 who were incapacitated by wounds and chronic illness, to say nothing of the unknown number of civilians whose health was wrecked by wartime privations. At the end of hostilities there was stark famine in some areas. "It is a common, an every-day sight," wrote one Federal official, "[to see] women and children, most of whom were formerly in good circumstances, begging for bread from door to door. . . . They must have immediate help or perish. . . . Some are without homes of any description." Among blacks who had left the plantations and crowded into towns and cities, the mortality rate was said to be enormous. Deaths from disease among black children were especially numerous; it was, said one observer, like Herod's slaughter of the innocents. By 1868 the danger of starvation was past, although widespread poverty became endemic. Charitable relief from Northern and border state organizations and the issuance of rations by the army and the Freedmen's Bureau were woefully inadequate remedies. Blacks were the principal recipients of assistance, which at best provided only temporary help for a tiny fraction of those in need. The general commanding at Atlanta reported in June 1865 that 800 bushels of corn and

30,000 pounds of meat would be required daily to feed the starving.

This suffering and impoverished people won the sympathy of many Northern soldiers and officials. Others heaped ashes upon their defeated enemies' heads by petty persecutions and humiliations that helped to shape the attitude of Southern whites toward Federal authority. General Henry Halleck ordered that no wedding be allowed in Richmond unless the bride, groom, and minister take the oath of allegiance. He did so, said the general jocularly, to prevent "the propagation of legitimate rebels." Even so stringent a Republican as Whitelaw Reid commented on "the almost painful efforts of the rebels, from generals down to privates, to conduct themselves so as to evince respect for our soldiers." He witnessed

> a brutal scene at the hotel in Savannah, where a drunken sergeant, with a pair of tailor's shears, insisted on cutting the buttons from the uniform of an elegant grayheaded old brigadier, who had just come in from Johnston's army; but he bore himself modestly and handsomely throughout it. His staff was composed of fine-looking, stalwart fellows, evidently intensely mortified at such treatment. They had no other clothes except their rebel uniforms. . . .

Federal military orders forbade the wearing of Confederate uniforms after the surrender, and some officers were arrested for so doing. The catalog of harassments could be lengthened almost indefinitely. Far more resented than any of them, however, was Jefferson Davis's imprisonment, for a time under cruel conditions. Other Confederate leaders were released within a few months, but Davis was incarcerated in Fort Monroe for two years in what, to Southerners, appeared to be a gratuitous display of malice and spite.

THE NORTH LOOKS SOUTH

For more than a generation abolitionists and then Republicans had stigmatized the South as an aggressive, brutal, backward, sinful society in need of punishment, repentance, and regeneration. The war, by magnifying fear and hatred of Southerners, seemed to prove the truth of that description. During the war, propaganda designed to fortify the martial spirit poured from private agencies such as the Union League of America, the Loyal Publication Society, and the Union Clubs. Some of it merely attempted to win support for the policies of the Lincoln administration. This unexceptionable type of political literature, however, was accompanied by a flood of hate propaganda concerning alleged Confederate atrocities. Newspapers and magazines seized avidly on this sensational material. They were encouraged by official agencies such as the War Department and the Joint Committee on the Conduct of the War. The main theme was Southern savagery. One woman recalled in after years how as a little girl she had thrilled with horror when told that the rebels had sent the governor of Massachusetts a box full of live copperheads. The first battle of the war, Bull Run, spawned numerous imaginary horrors, many of which were officially certified as true by the Joint Committee. Rebel soldiers were said to have butchered or tortured Union prisoners of war. The committee's witnesses told how the bodies of Northern soldiers were dissected for the purpose of making drum sticks of shin bones and drinking cups of skulls. *Harper's Weekly* later published sketches of a necklace made of teeth (around the neck of a sinister-looking Southern female), a cake basket made of a rib cage, and a reading desk constructed of an entire skeleton.

Even more inflammatory were the atrocity stories concerning Union prisoners in camps such as the one near Andersonville, Georgia. Pictures of living skeletons ultimately released from these impoundments appeared widely in Northern publications—irrefutable evidence, it was claimed, of rebel brutality. That the death rate of Confederates in Northern prisons equaled the death rate in Southern prisons was either not known or was ignored, as were the repeated requests by the Confederates for a prisoner exchange. The point was not so much to discover what really happened as to document Southern depravity. A congressional committee solemnly concluded that its investigation proved "there was a fixed determination on the part of the rebels to kill the Union soldiers who fell into their hands," and Union authorities ordered that Confederate prisoners be treated more severely in retaliation. Nor did interested parties let the prisoner issue die with the war. It continued to be the subject of many sermons, and in 1869 Congress issued yet another report on the subject. During the six years after

Appomattox, nearly 50 narratives by ex-prisoners appeared in book form. The political potentialities of the issue were obvious, and eventually it came to be a valued part of the Republican arsenal. Few things would stir up old animosities as well as "waving the bloody shirt."

The assassination of Lincoln put the finishing touch on the portrait of rebel brutality; the government immediately accused Jefferson Davis and other high-ranking Confederates of complicity. Obviously there could be no virtue in considering leniency for a defeated enemy who had shown himself to be beyond the pale of civilization. The fact that Lincoln was shot on Good Friday was the text of hundreds of Easter sermons, which were reported extensively in the Northern press. The main theme was not "Forgive them, for they know not what they do." Far from it. Just as the war and its outcome were willed by the Almighty, said the ministers, so had He removed the too-forgiving Lincoln to clear the way for the South's stern punishment, for its root and branch reconstruction.

Forgiveness was indeed in short supply among many Republicans at the war's end. If Lincoln was "a martyr in heaven," Davis was "a felon sunk into the lowest pit of infamy on earth" who deserved immediate execution. Hang Lee too, said others. Senator John Sherman, a major figure in his party, said it was not enough to place the mark of "infamy" on leading Southerners; "the whole rebellion should wear the badge of the penitentiary." On Memorial Day at Arlington Cemetery, armed guards prevented flowers from being placed on Confederate graves. On the Sharpsburg battlefield a controversy over whether Confederate dead deserved decent interment ended when, with hogs rooting the skeletons about, hygienic considerations dictated burial.

A great many Northerners did not hate the South or demand revenge. For a variety of reasons, Democrats favored leniency, as did those Republicans who were interested mainly in doing business in the South. The latter took a practical, unemotional view of Reconstruction. A speedy political restoration of the Union would clear the way for the colonization of the South by Northern capital and Northern settlers. This process would simultaneously make over the South in the Northern mold and bring about that moral regeneration so dear to the hearts of evangelical Republicans.

Emancipated blacks working for wages meant a new market for Northern goods. Southern land and other natural resources would be exploited by Northern capital employing a plentiful supply of cheap Southern labor. Optimists predicted that in the postwar South free labor would produce cotton at half the antebellum cost because paying wages cost less than supporting slaves. As a Boston congressman and manufacturer put it, "It would be difficult to induce us to agree with them, instead of paying their wages, to support them with their families — in sickness or in health — the young and helpless, and the old and decrepit, as well as those who are able bodied."

The conquered Confederacy became a promised land. The New England Loyal Publication Society published a series of articles on "The Resources of the South." Returning soldiers and other travelers told of vast, untapped wealth. Plans were laid in Boston, New York, and other centers of commercial and industrial power for the most profitable integration of the section into the national economy. Although businessmen, politicians, and reformers might differ as to the method of Reconstruction, all agreed that Northern enterprise was as essential to the process as religion or education or political reorganization.

Northern politicians, like Northern businessmen, regarded Reconstruction as an opportunity to get ahead. To Republicans, an essential part of any policy was the creation of a Republican majority. The Democratic South had been traitorous; a loyal South would be Republican. Then the party of patriotism, the Union, and Lincoln would rule the councils of the nation. To give conquered Southerners the vote before they had been Republicanized would be, as Senator Sherman said, to "renew the war." Republicanization could be achieved only if the Slave Power were utterly destroyed and its membership either transformed into true believers or excluded from the political process. This would take time, and most Republicans were suspicious of any plan for speedy readmission of the ex-Confederate states. Whatever doubts they may have had on this matter were resolved by the frank avowal by Northern Democrats that quick restoration was their "prime political necessity." By the spring of 1865 influential Republicans had concluded that Negro suffrage would eventually be required to entrench their party in power, although they approached the subject very cautiously to avoid antagonizing anti-Negro Northern voters.

A HISTORIOGRAPHICAL NOTE

The history of Reconstruction was largely rewritten during the three decades after World War II. As in the case of slavery, the civil rights movement influenced revisionist historians. Until the middle of the twentieth century, the prevailing interpretation held that Lincoln and Johnson were right in favoring a quick and relatively painless restoration of the Southern states, but that their plans fell afoul of a ruthless opposition under the domination of Radical Republicans in Congress who overthrew Johnson's system, tied his hands, and then attempted to remove him from office for political reasons. Congressional Reconstruction, involving military rule and Negro suffrage, was said to have produced state governments dominated by unscrupulous Northern adventurers (carpet-baggers), Southern turncoats (scalawags), and their incompetent black allies, resulting in shameful excesses against which the mass of native whites justifiably revolted. The latter ultimately prevailed, while the Federal government finally saw the error of its ways, withdrew its last troops from the South in 1877, and restored home rule.

The revisionist picture, on the other hand, saw Lincoln as "growing" toward a more equalitarian form of Reconstruction at the time of his death, whereas Johnson, besides being inept, was a racist motivated by partisan political considerations and deserving of impeachment. The distinction between Radicals and rank and file Republicans became blurred, and the idea of a Radical conspiracy aimed at furthering selfish political and economic ambitions by taking control of Reconstruction vanished. Congressional Reconstruction was now seen as inspired largely by an altruistic dedication to equal rights for Negroes. Revisionists praised the so-called carpetbag governments for their progressive programs of welfare and public education, and minimized or palliated their corruption by referring to similar conditions elsewhere in the country and by pointing to dishonesty in the successor "Redeemer" governments.

They regarded congressional Reconstruction as a noble experiment that should be criticized only because it was not radical enough. Southern resistance, far from being an understandable reaction to military rule and fiat government, was a brutal "white terror," inspired by race hatred and dealing in murder and other forms of violence and repression.

Some revisionist scholars appear to be primarily concerned with promulgating the moral, ethical, and ideological rightness of congressional Reconstruction and its more extreme proponents, whom they have infused with the same idealistic motives they see in the civil rights movement of their own times. Since the Republicans of the 1860s and 1870s pushed for at least limited equality for blacks, it is assumed that their motives must have been largely pure and their sins venial, whereas their opponents were mainly controlled by selfish or racist considerations. Some revisionists make much of the Southern birth or conservative politics of the scholars they have undertaken to correct, forgetting their own Northern, or at least non-Southern, birth and liberal proclivities. The parable of the mote and the beam comes to mind.

Even as revisionism reached flood tide, there were signs that its days as the new orthodoxy might be numbered. The preoccupation with race has led to the rediscovery of a Northern racism that was by no means a Democratic monopoly. More significantly, there are still some historians who believe that the Republican party of the Reconstruction years functioned much as parties have always done, with little to indicate either an unusual supply of idealism or a shortage of unsentimental calculation. The day may yet arrive when the prevailing interpretation of Reconstruction will conclude that Republicans acted on the commonplace political axiom that what was good for their party was good for the country.

JOHNSON'S PLAN OF RECONSTRUCTION

The man who succeeded to the presidency on April 15, 1865, had risen like his predecessor from humble and impoverished circumstances. In early manhood Andrew Johnson moved to East Tennessee, where he followed his trade of tailor. He was from the first intensely interested in politics. He became an alderman of his town at the age of 21, served as mayor, in both houses of the legislature, as governor, and in both houses of Congress; he was a senator when Tennessee seceded. Johnson was a strong Jacksonian and an inveterate foe of vested privilege, especially of what he called the "scrub aristocracy" of his own section. On the other hand, Johnson, like Jackson, held orthodox Southern views on slavery, and was himself a slaveowner. He supported the Fugitive Slave Act, protection for slavery in the territories, and in 1860 endorsed the candidacy of John C. Breckinridge. He favored compromise during the winter of 1860-1861, but refused to go with his state when Tennessee seceded. In July 1861 he introduced resolutions, passed by the Senate, denying that the North was engaged in a war of "conquest or subjugation" or desired to interfere with "the rights or established institutions" of the Southern states, and affirming that its only purpose was to put down the disunionist revolt.

In 1862 Lincoln appointed Johnson military governor of Tennessee; there he used arbitrary means and military force to organize a "restored" government. By early 1865 this rump regime had abolished slavery, repudiated secession, and elected a Unionist government. The Republicans' desire to add a Democratic dimension to their wartime label of "National Union" party led them to nominate Johnson as vice-president in 1864. With his accession to the presidency in April 1865, Johnson now had to face the questions that had tested Lincoln's political talents so severely: the nature, means, and purposes of Reconstruction.

Some militant Republicans thought Johnson was in harmony with them, and they rejoiced that he and not Lincoln would be in the White House. Senator Zachariah Chandler observed that God had left Lincoln in office until His purposes could be better served by someone else. Others regarded Lincon's death as a "Godsend" to their cause, and Senator Benjamin Wade, cosponsor of the Wade-Davis bill of the previous year, told the new chief executive, "Johnson, we have faith in you. By the gods, there will be no trouble running the government." Hours after Lincoln's death, Chandler, Wade, and others of like mind met to discuss "the necessity for a new Cabinet and a line of policy less conciliatory than that of Mr.

Lincoln." Johnson, whose inability to control his tongue was his most obvious fault, lent encouragement to these views by some ferocious remarks about making traitors pay for their crimes. However, on the day he took office he told the cabinet he intended to follow Lincoln's policy, especially in regard to an early restoration of home rule in the Southern states and a lenient policy respecting pardon and confiscation. The great difference between Lincoln and Johnson was the goal they sought. Here Lincoln and his party were in agreement: the creation of a Republican majority in the South. Johnson had no such purpose and therefore could not escape a collision with the Republican party. His policy of quick restoration without requiring Negro suffrage threatened to return political control to the South's antebellum leaders, who would then combine with their former Democratic allies in the North to create a majority party at the national level. To make matters worse, the Constitution's three-fifths ratio clause would lapse when slavery ended. All blacks who had been slaves now would be counted in apportioning representation, increasing by 11 the number of representatives and electoral votes from the ex-Confederate states.

Within six weeks of taking office, the President had formulated his Reconstruction policy. On May 29 he granted pardon and amnesty to those who had participated in the rebellion and were now willing to take an oath to uphold the Constitution and all wartime laws and proclamations concerning emancipation. All rights of property except slaves were restored unless proceedings had actually been instituted under the confiscation acts. The amnesty was not universal. In general, those excepted were the civil and military officials of the Confederacy or its states, civil and military prisoners, and participants in the rebellion with taxable property in excess of $20,000. Johnson's proclamation, however, allowed persons in the proscribed classes to apply for special pardons. The President was very busy during the ensuing weeks issuing such pardons, which finally totaled about 13,500.

Simultaneously with his proclamation of pardon and amnesty, Johnson announced the procedure to be used in establishing a restored government for North Carolina, a system subsequently applied to other states. He appointed a provisional governor who was to summon a convention that would amend the state constitution, take any other action needed to "restore said State to its constitutional relations to the Federal government," and establish a republican form of state government. Voters and delegates were required to take the oath prescribed in the President's amnesty proclamation, and also to be qualified as electors according to the state laws in effect immediately before the state seceded; in this respect Johnson imitated Lincoln's proclamation of December 8, 1863. Thereafter the question of suffrage would be decided by the convention or by the legislature — "a power the people of the several States have rightfully exercised from the origin of the Government to the present time." The President, in other words, did not intend to require the enfranchisement of blacks.

Although Johnson left suffrage to the states, he let it be known that he would consider no state ready for readmission until it had ratified the pending Thirteenth Amendment abolishing slavery, declared the secession ordinance null and void, and repudiated the Confederate debt. This process and these conditions applied to all the ex-Confederate states except Virginia (whose existing puppet government Johnson had recognized early in May), Louisiana, Arkansas, and Tennessee. There Lincoln had set up "restored" governments during the war, although they had never been recognized by Congress.

The Southerners who erected governments according to Johnson's plan showed no signs of converting to the Union (Republican) cause. Only reluctantly and sometimes with revealing circumlocutions did they fulfill Johnson's three conditions. Their hesitation in ratifying the Thirteenth Amendment was due largely to the well-founded suspicion that Congress might invoke section two, which gave it the power to enforce the amendment by "appropriate legislation," to give blacks political equality. Unwillingness to repudiate the Confederate debt doubtless originated in the states' wartime guarantee of that obligation. Especially shocking to Republican sensibilities was the election of prominent Confederate leaders as representatives and senators, and the enactment by several states, beginning with Mississippi in November, of the so-called Black Codes to control the freedmen and define their status. The origins, purposes, and nature of these laws were largely misunderstood and widely misrepresented; to many Northerners they seemed to threaten the revival of slavery in another guise.

Johnson knew how the North would react to this recalcitrance. He had urged prompt compliance with his terms, including recognition of the Negro's basic civil rights. He even went so far as to recommend limited Negro suffrage. He had no success on the latter score and only limited success otherwise. These Southern attitudes and actions led Republicans to sound the alarm: the Slave Power had revived and if not stopped would resume its domineering career in national politics. As many had feared from the first, the President's policy would throw away the fruits of victory. Under these circumstances the party could not consider admitting these still rebellious (that is, non-Republican) states to the fellowship of the Union.

Some modern scholars have argued that initially there was little opposition to the President's program among congressional Republicans and that the later estrangement between Congress and the chief executive was caused by the South's unrepentant behavior and Johnson's stubborn refusal to meet Congress halfway. They have emphasized that only a handful opposed Johnson from the outset, whereas the majority praised his policy or at least acquiesced in it. This theory overlooks or underestimates the importance of several factors. First, a reluctance to break with Johnson did not imply approval of his program. Few politicians with hopes for the future could leave completely out of their calculations the patronage at the President's disposal, at least until they believed there were more votes to be gained by defying him than by receiving his favors. It could also be a risky business for the party as a whole to break with its president unless the time and circumstances were propitious. These considerations help to explain the widespread tendency of Republicans to take a wait-and-see attitude toward Johnson's plan, to describe it as "an experiment" that the President was entitled to try. By so doing they committed themselves to nothing; they only awaited developments.

Finally, neither the number nor the influence of the early opponents of Johnsonian Reconstruction should be underestimated. These men wanted to guarantee Republican rule in the South either by Negro suffrage and white disfranchisement or, if that was not yet possible or politically prudent, to reduce the South's representation and electoral strength. Many influential Republicans backed the former solution in the spring and summer of 1865, including three members of Johnson's cabinet. However, the President's steadfast refusal to force Negro suffrage on the South, evidence that rank and file Republicans were reluctant to grant Northern blacks the vote, and the suspicion of some that black voters would be controlled by their former owners, led them to shelve the issue temporarily in the interests of party unity.

Meanwhile the Johnson state governments would not be recognized, and of course their representatives and senators would not be seated. The Republican caucus decided that question on December 2, 1865, two days before Congress was to meet, by resolving to create immediately a Joint Committee on Reconstruction to deal with the admission of congressmen from the ex-Confederate states. Thaddeus Stevens of Pennsylvania, who, the previous spring, had called the President's policy "insane," was selected to present the resolution in the House. It was further arranged that the clerk of the House would not call the names of representatives-elect from the Johnson states. The President hoped that this strategy would break down when Horace Maynard of Tennessee presented himself, because Maynard had been accepted as a lawfully elected representative from his state in December 1861 and had served thereafter in the 37th Congress. Apparently Johnson had not yet realized that neither consistency nor, in the long run, the Constitution would be suffered to stand in the way of Republican ambitions.

THE OPENING SKIRMISH

When Congress convened on December 4, all went according to plan. The names of the Southerners were exised from the roll in the House, and the protests of Maynard were brushed aside. In the Senate credentials of Southern members were tabled. Ignoring a Democratic protest that action should be deferred until after the reading of the President's annual message, which would explain his Reconstruction policy, the huge Republican majority in the House passed Stevens' motion for a Reconstruction committee. The Senate later agreed to a somewhat modified version, and the committee began what was to be a famous career. This was the real parting of the ways for Johnson and the Republicans, not, as often claimed, the President's subsequent vetoes of the Freedmen's Bureau and Civil Rights bills.

The President's first annual message was read to Congress on December 5. It had been written by George Bancroft, noted historian and longtime Jacksonian Democrat. The organization was skillful, the style graceful, the tone conciliatory and statesmanlike; for these qualities it was widely praised. But however pleasing its manner, its substance offered little comfort to Republican leaders. The theory of the Union it expounded was simple enough. Secession was a nullity. "The States attempting to secede placed themselves in a condition where their vitality was impaired, but not extinguished; their functions suspended but not destroyed." Military rule denied the states' indestructibility and undermined the cause of reunion. Therefore Johnson had gradually "sought to restore the rightful energy of the General Government and the States" by establishing provisional governments, resuming trade, the postal service, and reopening Federal courts so far as possible. The President's pardoning power had been used as a major instrument in reviving the states. The provisional governments had been invited to ratify the Thirteenth Amendment, which would eliminate "the element which has so long perplexed and divided the country" and would make "us once more a united people." When that was done, "it would remain for the States" to resume their places in Congress and "thereby complete the work of restoration. Here it is [for Congress] to judge . . . of the elections, returns, and qualifications of [its] own members." Turning to the 4 million ex-slaves, he said that "good faith requires the security of the freedmen in their liberty and their property, their right to labor, and their right to claim the just return of their labor." Furthermore, Americans must avoid "hasty assumptions" that the two races could not "live side by side in a state of mutual benefit and good will." Johnson opposed "forced removal and colonization."

The President maintained that he, like Lincoln, did not have the power to enfranchise Southern blacks; if he had the power, he would have to give the vote to blacks everywhere, not only in the

South. Nor had Congress even in the heat of civil war presumed to exercise that power. It was thus

> not competent for the General Government to extend the elective franchise in the several States. . . . In my judgment the freedmen, if they show patience and manly virtues, will sooner obtain a participation in the elective franchise through the States than through the General Government, even if it had the power to intervene.

As for white Southerners, Johnson said that treason had been committed and those charged with it should be brought to trial. He seems to have had in mind trying Jefferson Davis, and certainly did not contemplate a large-scale prosecution of ex-Confederates. On the contrary, he declared that "every patriot must wish for a general amnesty at the earliest epoch consistent with public safety."

Nothing could have been clearer: with the final approval of the Thirteenth Amendment ending slavery, the process of Reconstruction was, from Johnson's point of view, essentially complete, and the Southern states were entitled to be represented in Congress. The responsibility of the Federal government toward the blacks included a guarantee of liberty and the right to work for wages and to own property, but emphatically did not include the conferral of suffrage. The role of Congress in the whole process was limited to its power, conceded by Lincoln as well as Johnson, to refuse to admit those elected from the ex-Confederate states. And if all this was not sufficiently irritating, the economic portion of Johnson's message was a typically Jacksonian statement; it denounced monopolies, came out for hard money, fair taxation (a clear reference to the tax-exempt status of Federal bonds), a retirement of the national debt, frugality in goverment, and a revenue tariff. Even if Reconstruction had not been an issue, many of these views would have grated on the ears of powerful interests within the party.

Johnson's message was popular with the Democrats. Republicans, not wanting to lose the chief executive to the opposition or risk patronage reprisals, tried to put the best face on things and claimed to find much encouragement in it. Some genuinely believed the President would move in their direction. Even so, many reservations were expressed, to say nothing of the vehement of opposition of extremists.

Actions taken by the House during December sufficiently indicate the collective attitude of the party. On December 14 the

Republican majority resolved that all papers concerning Southern representation be referred without debate to the Joint Committee on Reconstruction. Four days later it tabled a resolution denying that either Congress or the President could confer the suffrage on anyone. On the same day it resolved that the "ironclad oath," which barred all ex-Confederates from Federal office, should continue in force. And on December 21 Republicans shunted aside a Democratic resolution complimenting the President's message and his program of Reconstruction.

On December 18 Thaddeus Stevens declared open war on Johnson's program. This formidable old man, whose last wish on earth was to grind under his heel the hated Slave Power and its apologists, feared not to say what others often thought but rarely said in public. He had taken the lead in committing the Republican caucus to its resistance to Johnson's policies, and for the next two years he would exert a significant influence on the general direction taken by his party.

> The chief weapons of his rule were the remorselessness with which he pushed the party on from the premises agreed upon to the full logical conclusion, and the vigour with which he laid on the lash. . . . His eye shot over the blackened Southern land. He saw the carnage, the desolation, the starvation and the shame; and, like a battered old war-horse, he flung up his frontlet, snuffed the tainted breeze, and snorted Ha! Ha!

To Stevens the Southern states were merely so many conquered provinces. As states they were dead, and they could only be revived by joint action of the President and Congress, but not by the President alone. He recommended that the defunct states be made territories. Before they were fit to be readmitted, they would have to "learn the principles of freedom, and eat the fruits of foul rebellion." The inhabitants of these territories would "necessarily mingle with those to whom Congress shall extend the right of suffrage," an obvious reference to enfranchising the black. The previous August, Stevens had recommended evading the matter of Negro suffrage for the time being and concentrating on reducing the Southern states to territories; then Negro enfranchisement would be easier to accomplish.

In the meantime, Stevens continued, these territories should never be recognized as states until the Constitution had been amended "so as to secure perpetual ascendancy to the party of the Union." Otherwise the South, strengthened in Congress and in presidential elections by the demise of the three-fifths ratio clause, would combine with

> the Democrats that will in the best times be elected from the North. . . . They will at the very first election take possession of the White House, and the halls of Congress. I need not depict the ruin that would follow. Assumption of the rebel debt, or repudiation of the Federal debt, would be sure to follow. The oppression of the freedmen . . . and the re-establishment of slavery would be the inevitable result.

To prevent the creation of a Democratic majority, Stevens proposed a constitutional amendment that would base a state's representation on the actual number of qualified voters. If Southerners disfranchised the blacks, their representatives and electoral votes would be reduced accordingly and so "render them powerless for evil." If they allowed the blacks to vote, the latter would combine with Southern Unionists "to divide the representation, and thus continue the Republican ascendancy."

Stevens also proposed amendments that would prohibit discrimination on account of race or color by either state or Federal laws, prohibit payment of the Confederate debt, and permit export tariffs, the purpose being to tax Southern cotton. These four amendments, together with the reduction of the Southern states to territories, Negro suffrage, and confiscation of the plantations for distribution to the freedmen, comprised Stevens' program of Reconstruction. They have been described here because recent scholarship, in attempting to establish the essential conservatism and reasonableness of congressional Republicans, has pictured Stevens as being far more radical than the party generally. Yet here in December 1865, less than seven months after the war ended, Stevens presented a blueprint that was very close to the party's consensus on Reconstruction. Virtually everything he proposed had been extensively discussed by party leaders during the months before Congress met. His colleagues had introduced amendments dealing with Southern representation and equal rights for blacks, both regarded as necessary to prevent the Slave Power's revival. Constitutional repudiation of the Confederate debt had also been proposed. All three measures would, in a more or less modified form, become part of the Fourteenth Amendment, which Stevens and the other members on the Reconstruction committee would hammer out during the spring of 1866. The party did not adopt Stevens' export tax amendment, which was a cleverly contrived scheme to make the South pay the cost of the war and the continuing expenses of the Federal government while clearing the way for a prohibitive import tariff. But it did continue the tax on Southern cotton through fiscal 1868, dropping it only after intensive lobbying by New England business interests and Southern Republicans.

As for the rest of Stevens' program, within 15 months Congress would begin the enactment of Reconstruction laws that would overthrow the Johnson governments, reduce the ex-Confederate states to something less than territorial status, and, among other things, enfranchise their Negroes. The Republicans did not accept Stevens' demand to break up the plantations into small farms for distribution to the freedmen. No doubt some were partly influenced by a conservative respect for property rights or by the hope of confiscating Southern land to help pay the Federal debt and lighten Northern taxes. Investors who coveted valuable Southern lands were perhaps the most important source of opposition. Not only would parcelling out farms to blacks reduce the amount of land on the market but, as one prominent Massachusetts investor complained, widespread black ownership would drive down property values generally. For these reasons Stevens' most radical proposal did not appeal to his party.

Thaddeus Stevens' plan of Reconstruction, when taken in the context of what had gone before and what was yet to come, shows that he and his party had the same overriding purpose: the establishment of a national Republican majority. The means to be used were a matter of tactics only. The benefits they bestowed on the Negro, however desirable otherwise, were incidental, as the party's abandonment of the Negro a few years later so clearly demonstrated.
An open break between Andrew Johnson and the Republicans could have been avoided only if Johnson had agreed that the purpose of Reconstruction was Republican hegemony. This he was unwilling to do, and therefore no accommodation was possible. Johnson and his restored states stood squarely between the Republican party and the fruits of victory.

Chapter XI

The Republican Party Versus Andrew Johnson

THE PRESIDENT WITHOUT A PARTY

Most Republican politicians wished to avoid open war with the President. To drive Johnson into the arms of the Democrats prematurely would be risky and would be better avoided altogether if possible. On his part, Johnson knew that the success of his program would be gravely jeopardized by a break with the party. In the beginning he tried to reassure congressional Republicans by giving them a sympathetic hearing and by assuming a conciliatory manner, yet without altering the stand he had taken on Reconstruction in his annual message. This uneasy entente could last only as long as Congress took no action. The truce was necessarily brief because the party was determined to put its impress on Reconstruction before the public came to believe that the Southern governments recognized by Johnson during the fall and winter met all requirements for restoration. The main features of the early congressional policy were a new Freedman's Bureau, the Civil Rights Act, and the Fourteenth Amendment.

As Northern armies pushed deeper into the Confederacy, large numbers of blacks came within Union lines. They were regarded mainly as a resource to be used in winning the war. Those not put in the army were under the control of officials who "functioned as quartermasters of black labor. They consolidated, categorized, and disposed freedmen as if they were mules or wagons." In March

1864 the House of Representatives passed a bill to deal with the management of the freedmen. Sent to the upper house, it was drastically changed by Senator Sumner, who wished to put the proposed Freedmen's Bureau under the Treasury Department instead of the War Department and to place greater emphasis on leasing Southern lands to Northern whites. Bureau officials would act as "advisory guardians" for blacks and as organizers of their labor. The bill went through various changes before finally winning passage in March 1865; in its final form it created a Freedmen's Bureau in the War Department, to continue for one year after the end of the rebellion. The new agency was to provide "immediate and temporary" food, shelter, and clothing for "destitute and suffering refugees and freedmen and their families." The Commissioner of Freedmen was authorized to rent them abandoned plantations or land acquired by the United States through confiscation, with an option to buy at the end of three years.

An estimated 238,000 blacks within the Confederate states were under the control of Federal officials by the time the above law was passed, and another 1 million were within Union lines. The collapse of the Confederacy tripled that number, not counting the border state blacks who would be freed when the Thirteenth Amendment became part of the Constitution in December 1865. If the Federal government was to assume responsibility for these people, there would have to be a new law giving the bureau expanded functions. Powerful political and economic influences, together with humanitarian considerations, combined to produce the necessary legislation.

The new Freedmen's Bureau and the Civil Rights Act helped to calm Republicans' fears that the Slave Power might revive by substituting peonage for slavery. But the Freedmen's Bureau also had an economic significance of the utmost interest to important segments of the business community. Many Northern business leaders agreed that the chief aim of any Southern policy should be to restore order and clear the way for the realization of maximum profits from the South. Some of them believed that private enterprise with a minimum of government interference was the best approach. Others demanded Federal action. The latter, with allies such as Thaddeus Stevens, wanted a continuation of the cotton tax and the expansion of the Freedmen's Bureau, the overall purpose being the enthronement of protectionism and the economic colonization of the South by Northern settlers and capital. The immediate object was the resumption of cotton production. There was some difference of opinion as to whether the Bureau should be a quasi-business operation or should merely protect the rights of black labor, but all agreed that the *sine qua non* was cotton. Finances as well as the prosperity of commerce and manufacturing were involved. Resumption of cotton exports on the vast scale of antebellum years would promote a favorable balance of trade; that in turn would hasten the resumption of specie payments, on which the value of Federal securities on the European market was said to depend. Federal bondholders were able to make Congress sensitive to their needs in this as in other matters.

By the first week in February 1866 Congress had passed and sent to the President a bill to continue the Freedmen's Bureau with enlarged duties and authority. It was indeed an extraordinary measure on which Johnson cast his eye. The existing law limited the bureau's jurisdiction to freedmen in the rebellious states or in areas of military operations. This new bill applied to freedmen everywhere, including the border states, and presumably the bureau would exert in peacetime the same pro-Republican influence that provost marshals had exercised in time of war. Furthermore, it would "continue in force until otherwise provided by law." The bill empowered the President to divide the South into districts of one or more states, and into subdistricts not exceeding the number of counties in the district. The commissioners, agents, and clerks presiding over this bureaucracy could number in the thousands, and none could be hired unless he could take the "ironclad oath," making a succulent patronage pie indeed. The terms "destitute and suffering" contained in the first Freedmen's Bureau Act were defined to exclude those who could "by proper industry and exertion avoid such destitution." No loafing while cotton was in the boll! The bill authorized the President to distribute in 40-acre plots up to 3 million acres of public lands in Florida, Mississippi, Alabama, Louisiana, and Arkansas to "loyal refugees and freedmen" at a rental to be agreed on, with an option to buy; land in non-Southern states and territories was not made available. The bureau's commissioner could buy land for asylums and schools provided Congress appropriated money for the purpose.

All employees of the bureau were placed under military jurisdiction and protection. More than that, it became the duty of the President, through the commissioner, to extend that same jurisdiction and protection to all cases in which blacks were deprived of any civil rights enjoyed by whites. It was made "the duty of the officers and agents of this bureau to hear and determine all offenses" of that nature, the maximum penalties being $1000 fine and one year in prison. Cases were to be tried according to rules promulgated by Secretary Stanton. As Johnson observed, "from these arbitrary tribunals there lies no appeal, no writ of error to any of the courts in which the Constitution of the United States vests exclusively the judicial power of the country."

Johnson vetoed the bill in a cogent and temperate message. From his point of view, it was completely at war with the Constitution and ill-adapted to accomplish its stated purposes. His point-by-point criticisms annoyed Republicans, but far more did his objection to the enactment of such legislation when the Southern states were unrepresented in Congress. The Constitution decreed that each state was entitled to two senators and at least one representative, and although he had no intention of challenging the congressional right to judge "of the election, returns, and qualifications of its own members," he did not believe that clause could be "construed as including the right to shut out" states from representation. Most of the Southern states were now, in his opinion, entitled to the full restoration of their constitutional rights.

The Senate vote (30 to 18) was not sufficient to override, but five months later a modified version of the bill would pass over a second veto. In response to Johnson's defiance, Congress adopted a joint resolution stating that no senator or representative from the ex-Confederate states would be admitted until Congress declared the state involved entitled to representation. Republican politicians were not the only ones angered and disappointed by the veto. The Boston *Advertiser* remarked pointedly, "We cannot afford to have several millions of men idle. We cannot afford to have the whole industrial interest of the South thrown into confusion." What Horace Greeley most regretted about the veto was "its tendency to unsettle the industry of the South." There were comments of a similar kind from other newspapers and party leaders, although the veto was commended by those capitalists, primarily in the Democratic stronghold of New York City, who favored a *laissez-faire* approach to Reconstruction. The latter wished to resume their traditional commercial ties with the South as quickly as possible; they suspected that the policy represented by the Freedmen's Bureau was designed to allow rival groups of capitalists from Boston and elsewhere to supplant their once dominant influence in the Southern economy.

On Washington's birthday Johnson spoke extemporaneously to a large crowd which had come to serenade him, as was the custom. He defended his policies and responded angrily to the insults and vituperation directed at him by the likes of Stevens, Sumner, and Wendell Phillips, among others. Johnson's irritation was understandable. These men had accused him of making proposals that "centuries ago, had they been made to Parliament by a British king . . . would have cost him his head," had referred to him as "an alien enemy," a traitor worse than Benedict Arnold, an "obstacle to be removed" (Phillips), and a whitewasher of "enormities" (Sumner). Although the President's speech was applauded by many Democrats and some conservative Republicans, it was undignified in manner, extravagant and self-serving in substance, and provided ammunition for his enemies.

The veto of the Freedmen's bill had alienated many Republicans, and the veto of a companion measure, the Civil Rights bill, antagonized even more. In brief, this bill declared blacks to be citizens of the United States with the right

> in every State and Territory . . . to make and enforce contracts, to sue, be parties, and give evidence, to inherit, purchase, lease, sell, hold, and convey real and personal property, and to full and equal benefit of all laws and proceedings for the security of person and property, as is enjoyed by white citizens, and shall be subject to like punishment, pains, and penalties, and to none other, any law statute, ordinance, regulation, or custom, to the contrary notwithstanding.

The enforcement apparatus was even more remarkable than that established by the Freedmen's Bureau bill. Federal courts were given jurisdiction over all cases involving persons "who are denied or cannot enforce" in state or local courts the rights guaranteed by the act, and over cases involving anyone being sued or prosecuted for "any arrest or imprisonment, trespasses, or wrongs done or committed by virtue or under color of authority" of the act or the Freedmen's Bureau Act. The power to arrest offenders against the act was given to Federal district attorneys, marshals, deputy marshals, officers and agents of the Freedmen's Bureau, and commissioners appointed by Federal courts, the number of such commissioners to be increased "from time to time." The commissioners were "authorized and empowered, within their counties respectively," to appoint "one or more suitable persons . . . to execute warrants," with authority to "call to their aid the bystanders or the *posse comitatus*," as well as the army, navy, and state militia. The commissioners were to be paid $10 for each case handled, and their agents $5 and "other fees" for each arrest made. Anyone attempting to obstruct these procedures was subject to fine and imprisonment. The bill's sponsor, Senator Lyman Trumbull, patterned the latter provisions on the Fugitive Slave Act of 1850. Fine and imprisonment were also the punishment for "any person" who deprived anyone of rights guaranteed by the law or, because of race, inflicted different punishment than that levied against whites. There was no time limit on the law, no provision that it would lapse when certain conditions were fulfilled. Indeed, it still survives in part in the U. S. Code. Trumbull cited the enforcement clause of the Thirteenth Amendment as giving Congress authority to pass the bill, the purpose of which, he said, was to make the freedman really free.

Like the Freedmen's Bureau bill, the Civil Rights bill was to be a safeguard against the revival of the Slave Power, whatever humanitarian ideals may have been involved. It was also intended to protect and reassure Northern investors and other businessmen who were afraid that they would be discriminated against or shut out from commercial opportunities by the hostility of Southern whites. And the bill was also to soothe those Northerners who feared an influx of Southern blacks. As one Massachusetts radical put it, "a just policy on our part leaves the Black man in the South where he will soon become prosperous and happy. . . . Justice and expediency are united in indissoluble bonds, and the men of the North cannot be unjust to the former slaves without themselves suffering the bitter penalty of transgression" (i.e., black immigration).

Johnson again used his veto. His main objections to the bill may be summarized as follows: (1) legislation of such importance should not be enacted when 11 out of 36 states were not represented in Congress; (2) the bill would invade the reserved rights of the states, which hitherto had exercised exclusive jurisdiction over race relations, and it implied a claim to plenary congressional jurisdiction, including the question of Negro suffrage; (3) the bill would make members of state legislatures and state judges who legislated or decided contrary to the proposed act liable to fine and imprisonment, a remedy Johnson believed to be unconstitutional, as he did the transfer of such cases from state to Federal courts; (4) the bill would create a "numerous . . . sort of police" with the power of arrest and with the army at their disposal, "agents irresponsible to the Government and to the people . . . in whose hands such authority might be made a terrible engine of wrong, oppression, and fraud"; (5) the system of fees for arrests and hearings "might convert any law, however beneficient, into an instrument of persecution and fraud"; (6) the terms of the bill appeared to anticipate a permanent military occupation of the South; and (7) members of the large bureaucracy thus created would have "a vested interest in fomenting discord between the two races, for as the breach widens their employment will continue." The President concluded his veto message by offering to cooperate with Congress "in any measure that may be necessary for the protection of the civil rights of the freedmen . . . by judicial process, under equal and impartial laws, in conformity with the Federal Constitution."

The Freedmen's Bureau and Civil Rights bills proposed to establish for an indefinite time an extensive, extra-constitutional system of police and judicature with the opportunity, as Johnson correctly pointed out, for enormous abuses of power. These measures have been summarized at length because some scholars have depicted them as eminently moderate and reasonable, and the President's vetoes as a "declaration of war," evidence of incorrigible obstinacy and pathetic obtuseness.

The bills speak for themselves. As for Johnson, his position was perhaps not as petrified as is sometimes represented. The previous July he had approved a Freedmen's Bureau circular giving that agency's officials jurisdiction over non-Federal cases in which "the Negro's right to justice before the law" was denied by not "allowing him to give testimony." The next month he told Governor Sharkey that if Mississippi extended the franchise to literate blacks and those who paid taxes on real estate worth at least $250, it would "completely disarm the adversary and set an example the other states will follow." In October, in an interview with abolitionist George L. Stearns, the President said that if he were once again in Tennessee, he "would try to introduce negro suffrage gradually," first to army veterans, then to the literate and to taxpayers, a position virtually identical to that taken by Lincoln in April 1865. Johnson told Stearns that he opposed immediate suffrage for all Negro men. There was hostility between them and the mass of whites who had never owned slaves that would "breed a war of races. . . . The negro will vote with the late master, whom he does not hate, rather than with the non-slaveholding white, whom he does hate." Furthermore, he suggested that within the next few years the constitutional basis for apportionment might be changed "from population to qualified voters, North as well as South, and, in due course of time, the States, *without regard to color,* might extend the franchise to all who possessed certain mental, moral, or other such qualifications as might be determined by an enlightened public judgment." His annual message to Congress contained the same sentiment in more general terms. In November, when the head of the Freedmen's Bureau suspended a large part of Mississippi's Black Code, and in December, when General Daniel Sickles suspended all of South Carolina's code, Johnson allowed both actions to stand.

In light of these facts, Johnson's offer to accept some alternative to the Civil Rights bill should not be dismissed out of hand. His veto may not have sprung from an unwillingness to do anything of importance to protect the freedmen so much as from a conviction that Congress had fallen under the influence of a ruthless faction that was determined to create a vast political machine subject to its manipulation. This belief, the growing personal attacks on him, and the general course of events made Johnson ever more rigid in defending his policies.

Republican reaction to the Civil Rights bill veto was vehement, to say the least. For instance Oliver P. Morton, the staunch wartime governor of Indiana soon to be elected to the Senate, a man who had warmly supported the President in 1865, warned Johnson that he would be breaking with the party and with Morton personally if he did not sign the bill. After the veto, Morton traced Johnson's policy to the Democratic party's influence, and then delivered himself of an often quoted opinion on that organization.

> Every unregenerate rebel lately in arms against his government calls himself a Democrat. Every bounty jumper, every deserter, every sneak who ran away from the draft calls himself a Democrat. Every "Son of Liberty" who conspired to murder, burn, rob arsenals and release rebel prisoners calls himself a Democrat. . . . Every man who labored for the rebellion in the field, who murdered Union prisoners by cruelty and starvation, who conspired to bring about a civil war in the loyal states . . . every wolf in sheep's clothing who shoots down negroes in the streets . . . and murders women and children by the light of their own flaming dwellings, calls himself a Democrat. In short, the Democratic party may be described as a common sewer and loathsome receptacle, into which is emptied every element of treason North and South, every element of inhumanity and barbarism which has dishonored the age.

This is a good example of "bloody shirt" oratory. It was a tested strategy — identify the Democrats with the treasonous Slave Power. And now, in the spring of 1866, the Republicans began to tar Johnson with the same brush, to denounce him as the leader of this band of inhuman cut-throats and filthy traitors.

The Senate had got word of the impending veto of the Civil Rights bill several days in advance; on the day the President's message was delivered, it unseated John P. Stockton, a New Jersey Democrat, and thus secured the two-thirds majority necessary to override. In the House there was no need for any such summary execution; on April 9, 122 Republicans crushed 34 Democrats and 7 lonely Republicans, and the bill became law.

FRAMING THE FOURTEENTH AMENDMENT

Not long after Congress created the Joint Committee on Reconstruction, an Ohio newspaperman composed a burlesque of the kind of report he expected the committee to write. In this version the committee, with a great show of impartiality, collected evidence as to conditions in the rebellious districts and, to make a long story short, concluded that rampant disloyalty in the Southern states proved they were not ready to be welcomed back into the Union.

The committee began its labors on January 6. Its first act was to appoint a subcommittee to call on President Johnson and urge him "to defer all further executive action in regard to reconstruction until this Committee shall have taken action on that subject." Johnson informed the deputation that "it was not his intention to do more than had been done for the present." This was the only official contact between the committee and the chief executive. Johnson had stolen a march on Congress during the long recess between March and December. Republican leaders were anxious that no more be done until they had developed their own plans and cultivated support for them. Meanwhile, they would not restore the Southern states to representation.

The great majority of witnesses interviewed by the committee gave testimony supporting continued military rule. This is scarcely surprising. More than half were Northerners, including army officers, Freedmen's Bureau agents, travelers, and so forth, and among the Southerners were Unionists and black "loyalists." The witnesses were often asked leading questions designed to elicit evidence, however tortured, of rebel intransigence. The investigation continued for about three months and yielded quantities of the kind of testimony that fulfilled the Ohio journalist's prediction.

Concurrently the committee began to devise several alterations to the Constitution that would eventually be reported to Congress as the Fourteenth Amendment. As pointed out earlier, after testing public sentiment in the North, the party shied away from open advocacy of Negro suffrage and fell back on the idea of reducing the basis of representation as a penalty for not enfranchising blacks, who were sure to vote Republican if they could. This apparently simple stratagem presented unexpected problems. Many Republicans, especially those from the trans-Appalachian states, favored using voters for a basis, but this posed a special problem for New England. The proportion of males in that section's population was significantly smaller than in Western states. Because women were not enfranchised, a voter basis would shift House seats and electoral votes from the former to the latter. Another problem was the large number of immigrants pouring into Eastern states such as Massachusetts and New York. To assign representatives in proportion to voters would immediately raise up a lobby for the immediate enfranchisement of these newcomers, the great majority of whom traditionally joined the Democratic party. There was little sense in creating black Republicans in the South while raising up white Democrats in the North. New England finally prevailed. Representation would be based on population, not voters; a state would be penalized only for disfranchising male citizens over 21 years of age, except for persons who had participated in "rebellion or other crime." Thus there would be no dangerous inducement to enfranchise aliens or women, and Southern states that might fall under Radical rule were free to exclude ex-Confederates from politics, as Missouri and Tennessee already had done. But the Johnson governments would be compelled to choose between diminished representation and allowing the blacks to vote.

Not satisfied with this safeguard, the committee also proposed to prohibit ex-Confederates from voting in Federal elections until July 4, 1870. Congress changed this provision so as to disqualify from state or Federal office anyone who had ever sworn to uphold the Constitution as "a member of Congress, or as [a Federal officer], or as a member of any State legislature, or as an executive or judicial officer of any State," and had then supported the Confederacy. Congress reserved the right to lift such disability by a two-thirds vote. At one stroke the entire office-holding class of the South was eliminated from public life, at least for the time being. Another section embodied the principles of the Civil Rights Act.

The committee's version forbade either the states or the Federal government to pay the Confederate debt or any compensation for emancipated slaves. In its final form, the amendment also put the national debt of the United States beyond the reach of repudiation by some future Democratic majority in Congress. So far the Democrats had done no more than to suggest taxing Federal bonds and to object to their redemption in specie, but the specter of repudiation apparently served the useful purpose of frightening influential bondholders into supporting the amendment. A final section gave Congress the right to enforce the amendment by 'appropriate legislation,' the same conveniently elastic phrase used in the Thirteenth Amendment.

The combination of several subjects into one amendment was a source of strength. It appealed to various fears and hopes. But most important to the Republicans was its usefulness as a political platform on which almost all of them could stand in the 1866 elections. And a platform was urgently needed, lest the President's policies win by default. Political survival was the prime issue; whatever disagreements there were among the faithful, few braved the whip of party discipline. The amendment was approved and sent to the states in mid-June.

Some conservatives, including the small Republican minority who still adhered to Johnson, hoped that the President would accept the amendment. Instead he promptly attacked it. In a special message of June 22, Johnson opposed the adoption of a constitutional amendment while 11 states were excluded from Congress and before the people had been given an opportunity to discuss the matter and register their will in legislative elections. Shortly thereafter, the Seward faction and a few conservatives called for a National Union Convention in an attempt to rally support for the President. This move received substantial Democratic support and made the gulf between Johnson and the Republican party as a whole unbridgeable. The identification of the President with the Democratic party was virtually complete by the end of the summer, and it was emphasized by the resignation of three cabinet officers who were in sympathy with the congressional program. Stanton stayed on at the urging of party leaders as a spy in the enemy's camp.

THE CAMPAIGN OF 1866

The Republican party gave the voters a distinct impression that the proposed amendment embodied their program of Reconstruction. Although some members were willing to readmit a state upon ratification, or at least after the amendment had become part of the Constitution, at no time did the party ever make such a commitment. True, on July 24 the majority in Congress admitted Republican-controlled Tennessee after it had allegedly ratified the amendment, and there were hints that other states would be similarly favored. No doubt the party would have been glad to settle for the amendment if it had done poorly in the fall elections. Since it did well, some important Republicans in and out of Congress saw the amendment as merely a first step toward a plan that would rest on black enfranchisement. When such things were suggested during the canvass, Republicans usually protested that they were not aiming at eventual black suffrage. Thaddeus Stevens assured the voters that the amendment did not 'touch social or political rights."

The emphasis, then, was on the amendment as an eminently moderate and reasonable settlement put forward by the party of the Union as the minimum safeguard that the nation could afford to accept, and as a protection against rank injustice. The equal rights section, said its author, John Bingham of Ohio, would prevent the state of Georgia from ever again imprisoning someone for teaching the Bible. The provision for reduced representation merely kept a voter in South Carolina from having more influence than one in Ohio. The disqualification of leading rebels from holding office was lenient treatment indeed. "They ought to thank God," said Bingham, "they are permitted to live anywhere on this side of the deepest hell." As for the section guaranteeing the debt, it was intended to protect the savings of widows and orphans.

The only alternative to the Republican party, the voters were warned, was a resurrected Slave Power which, with its Northern fellow-travelers, would once again take over the government. It would slaughter blacks and Unionists in the South and tyrannize over the North as of old. Johnson was the tool of these conspirators. Senator Chandler said the rebellion had only changed leaders and tactics. "Then it was under Jeff Davis, now it is under Andrew Johnson. They mean to overthrow the government. These unwashed rebels . . . propose to control your government." Next to Jefferson Davis, said Senator Sumner, the President was the country's "worst enemy." This identification of all Democrats with copperheads and rebels, with Andrew Johnson at their head, was a powerful campaign technique. Johnson himself was called, among other things, a "sot," a "dirty dog," a "beast," a traitor, a Benedict Arnold, a Judas Escariot, a "low white of the South," and an assassin. Widely circulated rumors alleged that the President intended to overthrow Congress by a military *coup d'etat*. Not surprisingly, many voters concluded that the Republic was endangered by Johnson and his policies.

Republicans also held the President responsible for what they described as a carnival of persecution and slaughter in the South, with Negroes and white "loyalists" the victims of vengeful rebels. These lurid tales gained credibility from a bloody riot in Memphis early in May and another one in New Orleans in late July, just after Congress had adjourned. Hitherto urban race riots had been a Northern phenomenon. Between 1832 and 1849, for instance, Philadelphia alone experienced five major anti-Negro disturbances, and, of course, there was the New York riot of 1863, which lasted three days, took over 100 lives, destroyed much property, and subsided only when confronted by Union troops, naval forces, militia, police, and West Point cadets. Although these occurrences were not taken as conclusive evidence of the incurable depravity of Northern society, the Memphis and New Orleans riots and other incidents, real or fabricated, were cited by Republicans as revealing a continuing rebellion and the utter failure of Johnson's system of Reconstruction.

The main protagonists in the Memphis riots were the Irish and the blacks. The disfranchisement of Confederate sympathizers by the state government and the influx of Irish immigrants into the city gave the latter control of most municipal offices. The police force was more than 90 percent Irish; the mayor and most of the aldermen were Irish. Blacks from the surrounding countryside also streamed into the city, which grew in population from 35,000 to 60,000 in 1866 alone. Competition for jobs between Irish and blacks was a continual source of friction and produced numerous fights. Another source of hostility was the garrison of 4000 Negro troops, whose camps became a focus of crime. The soldiers themselves, often when drunk, occasionally robbed shops and individuals, pushed whites off the sidewalk into the mud, and so forth. Some Memphians suspected that Stanton employed Negro garrisons in hopes of provoking violence that he could use to political advantage. As early as the fall of 1865, General Grant had warned that the use of black occupation troops would lead to trouble.

The explosion was touched off by a fight between two hack drivers, one white and one black, with a crowd of recently discharged black soldiers looking on. When police arrived and tried to stop the brawl, these onlookers stoned the officers. A shot was fired, by whom no one knows, and this was the signal for a general attack by police and laboring-class whites, apparently mainly Irish, on the black community. Before troops arrived to restore order, 48 persons had been killed, hundreds wounded, and five raped. There were hundreds of robberies and hundreds of buildings destroyed. The overwhelming majority of the victims were black. The sociology of the riot bore strong resemblance to the New York City disorders of 1863.

The New Orleans riot had a much greater political impact, coming as it did only two months before the 1866 elections. It was also much more political in its origins. The persons holding office under the Unionist government of 1864, which came to power through the patronage of General Banks and the army, were displaced by elections held in 1865. They decided to regain power by reconvening the constitutional convention of 1864. This had been another Banks' concoction, elected by a trivial vote and representing mainly the Union army's political followers in New Orleans. Those who tried to revive it intended to reverse the polarity of Louisiana politics by partial enfranchisement of blacks and disfranchisement of some ex-Confederates. When the convention's former president refused to summon it again, surviving members chose another president who traveled to Washington and received from Republican solons what he considered to be encouragement to proceed. J. Madison Wells, Louisiana's chameleonlike governor, sensed the shift in political coloration in Washington and ordered elections for September 3 to fill vacant seats in the convention. The convention, however, announced its intention of meeting on July 30 at the Mechanics Institute in New Orleans. At a rally on July 27, a proconvention speaker reportedly delivered an inflammatory harangue to a racially mixed audience, defying local authorities and warning them that if they interfered, "the streets will run with blood."

The mayor of the city as well as high state officials opposed this attempt to rewrite the state's fundamental law so as to sweep them out of office. A local judge, himself formerly a convention member, denounced the impending gathering to a grand jury, whereupon he was arrested for treason and violation of the Civil Rights Act. The mayor informed General Absolom Baird, commanding Federal troops in the absence of General Philip Sheridan, that the conventioneers would be arrested for unlawful assemblage. Baird denied the mayor's right to interfere and offered his soldiers to help city police protect the convention from mob violence. State officials then appealed to Johnson, who told them that the military was expected to support, not obstruct, court actions, a reply that was shown to Baird. The latter telegraphed to Stanton that he could not allow interference with the convention without orders from the President. "Please instruct me at once by telegraph." But Stanton neither replied nor showed Baird's message to Johnson, although he was aware of the explosiveness of the situation. Stanton's most recent biographers conclude that he feared Johnson would order Baird to help the local authorities suppress the convention.

On July 30 two dozen delegates met at the Mechanics Institute. While they were waiting for additional members to arrive, a procession of blacks with flag and drum marched to the Institute. According to General Sheridan, about one in 10 carried a gun and the rest carried clubs or sticks. Upon arriving at the convention hall, there was much hurrahing, a shot was fired, and then both marchers and delegates were attacked by city police and numerous special deputies. Crowds of spectators joined in the *mêlée.* No accurate account of casualties is obtainable; although city and state officials swore that 42 policemen and several onlookers were killed or wounded, there seems little doubt that the great majority of victims were blacks, some of whom were killed in cold blood out of sheer race hatred. It was an "absolute massacre," said Sheridan.

While there can be no palliation of the deliberate cruelty toward innocent blacks exhibited by both the Memphis and the New Orleans riots, blame was not entirely on one side. Nor were the riots indicative of any general breakdown of law and order in the South, although they were so represented in the 1866 campaign. Republican journals such as the *New York Tribune,* the *Chicago Tribune,* the *New York Times, Harper's Weekly,* with Thomas Nast's superbly malicious cartoons, disseminated the horrors of Southern brutality throughout the North, as did the hundreds of ministers who preached every Sunday against the Democrats. The latter fought back in kind, trading insults and raising the bogey of black equality, but they were badly outgunned. The prospects for Johnson's policies were further endangered by his being a man without a party. Democratic candidates were not willing to sacrifice themselves by stepping aside in favor of someone better able to win the votes of conservative Republicans. The latter, faced with voting for old enemies who often had been accused of Copperheadism during the war, stayed with their party.

Johnson toured the North during the campaign and undoubtedly hurt his cause. Although the trip's effect has perhaps been overestimated, the President's undignified exchanges with hecklers at various places provided valuable copy for the Republican press. Most of the people who actually saw and heard him apparently were on his side; the number was small, however, compared to those who read the picturesque stories in Republican newspapers.

It has been charged that Johnson's greatest strategic mistake in the 1866 campaign was his failure to emphasize economic issues. During the spring and early summer, Congress had enacted numerous laws granting public land and other favors to various railroads, modifying excise taxes for the benefit of Northern interests, and giving Congress a substantial pay raise. Except for the last, however, which Johnson did denounce during the campaign, these measures may have been more popular than otherwise. One question that would undoubtedly have caused the Republicans trouble was the tariff. A bill had passed the House late in the session after considerable intraparty wrangling, but it died in the Senate, and Johnson was thereby deprived of what would have been his best economic issue.

The elections are usually called a smashing victory for the Republicans, although their share of the votes was less than in 1860 or 1864. Counting only the states that did not join the Confederacy, the Democrats polled 44.9 percent of the vote in 1860, 44.1 percent in 1864, and 45.4 percent in 1866. Compared to 1864, the Democratic percentage increased in 14 states and decreased in 10. The Democrats actually gained seven seats in the House, although Republicans won all the governorships filled that year. Such apparent ambiguity in the results was more statistical than actual; the

Republicans retained their overwhelming congressional majorities. They could now take control of Reconstruction and present the South with a revised peace settlement.

Chapter XII

Congressional Reconstruction: The Second Peace Settlement

REPUBLICANIZING THE SOUTH

The Republican success in the elections of 1866 made a more stringent Reconstruction politically acceptable; (the Johnson state governments rendered it inevitable when, with the sole exception of Tennessee, they unanimously voted down the Fourteenth Amendment.)Their negatives and those of Kentucky and Delaware denied the amendment the necessary three-fourths majority. Immediately most congressional Republicans agreed that strong new measures were required. There ensued much complex parliamentary maneuvering among various factions of the party, with the Democratic minority acting as marplots. Many members were considerably confused about what they were doing, displays of ill temper and disorderly conduct were common, and there were disagreements between the House and the Senate. At length Congress muddled through and passed the First Reconstruction Act over Johnson's veto on March 2, 1867. Three additional acts were necessary to repair the law's practical defects and to cope with Johnson's narrow and unsympathetic interpretation of its provisions.

The preamble to the first act announced that ("no legal State governments or adequate protection for life or property now exists in the rebel states" and so it was "necessary that peace and good order should be enforced . . . until loyalty and republican State

governments" could be "legally established."/The ex-Confederate
states, except Tennessee, were assigned to one of five military
districts, each commanded by a general who was to have a garrison
to "enforce his authority." He was empowered to remove officials
of the existing governments and to substitute military commissions
for civil tribunals in order to "punish . . . all disturbers of the
public peace and criminals."[Johnson observed in his veto message
that "the power thus given to the commanding officer . . . is that
of an absolute monarch. His mere will is to take the place of law."/

The Reconstruction acts decreed the political reorganization of
the Southern states. Constitutional conventions were to be elected
under the auspices of the military authorities. All adult males, white
and black, were declared electors, except "such as may be disfranchised for participation in the rebellion," or who might fall under
the ban of section three of the pending Fourteenth Amendment,
which applied to former state and Federal officeholders who subsequently supported the Confederacy. Voter registration and supervision of elections were placed in the hands of persons who could take
the "ironclad" oath of 1862, that is, could swear that they had
never willingly given aid or comfort to the Confederacy. The regis-
trars were required, if they deemed it necessary, to go behind the
oath taken by the prospective voter, who was to swear that he was
not disfranchised by the Reconstruction acts.

The convention chosen by this constricted electorate then was to
draw up a constitution containing these same franchise provisions.
The completed constitution was to be submitted to the same voters
in a referendum and, if approved, submitted to Congress, which
would examine its provisions and make sure the elections had been
free from fraud and intimidation. If the constitution passed muster,
the legislature of this quasi-state government was next required to
ratify the Fourteenth Amendment. When that amendment had
become part of the Federal Constitution, and if the state had done
nothing in the meantime to antagonize the Republican majority in
Congress, senators and representatives would be allowed to take
their seats in Congress and the military regime would be ter-
minated.

Voter registration in the 10 states came to 703,000 Negroes and

627,000 whites. The total number of whites disfranchised has been estimated by one historian at 150,000, a figure that may be too high. Black registrants were a majority in five states, reflecting the great preponderance of the black population in South Carolina and Mississippi, probably a small majority in Louisiana, and near equality in Alabama and Florida. Where the black population was concentrated in a minority of counties, the ruling Republicans sometimes gerrymandered county lines so as to create black majorities.

All of the constitutions admitted blacks to the franchise, as the Reconstruction acts mandated. Some placed restrictions on ex-Confederates exceeding what the acts called for, and others omitted such restrictions altogether. Congress did not challenge the latters' omission, perhaps because the political outcome of its program seemed so satisfactory: Republicans took control of every state except Virginia. From the seven states restored in 1868, 30 of 49 senators and representatives and four governors were men who had come south after the war — a far cry indeed from what had happened under the Johnson governments. The other three states gained admission in 1870. In the 40th Congress, 20 of 22 senators from the 11 ex-Confederate states were Republicans, as were 44 of 58 representatives.

Congressional Republicans intervened repeatedly in an attempt to keep their Southern allies in power. In 1869 ratification of the Fifteenth Amendment, prohibiting disfranchisement on account of race, was required of those states not yet readmitted. During Grant's first administration, Congress did everything it could by statutory enactment to guarantee that blacks and Republicans not only were permitted to vote, but did vote. Three Enforcement Acts (May 31, 1870, February 28, 1871, and April 20, 1871) used Federal officials and courts in the manner of the Civil Rights Act, which was reaffirmed, in an attempt to protect every aspect of the electoral process from any kind of intimidation or economic pressure. In addition Congress provided up to six years imprisonment at hard labor and $5000 in fines as punishment for depriving anyone of civil rights, including the right to vote, and empowered the President to suspend the writ of habeas corpus and to use Federal troops to put down disorders. Congressional elections were placed under Federal supervision. These laws, in brief, included almost every conceivable method to protect the Republican majorities created by the Reconstruction acts. Their ultimate failure cannot be attributed to a lack of earnestness or ingenuity on the part of their backers.

Congress was determined to brook no interference from the executive branch. Since its program depended largely on military force, Congress reduced the authority of the commander-in-chief: Andrew Johnson. In riders written by Stanton and attached to military appropriation bills, Congress required the "General of the Army" (Grant) to maintain his headquarters in Washington. All orders to the army from the War Department or the President had to go through that officer, who could be removed or assigned other duties only with the Senate's concurrence. Any orders issued contrary to this law were declared to be void, and any officers issuing or obeying orders contrary to the act were made liable to imprisonment for as much as 20 years. This dovetailed with that section of the Third Reconstruction Act giving the General of the Army extensive powers over civil officials who held office under the lame-duck Johnson governments.

The Tenure of Office Act (March 2, 1867) accomplished several purposes. By compelling the President to secure senatorial concurrence before removing officials whose original appointment had required the Senate's approval, Congress apparently entrenched in the cabinet Secretary of War Stanton, their valued ally and agent. Furthermore, the law prevented Johnson from tampering with the Senate-approved bureaucracy that would preside over Reconstruction. Perhaps most important to congressional Republicans, it would lessen Johnson's power to retaliate against them by patronage reprisals, to which the President had at last resorted during the latter half of 1866. And some who supported the law hoped it might trap the President into committing an impeachable act. Congress also attacked Johnson's authority by repealing the section of the Second Confiscation Act that gave him power to proclaim pardon and amnesty for persons who had participated in the rebellion. Similarly, in the Third Reconstruction Act, it directed that no person be enfranchised "by reason of any executive pardon or amnesty."

Having hemmed in the President in this fashion, Congress took precautions against the Supreme Court. The Court's denunciation of trials by military commissions in *Ex parte Milligan* augured ill for a system of Reconstruction built on military authority. *Cummings v. Missouri* and *Ex parte Garland* (January 1867) gave rise to similar misgivings, even though the Court afterward declined the requests of Johnson governments in Mississippi and Georgia to enjoin the executive branch from executing the Reconstruction acts. Then the Court agreed to hear a case arising from the actual operation of the acts, *Ex parte McCardle*. McCardle, who had been tried before a military commission in Mississippi, brought his case before the Supreme Court by invoking the Habeas Corpus Act of 1867. Fearful that the Court would declare such military tribunals unconstitutional and thus sweep away the whole enforcement apparatus of congressional Reconstruction, the Republican majority deprived the Court of its appellate jurisdiction in such cases. Of necessity the Court then declined to hear McCardle's appeal.

JOHNSON FIGHTS A REARGUARD ACTION

The President was directed by the Constitution to see that the laws were faithfully executed. But what of laws that he believed to be patently unconstitutional? Refusal to enforce them would give the President's enemies a golden chance to impeach him. Therefore he chose a middle course: obey the letter of the law, but construe its provisions as narrowly as possible. Here he came into conflict not only with Stanton but also with Grant. Although Grant had supported presidential policies in 1866 and had urged that Stanton be dismissed from the cabinet, he began to move erratically toward an alliance with Stanton during the winter of 1866-1867; just why is not clear. Any effort to detect a consistent rationale behind Grant's zigzag course is bound to fail. The general's mind did not work in a very systematic way.

Johnson concentrated his efforts on preventing military commanders in the South from superseding existing civil governments, and on a circumscribed interpretation of the First Reconstruction Act's disfranchising clause. The attorney general prepared an opinion on these subjects in which most of the cabinet concurred, Stanton excepted. The opinion was then transmitted to the generals through Grant, who directed them to regard it as advisory only and to follow their own interpretation of the Reconstruction acts.

Congress joined Stanton and Grant in thwarting Johnson's strategy. The Third Reconstruction Act overturned the administration's position on disfranchisement and stated that neither military district commanders nor boards of registration nor any of their subordinates were "bound by any opinion of any civil officer of the United States," an injunction clearly directed at the attorney general. It asserted that the 10 Southern states were without "legal State governments," and upheld the military's plenary power to remove and appoint state officials pending the consummation of congressional Reconstruction.

With his power of interpretation so limited, Johnson began to use his power of removal. First on his list was the source of many of his troubles, Edwin M. Stanton. The President's friends had long been mystified at his tolerance of a man who had demonstrated hostility toward his chief's policies on so many occasions and who was ideally situated to obstruct those policies. Stanton's latest disloyal deed, collaborating in the authorship of the Third Reconstruction Act, plus his apparent approval of insubordinate behavior by General Sheridan, commanding in Louisiana and Texas, finally pushed Johnson to the verge of action late in July 1867. The last straw seems to have been his discovery that the military commission which tried the Booth conspirators had recommended clemency for Mrs. Mary Surratt, a recommendation withheld from him, Johnson believed, with Stanton's connivance. Mrs. Surratt, of course, was hanged.

On August 5, immediately after this revelation, Johnson asked Stanton to resign. Five months before, Stanton had ostentatiously denounced the Tenure of Office bill. According to Gideon Welles, Stanton had said then that "any man who would retain his seat in the Cabinet when his advice was not wanted was unfit for the place." These protestations were probably intended to reassure Johnson lest he remove the secretary of war before Congress could pass the bill over a veto. In this Stanton was successful. Now he invoked the act and declined to quit his office. The President then invited Grant to accept appointment as secretary of war *ad interim.* Grant opposed the removal of Stanton as contrary to the Tenure of Office Act, yet he accepted Johnson's offer and denied that there "was alienation, or substantial difference" between himself and the President.

By appointing Grant, Johnson forestalled his enemies; they could scarcely condemn him for removing Stanton without condemning Grant by implication, and the general was the hottest political property then extant. The dismissal, observed Welles, "creates no commotion." The President next transferred Sheridan, favorite of Grant and the more militant Republicans, from command of Louisiana and Texas to the Division of the Missouri. Daniel Sickles, commanding in the Carolinas, was likewise removed because of his lack of sympathy with the commander-in-chief's viewpoints. Johnson then compounded his sins by issuing a proclamation of pardon and amnesty embracing all but a small fraction of former rebels.

IMPEACHMENT

The state elections in 1867 were the first opportunity for the people to speak since congressional Reconstruction had begun. That issue, however, was in competition with others of more immediate interest to many Northerners. Since the end of the war there had been a steady economic decline that was often blamed on the postwar policy of contracting the currency by withdrawing greenbacks from circulation. Western Democrats tried to capitalize on the money question; the best-known proposal was put forward by Ohio's George Pendleton, who claimed that the principal on government bonds should be paid off in greenbacks, not in gold, thus lightening the burden of debt and halting contraction by keeping greenbacks in circulation. Republicans themselves were divided on the currency issue, most opposing inflation, others opposing both inflation and contraction, and some, among whom the high-tariff Radicals were prominent, favoring inflation. There was, in fact, a distinct correlation within the Republican party be-

tween Reconstruction extremists and currency inflation on the one
hand and on the other hand a disposition to regard the party's
Reconstruction policy as substantially complete, to support sound
money, and to repay the debt in specie. Following the election of
Grant in 1868, the schism would be resolved in favor of the latter
position. Another complicating factor was Negro suffrage, which
was put to the voters in three Northern states and rejected in all
of them.

The 1867 elections were a severe warning to the Republicans.
In many states their majorities were reduced or eliminated. The
lesson seemed clear: stop talking about suffrage for Northern
blacks, at least until the presidential campaign of 1868 was over,
and put an end to contraction of the currency. The Republican
setback was generally regarded as damaging to the Radicals, particularly with regard to their desire to impeach Andrew Johnson.
Certain Radicals had been aiming at impeachment since 1866, if
not before. Among them was James M. Ashley, an unscrupulous
spoilsman who tried to line his pockets by bartering Federal offices.
He also was a prime exponent of the conspiracy delusion so popular
with his ilk. He believed that Presidents Harrison and Taylor had
been murdered to allow their vice-presidents to succeed them, that
a similar attempt had been made on Buchanan's life, and that Johnson was behind the assassination of Abraham Lincoln. His allegations, which at first did not implicate Johnson in Lincoln's murder,
set in motion an impeachment investigation early in 1867. Ashley
raked the muck among convicted perjurers and professional liars
who provided the wild rumors and weird tales he used for "evidence."

The House Judiciary Committee scrutinized Johnson's "public
and private acts, . . . his household affairs, his domestic life, his
bank accounts, his social intercourse" and found no crime, not even
an indiscretion. On June 4, 1867, it divided five to four against
impeachment. Disappointed for the moment, the Radicals were
nothing if not persistent. They tried and failed to secure a fall
session of Congress so that impeachment could be pursued. The
outcome of the 1867 elections discouraged but did not daunt them,
and they reintroduced the subject when Congress met early in
December. One member of the Judiciary Committee reversed him-

self and now the vote was five to four in favor of impeachment. But the committee's case was very weak, and the Republican majority, although annoyed by a lecture in Johnson's annual message about the unconstitutionality of the Reconstruction acts, declined to impeach. Then Johnson played into his enemies' hands. First he resumed his purge of uncongenial military commanders in the South. Next he met the matter of Edwin M. Stanton head on.

The Tenure of Office Act stated that cabinet officers should hold office "for and during the term of the President by whom they may have been appointed, and for one month thereafter, subject to removal by and with the advice and consent of the Senate." Should the Senate not be in session, the President could suspend a cabinet member who was "guilty of misconduct in office, or crime" or who had become legally disqualified from holding his office or incapable of performing his duties. In such a case the President could appoint a temporary successor, explaining his action to the Senate within 20 days after it reconvened. On December 12, 1867, Johnson reported to the Senate his reasons for suspending Stanton four months previously. At the same time, he declared his belief that the Tenure of Office Act was unconstitutional, adding that when the bill was presented to the cabinet for discussion in February, it "seemed to be taken for granted" that it did not apply to Lincoln's appointees, of which Stanton was one. Moreover, no one in the cabinet, said Johnson, was more "elaborate or emphatic" than Stanton in denouncing the law with which he now sought to shelter himself.

On January 13, 1868, the Senate refused to concur in Stanton's suspension. Grant, the *ad interim* secretary, had promised Johnson either to resign before the Senate acted and give the President an opportunity to appoint someone else, or, if he did not resign and the Senate nonconcurred, to hold the office and force a court test. Instead he vacated his office, which Stanton promptly occupied. The latter claimed to be again secretary of war, but held no communication of any kind with Johnson nor did he attend cabinet meetings. This contretemps was a wholly logical outcome of the Republican attempt to nullify the President's constitutional prerogatives as commander-in-chief. Johnson had tried to use Grant's great reputation with the people to circumvent that attempt. He failed because the general accepted the office with mental reservations and surrendered it contrary to his understanding with the President.

Johnson was still determined that Stanton should not control the War Department; during the weeks following the Senate's action he cast about for a replacement. It was a time of great excitement and wild rumors. Some of the President's enemies claimed that he should be suspended from office as soon as the House impeached him, without waiting for the verdict of the Senate. Johnson had warned Congress in his annual message that he would resist any attack on a coordinate branch of government, but the rumors of a Republican *coup* persisted. Now that Grant had openly joined the opposition, Johnson tried to create a counterforce by making Sherman secretary of war, and then, when Sherman declined, by establishing a new military department of the Atlantic with Sherman in command, which assignment Sherman likewise declined. At the same time, the President's enemies were declaring publicly that another Pride's Purge was being plotted. Having been compared to Charles I in 1866, Johnson found he had now become Oliver Cromwell.

The President at last discovered someone willing to take the War Department temporarily: the army's elderly and bibulous adjutant general, Lorenzo Thomas. On February 21, a Friday, Johnson dictated an order removing Stanton, hitherto only suspended, and authorizing Thomas to serve as secretary *ad interim,* informing the Senate of his action. Shortly afterward Johnson nominated the highly respected Thomas Ewing as secretary of war. When General Thomas went to Stanton's office and delivered the notice of removal, Stanton asked for time to gather up his personal possessions. As soon as Thomas had gone, Stanton informed his friends in Congress of what had occurred. His partisans flocked to the office and urged him to hang on. Grant intimated that he would allow no soldiers to be used in evicting Stanton, and posted sentries to protect him. The Senate announced that Johnson had acted illegally. With such powerful backing, Stanton barricaded the office, had his meals sent in, and slept on the premises. Furthermore, he swore out a complaint against Thomas for violating the Tenure of Office Act. The old general was arrested before breakfast, having spent the previous evening (and the morning) at a masquerade ball and being rather the worse for wear. After being released on bail, Thomas again demanded that Stanton vacate the War Department, whereupon Stanton ordered him to return to his duties as adjutant general. Matters had evidently reached an impasse when Stanton, with unaccustomed amiability, put his arm around Thomas, playfully mussed his hair, and observed that he looked a little peaked — as indeed he did. Stanton then sent for some whiskey, and the contestants had a few drinks together — a curious interlude in a great constitutional crisis.

On Monday, February 24, the Radicals had their way. The House passed a resolution of impeachment accusing Johnson of having committed high crimes and misdemeanors, 128 Republicans overpowering 47 Democrats. The stakes were enormous, with ramifications far beyond the immediate issue of the Tenure of Office Act or even the future of Reconstruction. Should Johnson be removed, he would be succeeded by the Senate's president *pro tempore,* Benjamin F. Wade of Ohio, a man of coarse and brutal manners who was disliked by many of his Republican colleagues. He was a Radical, and like most of the Radicals he was a soft-money man; as President, Wade might challenge the candidate of the hard-money moderates, Ulysses Grant, for the 1868 nomination. Consequently there were Republicans who regarded impeachment as presenting a choice between rotten apples. On the other hand, Johnson's removal would certainly strengthen the party in the forthcoming presidential election by discrediting the Democrats, with whom the President was associated in the public mind, and by putting executive patronage in Republican hands. Furthermore, a Republican president could hasten the process of congressional Reconstruction and guarantee the admission of Republicanized Southern states in time for the fall elections. Such political considerations carried great weight. Finally, the action of the House partly reflected accumulated exasperation and a feeling that Johnson's direct defiance of Congress in attempting to remove Stanton a second time could not be passed over without making the party appear ridiculous, not to say pusillanimous.

The epithets applied to Johnson during the debate on the impeachment resolution and later were no worse than had been directed at him on other occasions, but some are worth quoting. He was described as "the great criminal of our age and country," as an "ungrateful, despicable, besotted, traitorous" man who had "dragged, as a demagogue, the robes of his high official position in the purlieus and filth of treason," and had "done every act a man can conceive, not only calculated to degrade himself, but to destroy the rights of the American people." He was ranked with the Emperor Nero, who had murdered his brother, wife, and mother. He was guilty of "a degree of perfidy and treachery and turpitude unheard of in the history of the rulers of a free people." He brought on himself "the opprobrium of both hemispheres" and "ineffable disgrace on the American name," and so forth and so on.

After these extreme diatribes, the articles of impeachment were a distinct anticlimax. Eight of them were variations on the same theme: Johnson had violated the Tenure of Office Act or the Conspiracy Act of 1861, or both, by removing Stanton and authorizing Thomas to act *ad interim.* The ninth article accused him of arguing with General William H. Emory that the law requiring the President to issue orders through the general of the army was unconstitutional. The tenth, proposed by Benjamin F. Butler, charged that the President "did . . . make and deliver with a loud voice certain intemperate, inflammatory, and scandalous harangues, and did therein utter loud threats and bitter menaces as well against Congress as the laws of the United States . . . amid the jeers and laughter of the multitude . . . ," all for the purpose of bringing Congress "into disgrace, ridicule, hatred, contempt, and reproach. . . ." The language was reminiscent of the Sedition Act of 1798. The last article, written by Stevens, charged Johnson with saying in public that because the Southern states were excluded from representation, Congress was incompetent to perform its constitutional functions. It also summarized the accusations made in all the preceding articles, spreading a net to catch as many votes as possible.

The Constitution provides that the President may be removed upon conviction by the Senate for having committed "treason, bribery, or other high crimes and misdemeanors." A two-thirds vote is necessary for conviction. The Tenure of Office Act declared that any "removal, appointment, or employment" contrary to its provisions was a high misdemeanor, a section doubtless written with Johnson in mind. The wording and legislative history of that law clearly show that Stanton, being a Lincoln appointee, was not under its protection — hence the insertion of the tenth and eleventh articles, which would appeal to those who regarded impeachment and removal as a political act instead of a finding that the accused had committed an offense indictable at law.

The House appointed a decidedly Radical delegation, including Stevens and Butler, to manage its case in the Senate. John A. Bingham, who had prosecuted Milligan and the Booth conspirators, was chairman. As a group, they were badly outclassed by counsel for the defense. The latter based their case on the unconstitutionality of the Tenure of Office Act, the contention that in any event it did not apply to Stanton, and, less convincingly, the argument that only by violating the act could Johnson test its constitutionality. The prosecution, Butler in particular, maintained that impeachable offenses need not be indictable at law, and that the Senate was not a court and hence was not bound by conventional rules of evidence. On May 16 the Senate voted on article eleven, the omnibus charge calculated to attract the most support. Thirty-five senators voted guilty, 19 not guilty, the majority lacking one vote of the two-thirds needed to convict. Seven Republicans, six of whom represented border or Midwest states, voted not guilty. The Senate then adjourned for 10 days; it reconvened on May 26 and voted on articles two and three with the same result. It then adjourned *sine die,* and the trial was over.

A recent constitutional history of the period portrays the trial as a moral victory, not because Johnson was acquitted, but because it allegedly demonstrated, in "one of the great legal cases of history," that the country's political institutions were strong enough to "give a political officer a full and fair trial in a time of political crisis." This view of the matter is difficult to square with the managers' wild and inflammatory attacks on Johnson, with Butler's frantic waving of the "bloody shirt" during the trial, and with the shameless use (during the 10-day recess) of political and popular pressure to force the seven Republican senators who voted not guilty to reverse themselves. Then there was the unsavory Alta Vela affair. Shortly after the House voted to impeach, four of the seven managers

(Butler, John A. Logan, Stevens, and Bingham) joined in an attempt to persuade Johnson to have the Navy occupy a guano island belonging to Santo Domingo, the beneficiaries being a group of speculators who claimed to own it. Johnson indignantly rejected these overtures, believing them to be a blatant attempt to bribe him with acquittal in exchange for enriching a few corruptionists and their friends. And then there was General Grant, who procured the services of a White House janitor to filch the contents of the President's wastebaskets for perusal by the impeachment managers. Finally, many of the impeachment articles were themselves contemptible, and the rest, given the well-known legislative history of the Tenure of Office Act, were shabby and thin. These things are not the hallmarks of a moral victory.

Stanton admitted defeat when the Senate failed to convict. Johnson had selected his replacement while the trial was in progress. He was General John M. Schofield, whom Johnson chose to reassure conservative Republican senators that the War Department would not be ruled by an anticongressional extremist should he be acquitted. As Schofield regarded the Reconstruction acts with distaste, Johnson in fact made no substantial concession to Congress by choosing him. After the acquittal the Senate grudgingly confirmed Schofield, in the same breath denying that Johnson could remove Stanton without its consent.

Neither during nor after his trial did Johnson do anything to show that he had been cowed by his enemies. In the midst of the proceedings he vetoed the bill that took away the Supreme Court's jurisdiction over the McCardle case. On July 4 he pardoned all former rebels except those under Federal indictment, and on Christmas Day he pardoned the latter. He vetoed bills admitting several Southern states under their new Republicanized governments and denounced the whole system under which they had been created, a denunciation he repeated in his annual message to Congress. He vetoed a bill excluding the electoral votes of the Southern states "which shall not have been reorganized" by the time of the presidential election. And, on his departure from office, March 4, 1869, Johnson issued a public statement accusing the "servants of the people" of betraying their trust, of exposing "to the poisonous breath of party passion the terrible wounds of a four years' war," of legislating for special interests so that "the few might be enriched at the expense of the many." The pugnacious tailor from East Tennessee went out with a bang, not a whimper. Nor did he stay away. Six years later he won election to the Senate, where he shook hands with men who had voted to convict him of high crimes and misdemeanors.

THE ELECTION OF 1868

The Republican convention met in late May during the adjournment of the impeachment trial. Grant's nomination for the presidency was insured, if it ever was in doubt, by Democratic gains in the elections of 1867 and by the general's final break with Johnson early the next year. Grant had been vaguely Democratic in his leanings in bygone years. He had voted for Buchanan in 1856 and favored Douglas in 1860, but in politics as in war he tended to drift from expedient to expedient; to be the Republican candidate in 1868 entailed no crisis of conscience for the general. The vice-presidential nomination went to Schuyler Colfax for services rendered as Speaker of the House.

The platform defended congressional Reconstruction and denounced Johnson. It revealed that the Republicans had learned their lesson about handling the question of Negro suffrage:

> The guaranty by Congress of equal suffrage to all loyal men in the South [i.e., black and white] was demanded by every consideration of public safety, of gratitude, and of justice, and must be maintained; while the question of suffrage [i.e., Negro suffrage] in all the loyal States properly belongs to the people of those States.

On the leading economic issue of the day, the redemption of Federal bonds in Greenbacks, the platform adopted the views of the party's mainstream and denounced any form of "repudiation," leaving room, however, for stretching out repayment of the debt and possible renegotiation of the interest rate. The volatile tariff question was not mentioned, but pensions to soldiers and their widows and orphans were heartily endorsed, as was the Declaration of Independence. Other planks dealt with matters such as the encouragement of immigration and sympathy with oppressed peoples.

The Democrats assembled on July 4. As expected, their platform denounced congressional Reconstruction as unconstitutional, demanded immediate restoration of all states to full equality, and called for universal amnesty. Negro suffrage received oblique mention when the platform said that the regulation of the elective franchise should be left to the states.

If the Democrats' neglect of economic issues contributed to their losses in 1866, the same cannot be said of this election. There were planks advocating a revenue tariff, redemption of government bonds in greenbacks, elimination of tax exemption for Federal obligations, early retirement of the national debt, and the reservation of public lands for actual settlers instead of railroad companies. Unfortunately for the party, the issues of greenback redemption and taxation of Federal bonds were clouded by the nomination of a hard-money Easterner, Horatio Seymour of New York, who did not want to be the nominee and who did little to advance his candidacy. The vice-presidential candidate was the intemperate Frank Blair, Jr., who had deserted the Democrats before the war and now deserted the Republicans, antagonizing voters in both parties. Left waiting at the church was President Johnson. He had not actively sought the nomination, but he was disappointed when his long and bitter struggle did not receive what he saw as its fitting reward. And there was the ever-hopeful Salmon P. Chase. Shunted aside by Grant's enormous popularity, Chase readjusted his political principles to attract Democratic support, only to be mystified again, as he was every four years, at the obtuseness of his fellow citizens.

The campaign was conducted on a low level. Grant was attacked as a drunkard, an inept and callous general, and a bigot who expelled Jewish traders from his lines while he connived at his father's illegal dealings in Southern cotton. Republicans retaliated by charging that hereditary insanity ran in Seymour's family and that Seymour himself once had been put away for several months, none of which was true. They also called Seymour a nullifier and a Copperhead. Republicans energetically waved the "bloody shirt," claimed that "Democracy is Revolution," and managed to obscure economic issues by extolling Grant and appealing to war hatreds.

To make insurance doubly sure, the Republican majority in Congress admitted several Reconstructed states to swell their total of electoral votes, while excluding the votes of the three states still under Johnson governments. They also met in September to assess the campaign and agreed to meet again in October, if necessary, after the elections in certain bellwether states. According to one authority on the election, if the October state elections had gone badly, the Republicans were "prepared to adopt some revolutionary measure to check the rising spirit of 'disloyalty' in the North."

Grant's fame and Democratic ineptness brought a sweeping victory for the Republicans in the electoral college: 214 votes to 80. Seymour carried only eight states, Georgia and Louisiana among them; Grant took the rest, including six of the eight "restored" ex-Confederate states, although he would have won even without the latter. Still, the Democratic party was far from defunct. Seymour polled 46.5 percent of the North's popular vote. He ran behind his party's state tickets, which polled 48.1 percent. Grant's nationwide popular majority was made possible by the enfranchisement of Southern blacks.

TWO CONSTITUTIONAL AMENDMENTS

During the summer of 1868, the Fourteenth Amendment was ratified in a manner that remains a curiosity in constitutional history. The governments set up in the South pursuant to Johnson's executive orders had been compelled to ratify the Thirteenth Amendment. There were then 36 states, including all the ex-Confederate states; if three-fourths of that number were regarded as necessary to validate an amendment, then the ratifications of at least two of the latter states (still not admitted to participation in the Federal government) were essential, and their ratifications were, in fact, counted. These were the same states that Congress declared, in the First Reconstruction Act, did not have legal governments. In 1866 and 1867, it will be recalled, all the Southern governments except that of Tennessee refused to ratify the Fourteenth Amendment. Congress thereupon required them to do so in the First Reconstruction Act. On July 20, 1868, Secretary of State Seward, performing a purely ministerial duty, announced that the amendment had been ratified by 21 Northern states, plus Tennessee and West Virginia, and by six "newly constituted and newly-established bodies avowing themselves to be legislatures of six Southern states." Meanwhile, he continued, two of the 21 Northern states had rescinded their ratifications. But if the original actions of those two states were considered "as remaining in full force and effect," then, said Seward, the amendment had received the necessary three-fourths majority.

On July 21 the Senate approved a concurrent resolution listing 29 states as having ratified. Yet, when the resolution arrived at the House that same day, South Carolina and Alabama had somehow disappeared from the document, and the House approved the resolution with only 27 states listed. Later in the day the clerk of the House notified the Senate that the House had agreed to the Senate's concurrent resolution. In response to Congress' pronouncement that the amendment had been ratified, Seward issued a second proclamation on July 28, listing the 29 states contained in the original Senate resolution, plus Georgia, which did not appear in either resolution. Yet the House clearly did not concede that more than 27 of 37 states had ratified. It has been conjectured that the House deducted from the total number of states those ex-Confederate states that had not completed the congressional requirements for Reconstruction, in which case 27 ratifications would constitute three-fourths. But the status of those states was the same as it had been when their ratifications had been counted in connection with the Thirteenth Amendment. Finally, the amendment would have failed without the forced ratifications of quasi-legislatures operating within military districts occupied by the Federal army. These non-states had to perform an act only a state could perform in order to become states once more. Such was the manner in which the Fourteenth Amendment, in modern times the most important part of the Constitution, became part of the nation's fundamental law. No incident more clearly illustrates the extraordinary means employed to enact the congressional program.

Not until Grant had been safely elected did the Republicans dare to propose a constitutional amendment dealing with Negro suffrage. As usual, their motives were mixed, but their actions were essentially political in nature and intent. The Fifteenth Amendment said that neither the United States nor any state could deny or abridge a citizen's right to vote because of "race, color, or previous condition of servitude," and that Congress could "enforce this article by appropriate legislation," echoing the enforcement clauses of the Thirteenth and Fourteenth Amendments. This proposition was ingeniously constructed so as to elicit minimum hostility from non-Southern whites, to prevent positive disfranchisement of blacks should the opposition regain control of the Federal government or of the Southern states, and to permit flexible implementation. Republicans had to take into account not only anti-Negro (and, in the Far West, anti-Chinese) sentiment within the party, but the desire to apply property and literacy tests to immigrants, such as the Irish, most of whom tended to vote the Democratic ticket, and to police elections in metropolitan strongholds of the Democrats such as New York City. In other words, the amendment would be of maximum use when the Republicans were in power. Then they could apply it selectively in both North and South. Great reliance was placed on the enforcement section. In the case of the Thirteenth Amendment, that wording, among other things, had been cited as authority for the sweeping enactments of congressional Reconstruction, including the enfranchisement of blacks in the former Confederate states. Likewise, the Enforcement Acts of 1870 and 1871, designed to enforce the Fifteenth Amendment, could scarcely have been more sweeping, and from them one may reasonably infer the intentions of the amendment's advocates, even though enforcement proved to be impracticable.

Caution was in order, since adoption was by no means a foregone conclusion. At the time of submission only seven Northern states had voluntarily enfranchised blacks. Republican arguments for ratification ranged from idealistic exhortations to frankly political appeals, usually accompanied by assurances that the amendment said nothing about black officeholding and would not promote social equality. Even with the automatic approval of carpetbag governments in the South, the prospects for the amendment seemed so bleak that Congress, as mentioned, made ratification a condition of admission for Virginia, Mississippi, Georgia, and Texas. By March 1870, 29 states, including three of the four just named, had ratified and the amendment was adopted. It was, however, a hollow victory. By the end of the century Northern indifference, Southern hostility, and a conservative Supreme Court had nullified the Fifteenth Amendment for most Negroes.

Chapter XIII

Reconstruction Abandoned: The Third Peace Settlement

THE SOUTH DURING RECONSTRUCTION

When the constitutional conventions ordained by the Reconstruction Acts were chosen late in 1867 or early in 1868, Republicans controlled them all. There were black delegates in all of them, although they were in a majority only in South Carolina. Some of the blacks were illiterate and incompetent, a fact that hostile white conservatives exaggerated and publicized widely. The conventions were sometimes marked by extravagance, if not fraud, and on occasion their proceedings were grotesquely inappropriate. Yet they produced constitutions that from the standpoint of the late twentieth century were distinctly better than the ones they replaced. Manhood suffrage was the rule, discrimination against the backcountry in legislative apportionment was eliminated, penal codes were revised to make them less Draconian, and the legal status of women was improved. Provision was made for insane asylums, homes for the poor, and other services that, so far as the black population was concerned, had previously been the responsibility of the slave owner. Most importantly, public education was established; except for a brief time in parts of Louisiana, the schools were racially segregated. Most of the constitutions were silent on the subject of social equality between the races, and only a few imposed political disqualifications on ex-Confederates beyond those stipulated by the Fourteenth Amendment. There were clauses intended to facilitate the formation of corporations and encourage industrialization. Seven of the new constitutions were approved by the voters in 1868 and the other three in 1870; state and Federal officers were elected at the same time, and congressional Reconstruction was at last under way.

For a long time Southern folklore pictured the period of carpetbag rule as the darkest chapter in the section's history, even worse, said some, than the war itself. And historians, also for a long time, tended to agree. Southern resentment sprang primarily from the seizure of power by Northerners with the help of their black allies and a minority, sometimes substantial, of native whites. In the estimation of Southern whites, nothing that these Republican organizations could have done would have been sufficient to overcome their tainted origins or the "crime" of Negro suffrage and officeholding, and so they were characterized as the worst of all possible governments. Since about 1950, modern scholars, often writing under the influence of the civil rights movement, have tended toward the opposite extreme, praising the carpetbag regimes as forward-looking, constructive, and democratic. The truth probably lies somewhere between.

Some traditional stereotypes are easily shown to be false. Radical Reconstruction was not the eternity it seemed to Southern memories; the average tenure of the Republican carpetbag regimes was about five years. Nor was any state ever controlled by blacks, who did not even hold office in proportion to their numbers. The Negroes' prime political function was to provide votes to put their white leaders in office. From 1868 to 1870 two blacks served in the U.S. Senate and a dozen others in the House. Several became lieutenant governors, and substantial numbers served in the state legislatures and in other positions at the state and county level. They were not a picturesque pack of peanut-crunching barbarians making a mockery of civil government, although there were enough misfits to give verisimilitude to that caricature. The majority worked earnestly and soberly despite their inexperience and the handicaps of defective education, and some were men of education and respectable attainments. It is worth noting that during this period and for many years to come, in the North black legislators and officeholders were conspicuous by their absence.

Negro voters overwhelmingly supported the Republicans, of course. Most were unable to read; many had no understanding of the political process and cast their votes for they knew not whom. They were often cynically manipulated by their white leaders, being registered, organized, and encouraged, not to say ordered, to vote by the Loyal Leagues, some military commanders, and the Freedmen's Bureau, which "as a whole became a Republican agent." Supposedly a relief and educational institution, the Bureau "materially assisted no more than 0.5 per cent of the four million ex-slaves." A more obvious economic function of the Bureau was helping planters keep the blacks at work in the fields. Nor did it preempt the field of black education. Before the advent of public education, blacks themselves built and supported many scools under very difficult circumstances, often with little or no help from the Bureau. Although some native whites sympathized with the blacks' efforts, others did not, and sometimes the whites burnt school houses and attacked teachers. They especially resented teachers from the North, who were inclined to mingle political indoctrination with the ABCs.

State militias became another important vehicle of political action. Under the Johnson governments the militias had fallen into the hands of conservative whites, many of them ex-Confederate soldiers, and so they were abolished by Congress in 1867. They were, however, reestablished under the carpetbag governments. Then the membership became heavily black, and the militia's main functions were to overawe hostile whites, who found that the shoe was now on the other foot, to promote the Republican cause at elections, sometimes by heckling the opposition and intimidating voters, and to enforce martial law. Both the white militia of 1865-1866 and the carpetbag militia were accused of committing acts of lawlessness and violence, including murder; probably both were guilty, although the truth is difficult to ascertain.

The picture of the black masses roaming aimlessly across the South and refusing to work is a considerable exaggeration. A great many did move about, primarily to test the fact of freedom, but usually they did not move far and often returned to their old neighborhoods. They were reluctant to work for their former masters, and Negro husbands were unwilling to have their wives and children work in the fields as they had done under slavery. They were likewise unwilling to work under yearly contracts, which the whites preferred as giving them greater control over their laborers than did the wage system. Dislike for contracts and a shortage of capital led to sharecropping: renting land in exchange for a part of the crop. Many blacks became sharecroppers. They were soon followed by a great many whites. Within 15 years of Lee's surrender, the best Southern land was owned by Northern investors or by resident merchants, themselves dependent on Northern banks for credit. The agricultural population, whites as well as blacks, rapidly slipped into sharecropping or tenancy. Not only were the freedmen denied the land promised them, but many independent white farmers lost their land, and the whole section sank into an era of grinding and unrelieved poverty without parallel in the nation's history.

In summary, legend notwithstanding, blacks neither ruled, robbed, ravaged, nor ruined the South during Reconstruction. Except for a small fraction, they received few political plums and little graft from the Carpetbag regimes, and after the latter were gone, they shared — and more than shared — the destitution and hopelessness that was the lot of most Southerners in the late nineteenth century. Blacks like whites had become colonials in the service of Northern capital, and they discovered how little legal freedom could mean when accompanied by economic bondage.

Aside from the unforgiveable sin of being controlled by an unholy alliance of carpetbaggers, scalawags, and blacks, Republican governments were most often criticized for imposing crushing taxes on the mass of whites so as to raise money for graft and extravagances. There is no doubt that taxes went up sharply; the sum of state and local taxes doubled between 1860 and 1870, although property values had declined substantially during the same decade. Already impoverished by war, drought, and debts, many landowners lost their property when they could not pay the taxes. At one time about 20 percent of the land in Mississippi was up for sale because of tax defaults. Arguments about the need for higher taxes to repair war damage, finance public education, and provide other social services were naturally not convincing to people already faced with penury and embittered by undoubted instances of dishonesty and waste. Many examples of the latter could be given. The cost of public printing in Florida in 1869 exceeded the entire cost of state government in 1860 and the total cost of printing from 1789 to 1868. The cost of a legislative session in Louisiana before the war was about $100,000; under the Republicans it rose to about $1 million, much of which went for members' salaries and "travel expenses." Lousiana's printing bill, a favorite cover for theft, rose from $50,000 to $500,000. And so the story goes.

Far more important than simple graft was the granting of special privileges to corporate interests in exchange for bribes. The principal beneficiaries were railroads, and some of the major political battles of Reconstruction were rooted in railroad rivalries. Conservatives might play "Dixie" and appeal to white supremacy, and Republicans might talk of rebel atrocities and warn blacks of the danger of reenslavement, when the real question was quite different. In Alabama, for instance, the struggle was between railroads financed by August Belmont and other Democratic capitalists from New York, and those backed by Republican investors from Philadelphia led by Jay Cooke and Company. The latter's bankruptcy in 1873 was followed by Republican defeat in Alabama. Similar contests occurred in other states.

Modern scholars acknowledge the existence of corruption in the carpetbag governments, but point out that the culprits were conservative whites as well as Republicans, and that when the former replaced the latter in control of state governments, dishonesty continued. They also object to singling out the carpetbag regimes for opprobrium when corruption had become a nationwide phenomenon, exemplified at the national level by the scandals of Grant's presidency. While all this is undoubtedly true, it would appear to be more to the purpose to discover why the corruption of American politics became so much worse after the victory of the Republican party at the polls and of the North in the Civil War. The seeming paradox of crooked idealists and a corrupt crusade encountered during the war is also present during Reconstruction. It may be, as Kenneth Stampp wrote in his history of Reconstruction, that "we are here confronted with a group which pursued objectives that were morally good [i.e., Negro rights] for reasons that were morally bad." Idealistic means, in other words, could be incidental to the pursuit of corrupt ends.

REDEMPTION: THE COUNTERREVOLUTION

The reaction of the white majority to congressional Reconstruction was a complex phenomenon arising from longstanding political divisions within the South as well as from the events of the 1860s. Before the war the Whig party had been a substantial minority, and sometimes a majority, in all Southern states. The estrangement between Southern and Northern Whigs in the early 1850s and the growing importance of slavery and sectionalism in national politics had combined to submerge the Whigs as an identifiable party. In the North they became Republicans. In the South, after voting the Constitutional Union ticket in 1860, they abandoned party labels and joined their old Democratic antagonists in resisting the Northern invader. As a group, they continued to be identified with a reluctance to secede; as the war began to go badly, the people tended to turn toward them and away from the Democrats, who were regarded as the secessionist party. Former Whigs were elected in large numbers to the Second Confederate Congress in 1863.

This trend continued after the war. In 1860 there were no Whig governors in the states soon to become the Confederacy, with Whigs holding only two Senate seats and about 20 percent of the House seats from the South. Five years later, in elections held by the Johnson state governments, former Whigs won eight governorships, 11 Senate seats, two-thirds of the House seats, and large majorities in the constitutional conventions. They now called themselves Conservatives. Many of them still saw eye to eye with their former colleagues and hoped for a revival of the old intersectional Whig coalition. If Lincoln had lived they would have found a friendly welcome. With the overthrow of the Johnson governments by Congress, however, the Conservatives gradually came to see that the Republican party was intent on guaranteeing its political supremacy and on the economic and political exploitation of the South, not on a reconciliation with Southern Whiggery. The black populace, not former Whigs, were to be the party's Southern allies.

Lincoln had correctly foreseen that Confederate defeat would bring the old Whigs to the top. He had also realized that premature enfranchisement of the black would inevitably force Southern Whiggery into the arms of the Democrats, uniting the great majority of whites against the Republican party. And so it happened. As they had been driven under by the slavery issue and secession, once again the Whigs would be submerged, this time by Negro suffrage and officeholding. They would surface in the 1870s after the overthrow of congressional Reconstruction and become the dominant political force in Southern politics for many years. Now calling themselves Democrats, these "Redeemers" represented the same business-oriented conservative philosophy that Lincoln had relied on early in 1865 to Republicanize a restored South.

The advent of congressional Reconstruction threw the Conservatives into disarray. Some of them were, of course, disqualified from officeholding by the Fourteenth Amendment; some of the rest tried to work within the new situation, hoping to control the black vote. But the Reconstruction acts called into existence a rival group of political aspirants, the carpetbaggers. Under the Johnson governments Northerners had enjoyed almost no political opportunities. Now they could bid higher for the new black vote than could the Conservatives, who were unable for a variety of reasons to face the prospect of Negro equality.

Opposition to congressional Reconstruction should not be seen as merely a matter of vindicating white supremacy. That was, of course, an ingredient of major importance. A substantial portion of Southern whites, especially the ex-Whigs, were willing to make use of enfranchised blacks to accomplish ulterior purposes; in this they imitated their Republican cousins in the North. But in most states even this group was unwilling to admit blacks as equal partners. At the other extreme were the great majority of whites who wished to concede little or nothing to blacks — neither votes, nor officeholding, nor (most certainly) social equality.

Economic rivalries between railroad interests figured in the opposition to the Republican regimes, as did a desire to acquire the offices and spoils enjoyed by carpetbaggers. Those people most injured by new tax policies and skyrocketing expenditures had an obvious motive for wanting to restore home rule, and even those not directly affected were often shocked by the startling change in the whole theory and practice of state government as compared with the antebellum years.

But besides motives deriving from self-interest, there can be no doubt that the conservative counterrevolution drew great strength from a genuine and widespread disgust at what was seen as corrupt misrule. If carpetbag corruption is to be regarded as only one aspect of a nationwide phenomenon, then the reaction to it can likewise be seen as part of the nationwide revulsion at the prostitution of public office by the spoilsmen. In other words, there is no reason to think that Southerners valued honest government less than did Americans generally.

The anti-Republican forces used conventional political methods to restore home rule. They also used economic retaliation against blacks, social ostracism against whites, fraud, intimidation, and many forms of violence, including cold-blooded murder. This was scarcely surprising. The new order against which this violence was directed was itself the offspring of four years of killing that had left the South bled white, impoverished, and demoralized. It had come to power at the point of a bayonet. Added to these circumstances were the sudden emancipation and enfranchisement of millions of untutored blacks in a society that for generations had regarded white supremacy as a condition of survival. Such a hell's brew of war's aftermath and social and political disruption was bound to produce violence.

Lawlessness was often blamed on sinister, mysterious societies such as the Ku Klux Klan, which caught the imagination of the people and won the gratitude of Republican opportunists. A recent study of the Klan has revived the notion of a gigantic Ku Klux conspiracy and claims that the "Conservative community" encouraged a "reign of terror" that covered "much of the South." The author, however, was able to find virtually no "contemporary inside evidence" about the Klan and used for his main source witnesses called before the extremely partisan "Ku Klux" committee of Congress.

It is, in short, the problem of "bleeding Kansas" all over again: allegations of violence were made a prime weapon of political propaganda. The "facts" were usually produced by a partisan press or by partisan investigations, and were often based on hearsay or were invented altogether. The same problems of evidence are present with respect to Reconstruction. There was certainly violence in Kansas and in the postwar South, and in some instances a reasonable approximation of the truth can be glimpsed amid the clouds of propaganda. But thus far no body of reliable information has been unearthed or assembled that will answer questions such as: How much of the South was lawless and for how long? How many persons were beaten or killed or driven out? Were white conservatives always the aggressors? If not, how often were Republicans the attackers? How much of the violence was carried out by organizations such as the Ku Klux Klan, and how much by individuals? How much was politically motivated, and how much the result of ordinary criminality? How many Southerners approved of lawlessness? Merely asking such questions illustrates the impossibility of answering them except in the most unspecific way.

It is not even certain that the South was more violent than the North in the 1870s; like corruption, lawlessness was by no means a Southern monopoly. Violence is at least as easy to authenticate in the North as in the South. During the hard times that followed the Panic of 1873, newspapers told of swarms of homeless, jobless men who wandered over the Northern countryside and sometimes engaged in "organized brigandage, associating with professional criminals and beggars, camping in the woods, stealing, drinking and fighting. . . . From all over the East came reports of thefts, incendiary fires, rapes and even murders committed by vagrants." Repression of labor by business led workers to join societies that, like the Ku Klux Klan, had secret rituals, grips, and passwords. In the coalfields a wave of assassinations was blamed on a sinister conspiracy of "Molly Maguires." In 1877 strikes by railroad workers, joined by other laborers, paralyzed major trunk lines and led to looting, burning, and battles between workers and troops. The violence was so extensive that a general strike and widespread anarchy appeared imminent. Some Northerners came to regard unions and strikes the work of a Communist conspiracy. Several states outlawed strikes and unions. Employers blacklisted workers they regarded as troublemakers, and made others sign "ironclad" oaths not to join unions. All this suggests that violence in the South, as well as official reaction to it, should be examined in its national setting.

In 1869 the Conservative-Democrat coalition overthrew the Republicans in Tennessee, which had been the first state to fall under Republican rule. Virginia and North Carolina followed in 1870, Georgia in 1871, Arkansas, Texas, and Alabama in 1874, and Mississippi in 1876. The last three, Florida, South Carolina, and Louisiana, were "redeemed" in 1877 in the aftermath of the disputed election of 1876. There was a similar, and earlier, shift away from the Republicans in the five border states, Maryland, Delaware, West Virginia, Kentucky, and Missouri. The Republican-Unionist parties that had grown up during the war in this section under the fostering care of the Federal army had in several instances disfranchised Confederate sympathizers and barred them from a number of occupations. Disfranchisement was intended to do the job that Negro voting did further South; many border state Republicans looked on black voters with distaste. Despite occasional intervention by Federal authorities, the Democrats, many of whom were ex-Confederates, made substantial gains in all these states during the late 1860s and early 1870s. Once again, what was happening in the South was not unique. There was a nationwide shift away from the Republicans in the 1870s, with the Democrats winning control of the House in 1872 and a popular margin of 250,000 votes in the presidential election of 1876.

Republican leaders soon realized that their system, based on black suffrage, was not working as intended: within two years white conservatives had either triumphed or appeared to be on the verge of victory in several states. Therefore they tried to protect the blacks' right to vote by a sweeping extension of Federal authority in the Enforcement Act of May 21, 1870. Republican losses in congressional elections later that year led to the Second Enforcement Act (February 28, 1871), strengthening the first with respect to Federal elections. This was followed two months later by a law to suppress terrorist organizations such as the Ku Klux Klan, which was believed to be a major cause of Republican difficulties. It authorized Grant to suspend the writ of habeas corpus and to put down disorders by armed force. There ensued a vigorous use of

Federal power that is often credited with breaking the back of the Klan movement, although it did not put an end to politically motivated violence directed at the carpetbag regimes.

The Enforcement acts were, of course, damned by Southern conservatives and Northern Democrats, as well as by some Republican moderates. The latter were men who believed in conciliation instead of repression. They saw the acts as evidence of the failure of congressional Reconstruction, which in turn was evidence of a more general failure that proved the need for reform within the Republican party. The acts were reasonably effective in the South for a few years. After 1874 popular resistance, inadequate enforcement machinery, lack of financing, and adverse Supreme Court decisions made them a dead letter. In fact, the government spent more money implementing these laws in urban Democratic strongholds such as New York City than in the South.

REPUBLICANS ON THE DEFENSIVE: THE NORTHERN RETREAT FROM RECONSTRUCTION

The election of General Grant no doubt seemed to many the triumphant climax to Republican policies, a joint victory by the man who won the war and the party that saved the Union. Yet things began to go wrong very soon. Issues once set aside in favor of more urgent matters now claimed attention. Republicans were again divided by the tariff question. Duties had remained high during the postwar years, and a determined tariff reform minority within the party became ever more vocal. Money policy continued to be vexing and divisive, with inflationists drawing strength from a variety of economic groups. The Republican majority sided with "sound money," that is, providing for the redemption of greenbacks in gold and maintaining the sanctity of the national debt without scaling down interest payments. In the agricultural regions there were loud complaints about extortionate railroad rates. Members of the Patrons of Husbandry (the Grangers) turned from social and self-help purposes to political action, evincing little patience with Republicans who shied away from the regulation of corporate interests.

The surfacing of such economic divisions was inevitable once the common enemy had been defeated. But if these difficulties were no fault of the party leadership, the same cannot be said of others that arose during Grant's presidency. For some the President was at least partly responsible. His ignorance of government and politics allowed him to become the cat's-paw of dishonest sharpers, as did his obstinancy and his blind loyalty to friends unworthy of his trust. His every mistake injured the party by alienating or disillusioning important persons or interests.

Grant's strange enthusiasm for annexing Santo Domingo is a case in point. This underpopulated, underdeveloped, yet naturally rich little country had excited the appetites of its own petty tyrants as well as those of a number of American adventurers who had been buzzing about it ever since the 1850s. Rival groups of speculators in New York, apparently including Seward's mentor Thurlow Weed, were involved. At Seward's instance Johnson recommended annexation in his last annual message to Congress. Grant's conversion to the cause was mainly the work of his former staff officer and now private secretary, Orville Babcock, who in turn was taken in hand by the leading speculators. Once he made up his mind to have Santo Domingo, Grant kept after it as if he were pounding Lee at Spotsylvania. As the facts came out, the scheme appeared for what it was: hasty in contrivance, ill-conceived, and malodorous. Grant used all his influence to whip up support for a treaty of annexation, but although he was able to get a majority of Republican senators to support him, including prominent militants such as Zachariah Chandler and Oliver Morton, as well as a strong contingent of Republicans from the carpetbag states, he could not get the necessary two-thirds. Important to the outcome was the opposition of Charles Sumner, chairman of the Foreign Relations Committee. Here began a feud between Sumner and Grant that the administration pursued with relentless rancor and that ended with Sumner's loss of his chairmanship. The Sumner feud damaged both Grant's reputation and the unity of the party, as did his callous treatment of cabinet members and other high Federal officials. The President often seemed to act from motives of personal spite or narrow party advantage.

Grant's poor judgment led him to hobnob openly with men

whose reputations were a public scandal. He consorted socially with the notorious "Jubilee Jim" Fiske and Jay Gould, who were trying to influence the Treasury Department's policy with respect to the sale of gold in order to "corner" the market and make a quick fortune. They were hand in glove with a brother-in-law of the President in causing the gold market crisis, popularly known as "Black Friday" (September 24, 1869), which led some people to suspect that Grant had connived at the whole scheme. He was innocent of that, but certainly guilty of a choice of associates that convinced the more principled Republicans of his unfitness for the office he held.

Grant's capitulation to the party regulars, men who put political and often pecuniary success above every other consideration, was illustrated by his intervention in Missouri affairs. A split developed in that state's Republican party between the regulars and the reformers, the latter led by Carl Schurz, German liberal, a Forty-Eighter, a Union major general, and once an advocate of stern treatment of the conquered South. Grant threw his influence behind the regulars by making John McDonald, an old friend, the party boss of Missouri. The reformers protested that McDonald's reputation for dishonesty would haunt the party, but Grant, who interpreted attacks on his friends as merely malicious snipings at himself, paid no heed. With money defrauded from the government by the collusion of whiskey distillers and revenue officers, McDonald financed the anti-reform element of the party in 1870. Thereafter the "Whiskey Ring" continued its operations for private profit. Tactics of this sort helped to cause a revolt of the party's reform minority, a revolt that began in Missouri and in which Schurz played a prominent part.

Anyone concerned about machine politics, the spoils system, and corruption was bound to have reservations about the carpetbag governments in the South, and indeed about the whole Republican approach toward Reconstruction. There was also a growing weariness in the North with atrocity propaganda. Years of overstimulation by horror stories from the South bred both scepticism and indifference. More important was the increasing dissatisfaction of the Northern business community, which had always wanted the kind of Reconstruction that would promote political stability and favorable conditions for investment. Republican politicians had also wanted political stability, by which they meant giving the party a firm grip on the Southern states. Secondarily, they wanted to please Northern business interests. For a time the picture of a violent and unrepentant South rallied most of the people and many businessmen behind the congressional program. The politicians argued that their methods were essential to the protection of property rights and equal opportunity for Northern investors. Republicans on the Ku Klux investigating committee, for example, claimed that one of the Klan's purposes "must have been to close the South against northern men and capital."

But the shabby reputation of the carpetbag governments, their tax policies, and continued turmoil led an increasing number of businessmen to conclude that congressional Reconstruction had been a mistake. They were not convinced when Grant blamed social ostracism and violence for impeding the flow of immigrants and capital to the South. They believed that Republican policies were prolonging such conditions. End those policies, and ostracism and violence would disappear; then the economic penetration of the South could proceed apace.

LIBERAL REPUBLICANS AND THE FIASCO OF 1872

The prospects for turning the Republicans out of office seemed good as the election of 1872 approached. With congressional Reconstruction an accomplished fact, the Democrats now stopped trying to turn the clock back and began to concentrate their attacks on corruption and Republican economic policies. They made substantial gains in the state elections of 1869 and cut deeply into the Republican majority in the House in 1870. By now the Republicans were quarreling among themselves. Early in January 1872, Missouri liberals sent out a call for a convention of reform Republicans to meet in May.

The heterogeneous throng that gathered in Cincinnati was somewhat reminiscent of antebellum Republican conventions, with their collection of reformers of every kind, old political enemies, and representatives of conflicting economic views. Before the war, politicians had been able to create a viable party out of such a miscellany. Fear of the Slave Power then had justified the kind of horsetrading among opposing groups that was essential to the creation of a durable coalition. But the 1870s were not the 1850s. There was no national crisis, and the reformers could not resort to horsetrading without assuming the role of pious hypocrites. The platform adopted by the Liberal Republicans at Cincinnati accepted the finality of the Reconstruction amendments and the principle of legal equality regardless of race, but it also called for the removal of political disabilities from ex-Confederates, the abandonment of military rule, and a return to local self-government. It came out for "sacredly" maintaining the national debt, the resumption of specie payments, fair taxation, giving public lands to settlers, not corporations, and reform of the civil service. This part of the platform passed without debate, but on the important question of tariff policy agreement was impossible. The free traders and the protectionists were alike immovable, and so the convention referred the question to the people and their elected representatives. This had a demoralizing effect. To many delegates tariff reform and political reform were inseparable; they did not believe corruption would cease until the bribery and logrolling that accompanied tariff legislation also ceased.

Even so, a strong leader might have rallied this hodgepodge. The convention could have chosen one of several able candidates who were experienced in public affairs. Instead, in a scene of utter confusion, it picked Horace Greeley of the New York *Tribune*. A worse choice was scarcely possible. Whatever Greeley's skill as a journalist, as a politician he was a joke. Over the years he had seemingly embraced almost every fad and reform that had come along, from vegetarianism to communitarian socialism, acquiring a reputation for being flighty, if not downright silly. He was tolerated affectionately because of his obvious sincerity, but the same people who regarded him with fondness often found the idea of "President Greeley" ludicrous. Southerners remembered his relentless animosity of the antebellum years, and free traders could not forget that he was still a "ferocious" protectionist. Many Liberal Republicans were so disgusted by Greeley's nomination that they left the movement altogether.

Regular Republicans were naturally delighted by the dissidents' blunders. They, of course, renominated Grant. In their platform they insisted that the Reconstruction amendments should be vigorously enforced by "the party that secured those amendments." They made a gesture toward civil service reform and opposed further grants of public land to corporations, thus stealing some of the Liberals' thunder. There was even a vague mention of the rights of labor and women. Otherwise the platform contained the customary flexible — but really protective — tariff plank, upheld the national debt, and pointed with pride to the accomplishments of the party that had saved the Union.

The Democrats brought up the rear, meeting in Baltimore in July. In a brief convention dominated by party professionals, they, too, nominated Greeley and adopted the Liberal Republican platform. They thereby repelled Republicans who might otherwise have deserted to Greeley and the reformers, and simultaneously antagonized Democrats who would have voted for their own candidate, but who could not stomach Greeley.

The Grant forces had everything their own way. Most of the scandals of the General's administration had yet to be discovered, and those that had come to light did not prove dishonesty on Grant's part. In foreign affairs the administration could point to the Treaty of Washington (1871), a reasonable and satisfactory settlement of American claims against Britain arising from the depredations of the *Alabama* and other Confederate crusiers built in British shipyards. The business community, suspicious of Greeley's Democratic support, was heavily on Grant's side and contributed generously to the campaign. During the spring Republicans made token cuts in tariff duties, which they restored soon after the election, and relieved most ex-Confederates from Fourteenth Amendment disabilities. At the same time they used the Enforcement Acts to help them keep all but two ex-Confederate states in the Republican column. The "bloody shirt" was flapped energetically, and personal attacks on Greeley descended to new depths of scurrility. Thomas Nast's malevolent cartoons showed the hapless Horace in the form of a vulture, perched on the ruins of Negro orphan asylums, or shaking hands with a Ku Klux murderer. But probably more persuasive to the voters than the issues and the mudslinging was the fact that, except for the South, the country was generally prosperous. In good times the incumbent party is rarely turned out of office.

The Republican triumph was crushing. Grant polled 55.6 percent of the popular vote, Greeley 43.8 percent. Counting only those states that voted both in 1868 and 1872, the Republicans picked up 343,000 votes, while the Greeley ticket polled 90,000 fewer votes than Seymour, showing that Greeley's candidacy turned away many Democrats. Greeley carried only three border states and three or four from the old Confederacy, depending on which set of returns from Louisiana is accepted. The unfortunate editor lost the election, his wife, and control of the *Tribune* in quick succession, and he died before the end of November. The Liberal Republican party never ran another presidential campaign. Its members drifted back into the two major parties or into third parties such as the Greenbackers or Populists.

PANIC, DEPRESSION, AND SCANDALS

If the presidential election of 1872 had been held a year later, even Greeley might have won, such were the disasters of the mid-1870s. Most important was the financial panic that began in the late summer of 1873, and that touched off perhaps the worst depression in the nation's history. The causes were complex and international in scope. A worldwide increase in land under cultivation and in the use of machinery led to a decline in agricultural commodity prices and an increase in both agricultural capital requirements and debt. Each year from 1869 to 1872 total imports exceeded exports, producing a steady growth in the nation's foreign indebtedness, a problem that was aggravated by the debt-financed overexpansion of American industry, especially railroads. This mortgaged economy was still heavily dependent on European, especially British, credit, and the stage was set for the usual sequence of events: contraction in Europe, panic in the United States. The European contraction began in the spring of 1873; the panic began with the failure of Jay Cooke and Company in September. The ensuing depression lasted for five years. Bankruptcies numbered in the tens of thousands.

Unemployment rose to 3 million, mostly among the nonagricultural laboring population of about 7 million. An unprecedented wave of strikes and industrial disorders reached its peak in 1877, the "year of violence."

The elections of 1874 transformed an overwhelming Republican majority in the House of Representatives into the first Democratic majority since the 1850s. Many new members from the South and West were swept into office by demands for monetary inflation. Therefore early in 1875 the lame-duck Republican Congress hastened to protect sound money by passing a law that, among other things, provided for the resumption of specie payments (redempton of Greenbacks in gold) by 1879. Congress also passed a revenue act that restored the nominal cuts in tariff rates on manufactured goods made in 1872 and raised rates on other articles. From this time forward, the Republican party took its stand on "sound money" and a thoroughgoing protectionism.

At this same session, Congress debated bills that both epitomized and wrote *finis* to congressional Reconstruction. One was an enforcement bill designed to help carry the South in the election of 1876. House Democrats managed to delay the bill until near the end of February, leaving too little time for the Senate to take action before the session ended a few days later. The other was a civil rights bill, the favorite project of the late Charles Sumner who, on his deathbed the previous year, had asked his friends to shepherd the measure through Congress. In its original form it would have outlawed racial discrimination in public accommodations, including public schools. Before it was passed, however, Republicans and Democrats joined to delete the reference to schools, some of them reasoning that to require racially mixed schools would doom public education in the South to early extinction. Even this diminished monument to Sumner's long struggle for racial justice was overturned by the Supreme Court eight years later.

The appalling hardship that accompanied the depression was not the only burden the Republican party had to bear when it faced the voters. During Grant's second term it was staggered by one spectacular scandal after another. Some of them touched the intimate friends of the President. The suspicions aroused by Grant's social relations with Fiske and Gould were revived by the discovery that

Orville Babcock was a member of the "Whiskey Ring." Then Secretary of War W.W. Belknap, an old friend of the President's, turned out to be a bribetaker and had to resign to escape impeachment. Also accused of fraud were Orvil Grant and Fred Dent, brothers respectively of the President and his wife. The scandals extended far beyond Grant's circle, besmirching the reputations of diplomats, judges, the vice-president, and congressmen (including a future president and a presidential nominee), some of whom had accepted bribes from Crédit Mobilier, a construction company connected with the Union Pacific Railroad.

George William Curtis, editor of *Harper's Weekly,* whom Grant had appointed ostensibly to institute civil service reform, resigned in 1875 when the President ignored his recommendations. The next year he addressed the New York Republican convention.

> The corruptions of the administration exposed in every direction, and culminating at last in the self-confessed bribery of the Republican Secretary of War, the low tone of political honor and of political morality that has prevailed in official Republican service, the unceasing disposition of the officers and agents of the administration of this country to prostitute the party organizations relentlessly and at all costs to personal ends, has everywhere aroused the apprehension of the friends of free government, and has startled and alarmed the honest masses of the Republican party.

And George F. Hoar, Massachusetts Republican and one of the managers of the Belknap impeachment, lamented that he

> had heard in highest places the shameless doctrine avowed by men grown old in public office that the true way by which power should be gained in the Republic is to bribe the people with the offices created for their service, and the true end for which it should be used when gained is the promotion of selfish ambition and the gratification of personal revenge.

The Republican party was not responsible for the depression, nor did it have a monopoly on corruption, but as the party in power it was the target for popular wrath. To Democrats, the omens for 1876 appeared auspicious indeed.

THE LAST COMPROMISE

By the mid-1870s the revolutionary impulse that had swept over the nation had largely spent its force. The Republican party was now concerned with consolidating the political and economic gains

of the past 15 years. The zeal that had once inspirited the party —
to combat the aggressions of the Slave Power, to preserve the
Union, to safeguard the rights of the freedmen — that zeal had all
but disappeared. Men like Sumner and Stevens who had tried to
keep the party close to principle were either dead or ignored or
disillusioned. Far from being the party of idealism, it was now
notorious for its materialism, cynicism, and corruption, traits its
opponents summed up in the epithet "Grantism."

The unlucky man who gave his name to that "ism" was perhaps
more sinned against than sinning; his greatest disservice to the
nation had been to accept a position for which he was completely
unfit. And yet he flirted with the notion of seeking a third term even
after he had become a heavy political liability — especially in the
eyes of those Republican leaders who aspired to their party's nomination. Foremost among these was James G. Blaine, speaker of the
house from 1869 to 1875, who touched off his campaign early in
1876 by a brilliant "bloody shirt" attack on the South. But at a
crucial moment Blaine was touched by scandal, and although he led
all contenders for six ballots at the Republican convention, the
nomination went to Rutherford B. Hayes, governor of Ohio. This
otherwise undistinguished individual had a creditable war record,
a reputation for personal integrity, a generally conservative outlook
(he was a former Whig), some interest in reform, and, of course,
he came from a strategic state. The Republican platform rejoiced
in "the quickened conscience of the people" and promised to punish corrupt public officials. It made a thinly veiled appeal to anti-
Catholic feeling, promised to crush out polygamy, and agreed to
give "respectful consideration" to additional rights for women.
Otherwise it was a conventional Republican platform, favoring a
protective tariff and resumption of specie payments, claiming to
represent the party of patriotism, and charging the Democratic
party with being "the same in character and spirit as when it sympathized with treason."

There was no real contest for the Democratic nomination. Governor Samuel J. Tilden of New York, touted as a reformer, won on
the first ballot. There was considerable dissension on the money
question, and the platform revealed the party's split personality by
denouncing the Republicans' failure to resume specie payments

while simultaneously demanding repeal of the Resumption Act! Otherwise the document contained no surprises. It attacked the tariff, government extravagance, and the huge increase in taxation since 1860. Most of the platform was devoted to the need for sweeping reforms. It listed the Republicans' misdeeds at length, even accusing them of reviving "the coolie-trade in Mongolian women for immoral purposes."

The character of the campaign was predictable. The Democrats concentrated on hard times, corruption, and the failure of Reconstruction. Under the circumstances, the Republicans were left with few weapons. They attacked Tilden personally and accused the Democrats of being unreliable on the money question, but most of all they appealed to sectional hatreds. As Hayes wrote Blaine, "Our strong ground is the dread of a solid South, rebel rule, etc., etc. I hope you will make these topics prominent in your speeches. It leads people away from 'hard times' which is our deadliest foe." This was congenial to Blaine, who advised Union veterans to "vote as they shot." Unfortunately for the Republicans, there was a relative shortage of "Southern outrages." There were some, of course, such as the killing of several black members of a militia unit in South Carolina, and others were invented, but the total effect was not as persuasive to Northern voters as in other election years.

At first Tilden had apparently won a clear victory. He had a popular vote larger by 250,000 than Hayes' and he had undisputed possession of 184 of the 185 electoral votes needed to win; Hayes had only 165, with 20 others contested. One of the latter was in Oregon, which Hayes carried, where one elector was ineligible because he was a Federal employee. This vote ultimately went to Hayes, as it should have. The other 19 consisted of eight from Louisiana, seven from South Carolina, and four from Florida. These were the last three ex-Confederate states controlled by the Republicans. Both parties claimed to have carried them, and two sets of votes were returned from each. Which votes were to be counted? The Constitution merely said that the President of the Senate "shall, in the presence of the Senate and the House of Representatives, open all certificates, and the votes shall then be counted." Some new method was obviously required. Time was running out. As the days passed, tempers grew hotter, and Democrats cried out against attempts to steal an election they claimed was clearly theirs. Congress convened early in December, but with the House controlled by Democrats and the Senate by Republicans, the deadlock dragged on into the new year. There was even talk of civil war, and some Northern Democrats sounded as ferocious as the fire-eaters of 1861.

At length congressional moderates of both parties, with Democrats predominating, established an electoral commission of 15 to decide between the two sets of votes. There were to be five members from the Supreme Court and five from each house of Congress. As planned, there would be seven Democrats and seven Republicans, with the deciding vote resting with Supreme Court Justice David Davis, an old friend and associate of Lincoln and more lately a Liberal Republican. The Democrats had hopes Davis would see things their way, but before the commission could begin its work, Davis was elected to the Senate by a Democrat-Greenbacker coalition in the Illinois legislature, and his place was taken by a Republican justice. When the commission decided by a strict party division of eight to seven that Florida had been won by Hayes, the Democrats knew that they had lost the presidency. Feelings ran very high, especially among Northern Democrats in Congress, who now proposed to prevent the completion of the electoral vote count by a filibuster in the House. This would prevent Hayes' inauguration, of course, with consequences that promised to be serious indeed. Violence or even anarchy seemed quite possible, given the excited state of public opinion.

The way out of the crisis lay through an investigation already undertaken by the Hayes managers of the realities that lay behind Southern politics. Many of the Dixie conservatives who had voted for Tilden had been Whigs before the war, as Hayes had been. They and their section had not been included in the largesse the Federal government had extended to business interests in the postwar years, and now, in the midst of depression, Northerners of both parties were demanding retrenchment. These ex-Whigs had likewise been shut out from political preferment at the national level because local necessities had compelled them to oppose the Republicans. Finally, like most other white Southerners, they wanted the last Federal garrisons withdrawn and a permanent end to intervention in Southern affairs, racial and political, by Washington. In a complex series of negotiations, the Hayes men promised to meet all of these needs if Hayes was elected. The Southerners agreed, refused to support the filibuster, and Hayes took office peaceably.

The Republicans' immediate purpose in agreeing to the Compromise of 1877 was to elect Hayes, but they also hoped for a resurrection of their party in the South under the leadership of native white conservatives. In other words, they were trying to do in 1877 much the same thing as Lincoln had attempted in 1865. They eventually discovered that the Reconstruction years had engendered too much additional bitterness for that strategy to work now. These hopes, however, were a continuing inducement for Hayes to keep his part of the 1877 bargain. He recommended Federal assistance for Southern internal improvements, including the Texas and Pacific Railroad, whose lobby had played an important role in bringing Hayes and the Southerners together. He chose an ex-Confederate army officer and ex-Whig for the politically powerful position of postmaster general. He withdrew the last Federal garrisons in the South, and with the troops the last carpetbag governments disappeared. "Redemption" was complete. Hayes himself toured the Southeast, speaking in conciliatory terms and advising the Negroes that their rights could be better protected by Southern whites than by Federal power.

The political honeymoon between Republicans and white conservatives was brief. Other than a small remnant, no indigenous Republican party took root in the South. The Stalwarts, those who believed in taking a hard line toward the South, pushed Hayes aside and revived the "bloody shirt," which still could sway a considerable fraction of Northern voters. Not until the 1890s was this banner finally laid to rest. During the intervening years there were occasional unsuccessful efforts to promote Federal intervention in the South, but there was no really dangerous threat to the Compromise of 1877 before the 1950s. Until then, politically and socially, the South was left to manage its own affairs. Blacks were systematically disfranchised, segregated, and relegated to the bottom rung of the economic ladder. This was done with the tacit and sometimes explicit acquiescence of the North, whose own black population could testify that prejudice was not a sectional phenomenon.

The passions of the war years weakened steadily after the compromise. By 1888 the Republicans could elect a president without appealing to old hatreds. That same year Jefferson Davis spoke to an audience of young men in Mississippi: "The past is dead; let it bury its dead, its hopes and its aspirations. . . . Let me beseech you to lay aside all rancor, all bitter sectional feeling, and to take your places in the ranks of those who will bring about a consummation devoutly to be wished — a reunited country." Ten years later the war with Spain carried reconciliation still further, and World War I extinguished the last embers of overt sectional hostility.

The years of Civil War and Reconstruction had witnessed many changes of the utmost importance. The nature of the Union was submitted to the arbitrament of the sword; state sovereignty and the right of secession were buried in a common grave. The political power of the agrarian interest was broken, the old mercantile capitalism was overwhelmed, and the nation was swept into the industrial age with dizzying speed. Rockefeller, Carnegie, and Morgan soon would stand in the place of Clay, Calhoun, and Webster. Slavery was destroyed, and although the Negro's dream of equal rights was not realized, adoption of the Fourteenth and Fifteenth amendments made possible the abolition of legal discrimination a century later.

Yet these changes raised questions that remain unanswered. Although relieved of legal oppression, socially and economically blacks are still an unassimilated minority, as Lincoln feared they would be. The limited and largely negative influence of the agrarian interest has been replaced by the enormous and pervasive power of financial empires, conglomerates, cartels, oligopoly — all the manifestations of concentrated capital in a technological society. A loose federal system of semiautonomous states has yielded to a gigantic central government far removed from the people, whose daily lives it nevertheless affects in countless ways. The drift away from the strongly held convictions of the 1860s toward the ethical relativism — or cynicism — of the late twentieth century may be due partly to the depletion of the moral resources so prodigally expended during the Civil War.

In short, the balance sheet no longer seems to be so overwhelmingly on the side of progress as it once did. History always speaks cautiously, warning the present that things often are not what they seem, that actions can produce the most unexpected consequences. As Lincoln said in his second inaugural, when the war began neither North nor South looked for such "fundamental and astounding" results. And it was beyond even Lincoln's vision to see just how fundamental and astounding they would be.

Chapter XIV

A Bibliographical Note

THE COMING OF THE CIVIL WAR

Writers contemporary with the Civil War had no doubts as to its causes. The prevailing Northern explanation blamed a wicked conspiracy of slaveowners who deliberately sought to destroy republican government while spreading and perpetuating their nefarious institution. Allowed by an all-wise Providence to drive on from one mad act of aggression to another, they finally went too far, started the war, and brought about their own ruin at the hands of a righteous, liberty-loving North. The titles of representative works sometimes reveal their point of view: *The Great Conspiracy, History of the Rise and Fall of the Slave Power in America, The Adder's Den,* and so forth.[1]

Southerners of the war generation, who had differed considerably in 1860 and 1861 as to the seriousness and causes of the crisis as well as to the best course of action, sank all such differences once the war was over. They of course completely rejected their opponents' interpretation. Slavery was not the cause of the war, merely the occasion. The real culprit was an aggressive North which was

---

[1] Henry Wilson, *History of the Rise and Fall of the Slave Power in America* (3 vols.; Boston, 1872-1877); John A. Logan, *The Great Conspiracy* (New York, 1886); John S. Dye, *The Adder's Den. . . .* (New York, 1864). For an excellent essay, see Chapter IV ("The Literature on the Background of the Civil War") in David Potter, *The South and the Sectional Conflict* (Baton Rouge, 1968). See also Thomas J. Pressly, *Americans Interpret Their Civil War* (Princeton, N.J., 1954).

using its superior power to overthrow the Constitution so that it could exploit the South at leisure. After years of provocations the South, exercising an undoubted right, resumed the powers formerly delegated to the central government and withdrew from the Union as the only way of saving the Constitution and protecting itself from Northern fanaticism and greed. Far from being responsible for beginning hostilities, it had stood wholly on the defensive, desiring only to be left in peace; but the North, led by Lincoln and Seward, determined on conquest, and the war came.[2]

The passage of time softened these asperities. Many ex-Confederates, while loyal to the "Lost Cause," adopted the tribal gods of the victors, proclaimed the death of slavery a blessing, and extolled the virtues of industrialization. The imprecations of die-hard sectionalists were drowned out by the voices of reconciliation. Agreement as to the natural superiority of the Anglo-Saxon was a bond between Americans everywhere as the racial interpretation of human affairs became an international cliché toward the end of the century. And new issues supervened; internal divisions now seemed to be more East against West or labor against capital, than North versus South. James Ford Rhodes, a Northerner, wrote a massive history[3] of the period 1850 to 1877 reflecting this changed climate. The immoral institution of slavery was still the cause of the war, but the South had not been willfully wicked. It was, rather, a victim of circumstances. And if the South was wrong in trying to perpetuate slavery, the North was wrong in its reconstruction policies, especially the enfranchisement of blacks. Yet the final result was a better country based on freedom and union.

Rhodes is often identified as the first of a group of historians called the "nationalist school."[4] Like Rhodes, they believed that a stronger country had emerged from the crucible of war, purged

[2] For three examples, see Jefferson Davis, *Rise and Fall of the Confederate Government* (2 vols.; New York, 1881); Edward A. Pollard, *The Lost Cause* (New York, 1866), Alexander H. Stephens; *A Constitutional View of the Late War Between the States* (2 vols.; Philadelphia, 1868-1870).

[3] James Ford Rhodes, *History of the United States from the Compromise of 1850 to the Final Restoration of Home Rule at the South in 1877* (7 vols.; New York, 1893-1906). Rhodes later added two volumes carrying his chronicle to 1909.

[4] For example, John B. McMaster, *A History of the People of the United States from the Revolution to the Civil War* (8 vols.; New York, 1893-1913); Woodrow Wilson, *Division and Reunion,*

as it was of slavery and particularism. And again like Rhodes, they forebore to apportion guilt; instead they looked for the forces that produced an "irrepressible conflict" between the sections. Where Rhodes was an amateur, the others were scholars trained in "scientific" history, and the causes of the war seemed more complex to them. The most persuasive and perceptive was Frederick Jackson Turner, who dealt with the coming of the war obliquely. He was impressed by the diversity of the country, by the intricate pattern of qualities that separated it into sections — North, South, West. To him the Civil War was the manifestation of an "extreme and tragic form of sectionalism."[5] Other themes stressed by Turner's contemporaries were the tensions produced by national growth and development and the clash of antagonistic societies, although much of what they said could be subsumed under Turner's sectional hypothesis.

The unity of interpretation that the nationalist school lacked was supplied by Charles A. Beard. In a masterly synthesis of American history written in collaboration with his wife, Beard promulgated his explanation of the coming of the war, which he called the "second American Revolution."[6] There had been, as Seward had said, an "irrepressible conflict." Its roots lay in "social groupings founded on differences in climate, soil, industries, and labor systems . . . rather than in varying degrees of righteousness and wisdom. . . ." The war was "a social war, ending in the unquestioned establishment of a new power in the government, making vast changes in the arrangement of classes, in the accumulation and distribution of wealth, in the course of industrial development, and

1829-1899 (New York, 1893), among other writings; Edward Channing, *A History of the United States* (6 vols.; New York, 1905-1925). James Schouler, although earlier than Rhodes, is often classed with the nationalists; see his *History of the United States of America under the Constitution* (7 vols.; New York, 1880-1913).

[5] Frederick Jackson Turner, *The Frontier in American History* (New York, 1963), p. 158. This was originally published in 1920. Turner is usually included among the nationalists, but it is not entirely clear why. See his *The United States, 1830-1850: The Nation and Its Sections* (New York, 1935).

[6] Charles A. Beard and Mary Beard, *The Rise of American Civilization* (2 vols.; New York, 1927). For a Marxist's indorsement of the "Second American Revolution," see Louis M. Hacker, *The Triumph of American Capitalism* . . . (New York, 1940), p. 339.

in the Constitution. . . . Merely by the accidents of climate, soil, and geography was it a sectional struggle." It was as much a revolution as the French Revolution; it was a "social cataclysm in which the capitalists, laborers, and farmers of the North and West drove from power in the national government the planting aristocracy of the South."[7]   Slavery and states' rights were but incidents of a struggle that was at bottom economic in nature.

Beard came to professional maturity at the height of the Progressive movement, which was characterized by battles against political corruption and capitalistic feudalism. Therefore it is not surprising that he was not as optimistic as the nationalist school. He did not sermonize about the ultimately constructive results of the Civil War or subscribe to the inevitability of progress. To this extent he provided a transition to the next major interpretive theme, which is usually called "revisionism." Appalled by the holocaust of World War I, which was to put an end to war and make the world safe for democracy and had done neither, revisionist scholars took a dim view of war as an instrument of human progress. They refused to believe that the Civil War had been inevitable, or at least they believed that it should not have been inevitable. It was a "repressible conflict," a "needless war," the work of a "blundering generation," of a defective political system, of an inability to see things as they were, all of which allowed scheming politicians and irresponsible fanatics to generate a runaway emotionalism that led to the unnecessary slaughter of hundreds of thousands of men.[8]   Revisionists tended to discount the substantive importance of slavery as a major cause of the war, especially since the question had been so narrowly defined in terms of the territories.

Once again, however, the coming of a major war led to a reinterpretation of the conflict of the 1860s. World War II seemed to prove that wars were sometimes inevitable and could lead to constructive results. Who could doubt that the overthrow of Hitler was

---

[7] Beard, *Rise of American Civilization.* Vol. II, pp. 51, 53, 54.
[8] Avery Craven, *The Repressible Conflict, 1830-1861* (University, La., 1939); see also his *Coming of the Civil War* (New York, 1942); George Fort Milton, *Eve of Conflict: Stephen A. Douglas and the Needless War* (Boston, 1934); James G. Randall, "The Blundering Generation," *Mississippi Valley Historical Review,* XXVII (1940); Roy F. Nichols, *The Disruption of American Democracy* (New York, 1948).

a good thing? Moreover, moral issues were obviously of great importance in rallying resistance to Nazi Germany. Then, soon after the Axis had been defeated, the Cold War with Russia and its communist satellites began, and the necessity of a unified country dedicated to freedom seemed beyond doubt. Next came the civil rights movement, which undertook to make good what some saw as the North's long-deferred commitment to the Negro.

This succession of events led to the development of a neo-nationalist interpretation that reaffirmed the centrality of slavery as a moral issue and the moral superiority of the Northern cause. To the neo-nationalist, the revisionists' belief that the war was avoidable was an expression of "historical sentimentalism." The important thing to realize was that evil can never be exorcised from human affairs, and that its existence imposes on us "the necessity for decision and for struggle."[9] The evil in this case was obviously Southern slavery. "To say that the Civil War was fought over the 'unreal' issue of slavery in the territories is like saying that the Second World War was fought over the 'unreal' issue of the invasion of Poland. . . . The extension of slavery, like the extension of fascism, was an act of aggression which made a moral choice inescapable." One scholar commented in a historiographical essay, "Presumably, to satisfy the new nationalists, one not only cannot consider the Civil War repressible, but also must write with righteous indignation against the South."[10] In his massive synthesis of the 1850s, Allan Nevins appeared to be close to the new nationalists when he said, "The main root of the conflict . . . was the problem of slavery *with its complementary problem of race-adjustment,*" a problem that Southerners refused to face and Northerners refused to share.[11] Revival of slavery as a moral issue led to a favorable reassessment

[9] Arthur M. Schlesinger, "The Causes of the American Civil War: A Note on Historical Sentimentalism," *Partisan Review, XVI* (1949). The quotations are from the reprint in Edwin C. Rozwenc, ed., *The Causes of the American Civil War* (Boston, 1961), pp. 188, 189. See also, among others, Harry V. Jaffa, *Crisis of the House Divided: An Interpretation of the Issues in the Lincoln-Douglas Debates* (New York, 1959); Peter Geyl, "The American Civil War and the Problem of Inevitability," *New England Quarterly, XXIV* (1951), pp. 147-168; Fawn M. Brodie, "Who Won the Civil War Anyway?" *New York Times Book Review* (August 5, 1962).
[10] Arthur S. Link and Rembert Patrick, eds., *Writing Southern History, Essays in Historiography in Honor of Fletcher M. Green* (Baton Rouge, 1967), p. 240n.
[11] Allan Nevins, *The Emergence of Lincoln* (2 vols., New York, 1950), Vol. p. II, 468.

of abolitionism, which was looked on as "roughly analogous" to the modern civil rights movement.[12]

The civil rights movement not only rehabilitated morality as the main issue between the sections, it inspired an investigation of racial attitudes in the North before, during, and after the war. In book after book[13] the North was shown to have been thoroughly anti-Negro, as much concerned, it sometimes seemed, with keeping blacks out of the North as with liberating them. Not the expansion of slavery but the migration of blacks was shown to have been uppermost in the minds of many Northerners. Even straight-out abolitionists were often tainted with ideas of white superiority. During the same decade in which most of these studies appeared (the 1960s), several major Northern cities were rocked by the worst race riots in the nation's history, riots that were blamed on the oppression of blacks by the white community. Such facts, historical and contemporary, raised doubts about the Northern commitment to human rights in the 1860s as well as the 1960s. As one thoughtful reviewer said, "After an excursion through revisionary historical literature, . . . it seems harder than ever to locate that legendary 'interlude of virtue' when Americans renounced racism and rededicated themselves to their ideals of equality. The present seems depressingly continuous with the past." It seemed more difficult, he said, "to be confident in justifying the sacrifice of those 600,000 lives."[14]   The latter conclusion was reinforced by the

[12] Martin Duberman, ed., *The Antislavery Vanguard: New Essays on the Abolitionists* (Princeton, 1965), p. ix. For a similar evolution of the historiography of slavery, see pp. 2-4 above. The most important (or controversial) books are: Ulrich B. Phillips, *American Negro Slavery* (New York, 1918); Kenneth M. Stampp, *The Peculiar Institution* (New York, 1956); Stanley B. Elkins, *Slavery: A Problem in American Institutional and Intellectual Life* (Chicago, 1959); Robert W. Fogel and Stanley L. Engerman, *Time on the Cross: The Economics of American Negro Slavery* (Boston, 1974); Eugene Genovese, *Roll, Jordan, Roll: The World the Slaves Made* (New York, 1974); Herbert G. Gutman, *The Black Family in Slavery and Freedom* (New York, 1976).

[13] Leon Litwack, *North of Slavery: The Negro in the Free States, 1790-1860* (Chicago, 1961); Eugene H. Berwanger, *The Frontier against Slavery: Western Anti-Negro Prejudice and the Slavery Extension Controversy* (Urbana, Ill., 1967); James A. Rawley, *Race and Politics: "Bleeding Kansas" and and the Coming of the Civil War* (Philadelphia, Pa., 1969); V. Jacque Vogeli, *Free but Not Equal: The Midwest and the Negro during the Civil War* (Chicago, 1967); Forrest G. Wood, *Black Scare: The Racist Response to Emancipation and Reconstruction* (Berkeley, Cal., 1968).

[14] C. Vann Woodward, "White Racism and Black 'Emancipation,' " *New York Review of Books* (February 27, 1969), p. 11.

revulsion of so many Americans against the war in Vietnam. Lincoln had preserved the Union because, he said, the United States was the last best hope of mankind. But Lincoln's role for the Union as the light of the world ill-suited a powerful nation that was savagely blasting a small agricultural country on the other side of the world in a war begun in ineptitude and continued out of stubborn pride. "It has become clear that we are a nation like all nations, that as a Great Power we are behaving no more morally than have other Great Powers."[15]

The new nationalists counterattacked, and the war of words still goes on.[16] Both sides in the debate just sketched are practitioners of what has been called the "whig" interpretation of history, which reconstructs the past in terms of the present.[17] For example, one historian who believed that the beneficial results of the war were insufficient to justify its cost wrote that his "new revisionism . . . may be invalidated . . . by future developments: if significant gains are made by Negroes, and those gains are seen as dependent upon emancipation in 1865, then perhaps the sacrifices of the war should be regarded as justified."[18] This view of history assumes that specific events in the past can be identified as the causes of specific results in the present. Therefore it necessarily produces a constantly fluctuating image of the past, which becomes a selection of those events presumed to be most important to the present,[19] because the content of the present is always changing. In times highly charged with conflicting ideologies, the presentism intrinsic to the whig interpretation can easily transform history into propaganda. From seeing the past in terms of the present, it is a short step to using a contrived image of the past to coerce the present.

[15] John S. Rosenberg, "Toward a New Civil War Revisionism," *The American Scholar,* *XXXVIII* (1969). The quoted passage is taken from the reprint in Gerald N. Grob and George A. Billias, eds., *From Jacksonian Democracy to the Gilded Age* (New York, 1972), p. 207.

[16] For a comment on Rosenberg's article and an assertion that the war was "worth it," see Phillip S. Paludan, "The American Civil War: Triumph Through Tragedy," *Civil War History,* *XX* (1974), pp. 239-250.

[17] Herbert Butterfield, *The Whig Interpretation of History* (New York, 1965), p. 11. This essay originally appeared in 1931.

[18] Rosenberg, "Toward a New Civil War Revisionism," 209.

[19] Butterfield, *Whig Interpretation,* p. 25.

In the 1960s and 1970s the "new political history" was thought by some to offer hope of escaping the circularity of the whig interpretation. As related to the antebellum period, the new political history is the demography of cultural and political traits derived from the mathematical interpretation of quantitative data, a method given great impetus by the availability of electronic computers. The technique of history by quantification, in this field as elsewhere, has certain built-in biases and inherent limitations that make sound generalizations difficult to formulate. But the studies completed thus far have raised questions about the dynamics of antebellum political behavior, some of which challenge the assumption that the Northern masses were deeply moved by slavery as opposed to other issues, especially religion.[20] This suggests the possibility of successful manipulation of the Northern masses by politicians — as charged by the revisionists.

Lee Benson, a pioneer of the "new political history," has recommended breaking out of old patterns of thought by the systematic study of the Civil War as one of many "separatist internal" wars between "territorial culture groups," as one of a class of phenomena that have many elements in common. This approach will, he says, "facilitate our developing a powerful general theory to help explain the Civil War." Then it may be possible, he believes, to deal with theoretical questions, such as how groups opposed to the war could have acted to prevent it. The insights thus derived may then be used to deal with contemporary instances of conflicts between territorial culture groups, Quebec separatism, for example.[21] Attempts to convert history into a science have never met with much success, and it may be doubted if the "new political history," even with the help of modern computer technology, can overcome difficulties that are philosophical in nature.

---

[20] Ronald P. Formisano, *The Birth of Mass Political Parties: Michigan, 1827-1861* (Princeton, N.J., 1971); Michael F. Holt, *Forging a Majority: The Formation of the Republican Party in Pittsburgh, 1848-1860* (New Haven, Conn., 1969); Frederick C. Luebke, ed., *Ethnic Voters and the Election of Lincoln* (Lincoln, Neb., 1971). For other titles and a discussion, see Eric Foner, "The Causes of the Civil War: Recent Interpretations and New Directions," *Civil War History, XX* (1974), pp. 198-201.

[21] Lee Benson, "Middle Period Historiography: What is to be Done?" in George A. Billias and Gerald N. Grob, eds., *American History, Retrospect and Prospect* (New York, 1971), pp. 168-174.

Certainly any way of making the study of the Civil War era less parochial in outlook is welcome. Marxian historians long ago laid claims to having done so, but it may be objected that they have merely substituted an ideological for a nationalist parochialism. Up to a point there are striking similarities between the Marxian and Beardian interpretations. For example, both Beard and Barrington Moore[22] called the Civil War a social revolution, and compared it explicitly to the English civil war and the French Revolution, and both Beard and the Marxists stress the influence of economic factors as a cause of the war. An approach as yet imperfectly defined, but that has a distinct Beardian ring to it, is the concept of "modernization," which promises to be more comprehensive and cosmopolitan than the Beard thesis. Aside from one excellent essay by Raimondo Luraghi,[23] however, the concept has not been directly applied to the coming of the Civil War.[24]

Sometimes historians have failed to distinguish between the causes of sectional antagonisms and the causes of the war itself, assuming that one necessarily leads to the other. However closely related, they are still two very different things. Fortunately, several scholars have examined the train of events subsequent to secession that led to the outbreak of hostilities. The view that the South was to blame for starting the war was challenged by Charles Ramsdell, who maintained that the real cause of hostilities was Lincoln's send-

[22] Barrington Moore, *Social Origins of Dictatorship and Democracy* (Boston, 1966) contains an account of the causes of the war that sounds Beardian in many ways. For a discussion of Marxist writers, including a comparison of their work with Beard's, see Thomas J. Pressly, *Americans Interpret Their Civil War* (New York, 1962), pp. 249-262.

[23] Raimondo Luraghi, "The Civil War and the Modernization of American Society: Social Structure and Industrial Revolution in the Old South before and during the War," *Civil War History, XVIII* (1972), pp. 230-250.

[24] For some other important books bearing on the question of the causes of the Civil War, see: Paul C. Nagel, *One Nation Indivisible: The Union in American Thought* (New York, 1964); Ernest L. Tuveson, *Redeemer Nation: The Idea of America's Millenial Role* (Chicago, 1968); Robert R. Russel, *Economic Aspects of Southern Sectionalism* (New York, 1960), originally published in 1924; David B. Davis, *The Slave Power Conspiracy and the Paranoid Style* (Baton Rouge, 1969); George M. Frederickson, *The Black Image in the White Mind: The Debate on Afro-American Character and Destiny, 1817-1914* (New York, 1971); Major L. Wilson, *Space, Time, and Freedom: The Quest for Nationality and the Irrepressible Conflict, 1815-1861* (Westport, Conn., 1974); Eric Foner, *Free Soil, Free Labor, Free Men: The Ideology of the Republican Party Before the Civil War* (New York, 1970); Phillip Paludan, *A Covenant with Death: The Constitution, Law and Equality in the Civil War Era* (Urbana, Ill., 1975).

ing a relief expedition to Fort Sumter. Lincoln had done so, said Ramsdell, in the full expectation that war would result, because only by provoking the Confederates into firing the first shot could he hope to unify the Radical and Conservative wings of his party and attract Northern Democrats to the cause of preserving the Union by force. In a book-length study of Lincoln and the Republican party in the crisis of 1860-1861, David Potter defended the President against the charge of knowingly provoking the attack on Fort Sumter.[25] A new dimension was added to the subject by Kenneth Stampp, who carefully analyzed what the North feared it would lose by acquiescing in an independent Confederacy, and how those fears were translated into powerful political pressure on Lincoln to do something decisive. He conceded that Lincoln was no pacifist, nor were the Confederates, and that he was willing to accept war rather than Southern independence. "Perhaps it was only Lincoln's good fortune that personal, partisan, and national interests could be served with such favorable coincidence as they were by his Sumter decision." As for the North in general, Stampp concluded:

> Yankees went to war animated by the highest ideals of the nineteenth-century middle classes, but they waged their war in the usual spirit of vengeance. . . . But what the Yankees achieved — for their generation at least — was a triumph not of middle-class ideals but of middle-class vices. The most striking products of their crusade were the shoddy aristocracy of the North and the ragged children of the South. Among the masses of Americans there were no victors, only the vanquished.[26]

THE WAR AND RECONSTRUCTION

For a generation or more after 1865 memoirs and biographies were the predominant forms of Civil War literature.[27] Otherwise,

---

[25] Charles W. Ramsdell, "Lincoln and Fort Sumter," *Journal of Southern History, III* (1937), pp. 259-288; David Potter, *Lincoln and His Party in the Secession Crisis* (2nd ed., New Haven, Conn., 1962).

[26] Kenneth M. Stampp, *And the War Came: The North and the Secession Crisis, 1860-1861* (Chicago, 1964), pp. 297-298. First published at Baton Rouge in 1950.

[27] The historical literature on the Civil War is so gigantic that the best that can be done in a brief essay is to refer the reader to some bibliographies. Perhaps the best is in James G. Randall and David H. Donald, *The Civil War and Reconstruction* (Lexington, Mass., 1969), a masterly revision by Donald of Randall's classic text, which was first published in 1937.

the publication by the Federal government of the *Official Records of the Union and Confederate Armies* (1880-1901), consisting of about 140,000 printed pages and 1000 maps, followed by the naval records (1884-1927) was easily the most important event ever to occur in Civil War historiography.[28] These volumes not only provided the raw material for innumerable military and naval histories, but were a mine of information about economic, political, and diplomatic matters.

After the turn of the century, writings on the war began to dwindle. The leading participants were almost all gone, the rank and file were now old men — those who were left — and the war with Spain and then with Germany overshadowed the great events of the 1860s. History was now largely professionalized, and its practitioners were interested in things that seemed more important than mere military chronicles. An increasing number of those who did write about the war turned their attention to economic, political, administrative, legal, diplomatic, and social topics. The most important work published between the two world wars was Douglas S. Freeman's exhaustive biography of Robert E. Lee, followed by his massive study of Lee's lieutenants.[29] Freeman's books and the spectacular success of Margaret Mitchell's novel *Gone with the Wind* (later one of the most popular films in the history of the cinema) helped to reawaken interest in the "American Iliad."[30] But far more important in this respect was World War II, which was followed 16 years later by the centennial of the Civil War.

See also Allan Nevins, Bell I. Wiley, and James I Robertson, Jr., eds., *Civil War Books* (2 vols., Baton Rouge, 1967, 1969), and Robert F. Durden, "Civil War and Reconstruction, 1861-1877," in William H. Cartwright and Richard L. Watson, Jr., eds., *The Reinterpretation of American History and Culture* (Washington, 1973). *Civil War History*, which appears quarterly, annually publishes a compilation of articles on the antebellum, Civil War, and Reconstruction years, as well as reviews of books. Reviews may also be conveniently consulted in *The Journal of Southern History*, *The Journal of American History*, and *The American Historical Review*.
[28] Robert N. Scott, chief comp., *War of the Rebellion: A Compilation of the Official Records of the Union and Confederate Armies* (70 vols. in 128, Index, and Atlas, Washington, D.C., 1880-1901), Richard Rush and others, comps., *Official Records of the Union and Confederate Navies in the War of the Rebellion* (30 vols., Index, Washington, D.C., 1894-1927).
[29] Douglas Southall Freeman, *R. E. Lee: A Biography* (4 vols., New York, 1934-1935); *Lee's Lieutenants: A Study in Command* (3 vols., New York, 1942-1944).
[30] Margaret Mitchell, *Gone with the Wind* (New York, 1936).

The ensuing flood of books and articles was vaster than anything of its kind ever seen before. A sizable part of it was opportunistic, especially with the approach of the centennial, and often of poor quality, but a surprisingly large fraction of the rest ranged from creditable to outstanding. Military history came into its own again. Besides accounts of individual campaigns and biographies of generals, several multivolume works were produced,[31] and monographs were written on subjects that, while not dealing directly with the fighting, were important to an understanding of what took place on the battlefield. Logistics, railroads, ordnance, medicine, engineering, naval construction, strategic planning, troop recruitment, and military education were among the topics studied.

The majority of historians who addressed the subject revived the laudatory view of Lincoln as a commander-in-chief with keen insight into military affairs; and, perhaps unavoidably, they identified the generals with whom Lincoln worked best, Grant in particular, as being far superior to the likes of McClellan and others whom Lincoln discarded along the way. Some of these same scholars attributed the Union's ultimate triumph to the nature of Northern society, which they saw as modern, progressive, and flexible when compared with the South. The Confederacy, an outdated, rigid society, fought an outdated and stereotyped war and so inevitably went down to defeat. These theories have not met with universal acceptance.[32]

Race, emancipation, and the Negro received considerable attention from the 1950s on. The fears of many Northerners when faced by emancipation and Negro enfranchisement were carefully documented, as were the ways in which the Federal government at-

---

[31] Kenneth P. Williams, *Lincoln Finds a General* (5 vols., New York 1949-1955); Bruce Catton, *Mr. Lincoln's Army* (New York, 1951), *Glory Road* (New York, 1952), *A Stillness at Appomattox* (New York, 1953), a trilogy on the campaigns of the Army of the Potomac. See also his *Centennial History of the Civil War* (3 vols., New York, 1961-1965).

[32] For a discussion of this subject, with reference to pertinent books and articles, see Ludwell H. Johnson, "Civil War Military History: A Few Revisions in Need of Revising," *Civil War History*, *XVII* (1971), pp. 115-130. For a recent statement of the triumph of a "modernizing" North over a South handicapped by "persisting rigidities," see George M. Frederickson, "Blue over Gray: Sources of Success and Failure in the Civil War," in George M. Frederickson, ed., *A Nation Divided: Problems and Issues of the Civil War and Reconstruction* (Minneapolis, 1975).

tempted to allay such fears by keeping blacks in the South or promising to settle them in other countries. Federal policies in occupied parts of the Confederacy aimed at maintaining the subordination of the Negro, who was regarded as a means to an end — winning the war — and who was frequently subjected to brutal treatment by his liberators. Even where Northern idealism had its fullest expression, such as at Port Royal, it revealed an attitude toward blacks that boded ill for the future.[33] The story seemed especially melancholy in the light of the Negro's staunch support of the Union cause.[34]

Confederate history shared in the publishing boom of the post-World War II years. Although there were many new military and naval accounts and biographies of Southern generals, the emphasis was on social, economic, and political studies. Almost every aspect of the Confederate South received attention. The membership of the secession conventions and the Confederate Congress were scrutinized and quantified. There were studies of individual states, of towns and cities; even the minutes of the Richmond City Council were published. Various aspects of Southern diplomacy were examined anew. There were books on the trials of Confederate women, on refugees, on newspaper reporters, and so forth. This formidable literary avalanche produced much valuable new information and shed light on many hitherto obscure aspects of the Confederate saga, but it did not generate any historiographical revolution, although there were some attempts in that direction.[35]

The history of the wartime North has been in many ways a much livelier subject. Towering over the landscape was Allan Nevins'

[33] See Forrest Wood and V. J. Vogeli, footnote 13; Willie Lee Rose, *Rehearsal for Reconstruction: The Port Royal Experiment* (Indianapolis, 1964); Louis S. Gerteis, *From Contraband to Freedmen: Federal Policy Toward Southern Blacks, 1861-1865* (Westport, Conn., 1973). See also the older but still valuable study by Bell I. Wiley, *Southern Negroes, 1861-1865* (New Haven, 1938).

[34] Benjamin Quarles, *The Negro in the Civil War* (Boston, 1953); Dudley Taylor Cornish, *The Sable Arm: Negro Troops in the Union Army, 1861-1865* (New York, 1956); James McPherson, *The Negro's Civil War: How American Negroes Felt and Acted during the War for the Union* (New York, 1965).

[35] Up to 1950, the best general treatment containing the best bibliography is E. Merton Coulter, *The Confederate States of America, 1861-1865* (Baton Rouge, 1950). For more recent scholarship see the essays on Confederate historiography in Link and Patrick, eds., *Writing Southern History,* and the Durden essay cited in footnote 27.

four-volume *War for the Union,* the theme of which was the accelerated modernization of the North when confronted by the necessity of mobilizing for a conflict of unprecedented dimensions. "A modern America was being born."[36] Nevins' work is a paean of praise to the united nation that emerged from the war as "one of the principal world powers, with a new set of responsibilities, challenges, and opportunities."[37] *The War for the Union* will long stand as the crowning work of the "new nationalist" view of the period.

Meanwhile other historians were busy modifying or questioning various traditional views of the Union. The stereotype of Northern Democrats as being mostly copperheads and of copperheads as being disloyal went by the board; instead, Democrats became the loyal opposition who supported the war while resisting the Republicans in the political arena.[38] The belief that the war speeded industrialization was sharply disputed by Thomas Cochran, who argued that the momentum of economic development in the antebellum period has been slighted and that the war, in fact, retarded industrial growth. The Cochran thesis has been subjected to searching criticism, and there is no consensus in sight. But the debate has raised important questions both methodological and philosophical, giving rise to fruitful new inquiries.[39]

Abraham Lincoln continued to fascinate historians despite the existence of Carl Sandburg's six-volume biography and James G. Randall's scholarly and discriminating *Lincoln the President* in four volumes.[40] The civil rights movement led to a reexamination of

[36] Allan Nevins, *The War for the Union* (4 vols., New York, 1959-1971), Vol. II, p. viii.
[37] *Ibid.,* Vol. IV, p. 404.
[38] Frank L. Klement, *The Copperheads in the Middle West* (Chicago, 1960). See also Richard O. Curry, "The Union As It Was: A Critique of Recent Interpretations of the 'Copperheads,' " *Civil War History, XIII* (1967), pp. 25-39.
[39] Thomas C. Cochran, "Did the Civil War Retard Industrialization?" *Mississippi Valley Historical Review XLVIII* (1961), pp. 197-210; Ralph Andreano, ed., *The Economic Impact of the American Civil War* (Cambridge, Mass., 1962); David T. Gilchrist and W. David Lewis, eds., *Economic Change in the Civil War* (Greenville, Del., 1965); Harry N. Scheiber, "Economic Change in the Civil War Era: An Analysis of Recent Studies," *Civil War History, XI* (1965), pp. 396-411; Jeffrey G. Williamson, "Watersheds and Turning Points: Conjectures on the Long-Term Impact of Civil War Financing," *Journal of Economic History, XXXIV* (1974), pp. 636-661.
[40] Carl Sandburg, *Abraham Lincoln: The Prairie Years* (2 vols., New York, 1926) and *The War*

Lincoln's attitudes toward blacks, with results not always flattering to the Great Emancipator. However, most of the accusations of racism leveled at Lincoln came from journalists and other nonspecialists, who made much of his defense of white supremacy in the debates with Douglas and of his seeming reluctance to face the prospect of emancipation. Lincoln scholars quickly rallied to the defense and tried to show that although he appears reactionary to the late twentieth century, he was really ahead of most Americans. His conservatism on matters of race, they argue, was the product of the political circumstances with which he was surrounded. Between these two interpretations there are various shadings of opinion.[41] The controversy probably has revealed more about the disputants than it has about Lincoln.

The attempt by some historians to capture Lincoln for the equalitarian cause has often been part of a sweeping attempt to revise the picture of the Republican party as divided between a bullying Radical faction on the one hand and the Conservatives, including Lincoln, on the other. Once stigmatized as a cynical and semi-conspiratorial pack of vindictives who made life difficult for the kindly President, the Radicals now were seen as the zealous keepers of the Republican conscience. They were "Lincoln's Vanguard for Radical Justice."[42] This flattering new view of the Radicals, some charged, was largely a function of their antislavery vehemence, an illustration of the common tendency to infer mo-

Years (4 vols., New York, 1939); James G. Randall, *Lincoln the President* (4 vols., New York, 1945-1955), volume IV being completed by Richard N. Current. The most recent biography is by Stephen B. Oates, *With Malice Toward None: The Life of Abraham Lincoln* (New York, 1977). For Lincoln's writings, the definitive collection is Roy P. Basler, ed., *The Collected Works of Abraham Lincoln* (8 vols., and Index, 1953-1955). A supplementary volume appeared in 1974.

[41] For two discussions of this subject see George M. Frederickson, "A Man but not a Brother: Abraham Lincoln and Racial Equality," *Journal of Southern History,* XLI (1975), pp. 39-58, and Don E. Fehrenbacher, "Only His Stepchildren: Lincoln and the Negro," *Civil War History,* XX (1974), pp. 293-310. A general treatment is Benjamin Quarles, *Lincoln and the Negro* (New York, 1962). See also Richard N. Current, *The Lincoln Nobody Knows* (New York, 1958).

[42] Hans L. Trefousse, *The Radical Republicans: Lincoln's Vanguard for Racial Justice* (New York, 1969). For discussions of the Radicals and radicalism, see David Donald, *Lincoln Reconsidered* (New York, 1961), Chap. 6, and the essays by Donald and T. Harry Williams in Grady McWhiney, ed., *Grant, Lee, Lincoln, and the Radicals: Essays on Civil War Leadership* (Evanston, Ill., 1964).

tives from the cause with which people are associated, when a close scrutiny of their personal behavior might give a very different result.[43] And while the Radicals were being upgraded, Lincoln and most other Republicans were said to have agreed with the Radicals on fundamental issues.

Much work has been devoted to defining terms such as "radical" or "conservative" and to attaching labels to individual Republicans on the basis of extensive statistical analyses of roll-call votes in Congress. These studies demonstrated that the terms had been used much too loosely in the past, and that differences between various groups in the party, as well as the relationship between the groups, have been overstated or misunderstood. In particular it has been shown that Radicals were not a unit on economic issues; their main focus of agreement was on slavery and Reconstruction.[44]   This approach to a better understanding of the nature of wartime Republicanism has the defects intrinsic to its method, and naturally not all historians will agree on what set of roll-call votes should be used to determine degrees of radicalism or conservatism.

The tendencies just described were even more important in the reinterpretation of Reconstruction history. A sketch of this subject can be found above on pp. 190-191 and will not be repeated here. The Dunning school,[45] which was highly critical of congressional (or Radical) Reconstruction, has been almost entirely eclipsed, and

---

[43] Cf. Potter, *South and the Sectional Conflict,* p. 108.

[44] For example, see the articles of Glenn M. Linden "Radicals and Economic Policies: The House of Representatives, 1861-1873," *Civil War History, XIII* (1967), pp. 51-65, and "Radicals and Economic Policies: The Senate, 1861-1873," *Journal of Southern History, XXXII*(1966), pp. 189-199.

[45] William A. Dunning of Columbia University. Dunning's seminar turned out a number of students who went on to write state studies of the Reconstruction period from a conservative (and sometimes strongly pro-Southern) point of view. Dunning's own works (*Reconstruction, Political and Economic,* [New York, 1907], *Essays on the Civil War and Reconstruction and Related Topics* [New York, 1907]) were better balanced, but still highly critical of congressional Reconstruction and the carpetbag governments. For useful historiographical essays, see Bernard A. Weisberger, "The Dark and Bloody Ground of Reconstruction Historiography," *Journal of Southern History, XXV* (1959), pp. 427-447; Gerald N. Grob, "Reconstruction: An American Morality Play," in Billias and Grob, eds., *American History: Retrospect and Prospect;* Richard O. Curry, "The Civil War and Reconstruction, 1861-1877: A Critical Overview of Recent Trends and Interpretations," *Civil War History, XX* (1974), pp. 215-238. See also Kenneth M. Stampp and Leon F. Litwack, eds., *Reconstruction: An Anthology of Revisionist Writings* (Baton Rouge, 1969).

the economic interpretation of Charles A. Beard and Howard K. Beale[46] has fared little better. Now in almost undisputed possession of the field of battle are the post-World War II revisionists who have made the Radicals their special heroes and conservative whites, including Andrew Johnson, their villains.

Major reinterpretations of the era of Civil War and Reconstruction so far have come at intervals of about a generation. If the cycle holds true in the future, the pendulum of interpretation is due to swing back around the turn of the century. One might expect, or at least hope, that the ever-increasing body of fact unearthed by historical research will reduce the extremes of disagreement; the arc of the pendulum should become always narrower. On the other hand, complete agreement, or even substantial agreement, may never be achieved. The events of the period have the power to arouse antagonisms that are apparently deeply rooted in the American temperament, if not in human nature itself. It is a power seemingly undiminished by the passage of years, and the time may yet be far off when Americans will no longer hear the sound of distant trumpets or the rumble of the guns.

[46] Howard K. Beale, *The Critical Year: A Study of Andrew Johnson and Reconstruction* (New York, 1930). For Beard, see footnote 6.

Index